# MUCH ADO ABOUT NOTING

## and
## Shakespeare's Secret Source

Henry Neville, 1599

by
# JOHN CASSON

Published by Dolman Scott Ltd

Copyright 2010© Dr John Casson

All rights reserved. No part of this publication may be reproduced, stored in a retrieval system, or transmitted in any form or by any means, electronic, mechanical, photocopy, recording or otherwise, without prior written permission of the copyright owner. Nor can it be circulated in any form of binding or cover other than that in which it is published and without similar condition including this condition being imposed on a subsequent purchaser.

ISBN 978-1-905553-57-0

www.dolmanscott.com

for Andy Smith,

a true hero who has saved lives and limbs,
the world expert on the accidents
people have during demining,
and my best friend.

# Contents

| | |
|---|---|
| Preface: Henry Neville and the Authorship Question | v |
| Introduction | viii |
| Chapter 1: *Leicester's Commonwealth* | 1 |
| Chapter 2: *Leicester's Commonwealth* as a Shakespeare source | 7 |
| Chapter 3: The Annotations of Worsley MSS 47 | 32 |
| Chapter 4: The Annotator of Worsley MSS 47 and the Annotator of Halle's *Chronicle* | 73 |
| Chapter 5: Neville's changes to vocabulary in his copy of *Leicester's Commonwealth* | 95 |
| Chapter 6: Annotator A: Worsley MSS 36 | 108 |
| Chapter 7: *Look About You* | 119 |
| Chapter 8: Hand D in *Sir Thomas More* and Worsley MSS 47 | 164 |
| Chapter 9: Ptolemy and Politike Pamphlets, 1588-9 | 176 |
| Chapter 10: A National Treasure | 183 |
| | |
| Appendix 1: The Annotations of *Leicester's Commonwealth*, Worsley 36 and 47 | 188 |
| Appendix 2: The Northumberland Manuscript Annotations | 230 |
| Appendix 3: The Annotations in Halle's *Chronicle* and Worsley 36 and 47 | 236 |
| Appendix 4: The Vocabulary of *Look About You* | 243 |
| Appendix 5: The Date of *Look About You* | 251 |
| Appendix 6: *The Famous History of George Lord Fauconbridge* | 254 |
| Appendix 7: *Mucedorus* and *Leicester's Commonwealth* | 260 |
| Appendix 8: Henry Neville's letter, 1601 | 265 |
| Appendix 9: *Edward IV*, Thomas Falconbridge, Essex and Neville | 268 |
| Appendix 10: Arbella | 271 |
| | |
| References | 274 |
| Authors' Index | 282 |
| Index | 284 |

# Preface

## Henry Neville and the Authorship Question

This book builds on the work of Brenda James who first identified Henry Neville as the author of the works of Shakespeare in 2005. For the sake of anyone who has not read her books I will summarise her discovery but this is only to provide a context for this book and I would encourage any reader to refer to her work for the fuller picture.

**The Authorship Question**
Doubts about whether William Shakespeare from Stratford wrote the works attributed to him have been around since his own lifetime. These doubts can be summarised as follows:

1) The works of Shakespeare contain evidence of wide reading, travel, ability in foreign languages. Shakespeare never travelled outside England and left no books in his will.
2) Despite being our greatest writer his daughters were illiterate at a time when women were educated. His parents were illiterate. None of his ancestors or descendants were writers or involved in the theatre.
3) No letters written by this great writer have ever been found. Only one letter written to him has been discovered, it was never sent but found in the posthumous papers of the person who wrote it. The letter was a request for a loan (Michell, 2000, 48).
4) Shakespeare shows intimate knowledge of the English and French royal courts, yet no courtier ever wrote about meeting him.
5) When he died nothing whatsoever happened. When Francis Beaumont died he was buried in Westminster Abbey and Ben Jonson had a state funeral. Shakespeare's first monument in Stratford (recorded in engravings of 1653 and 1709) shows a very different man with his hands on a sack of grain (see Michell, 2000, 89, 91).

Diana Price (2000), who has written the most scholarly book on the available evidence, concluded the man from Stratford could not have been the writer. She was unable to suggest who was. The Authorship Question fell into disrepute because the candidates suggested (Bacon, Oxford and others), whilst intriguing, were just not credible.

**Henry Neville**
When Brenda James discovered Henry Neville she was not looking for him: indeed, unlike all the other candidates, Neville was not discovered because a researcher had identified a plausible candidate and then sought evidence to fit. James was examining the dedication to the 1609 edition of the Sonnets. Having hypothesised that it was in code she set out, through a logical process, to decode it and thus discovered the unexpected name Henry Neville. James had never heard of him but as she researched his life she found more and more evidence pointing to him having been the hidden poet behind the front man/pseudonym 'William Shakespeare'. Why did he want to keep his identity secret? James discovered an interlocking series of reasons that made this secrecy essential.

1) It was not socially acceptable for a man of his position to be identified as a playwright.
2) The plays he was writing were political and at the time such writing could be punished by imprisonment and torture.
3) Neville's father and father-in-law were involved in secret diplomatic government business. Indeed Neville himself became ambassador to France in 1599.
4) Crucially Neville was illegitimate and had this been discovered he could have lost one of the largest fortunes of the day: the Gresham inheritance. This last point explains the references to bastards in the plays, one of whom (in *King John*) is called Faulconbridge: a Neville family name.

**Neville's Life and Shakespeare's works**
As James researched Neville's life she found it fitted what we might expect to find in the biography of the bard, like a glove. I will illustrate this with ten points:
1) **Italy:** Neville visited Italy in 1581, including Padua and Venice, gaining special knowledge of that country which we find in Shakespeare's plays.
2) **France:** Neville was Ambassador to France 1599-1600, at a time when Shakespeare wrote *Henry V*, which includes scenes in France.
3) **Holinshed:** Neville's father-in-law, Henry Killigrew, was one of the editors of the 1587 edition of Holinshed, used as a major source by Shakespeare.

4) **Nevilles in the history plays**: members of the family are disguised by being identified only by their titles (the Earls of Salisbury, Warwick, Westmoreland etc.), though the name 'Nevil' is mentioned 7 times in *Henry VI* part 2.
5) **Imprisonment:** Neville was caught up in the Essex Rebellion and imprisoned in the Tower of London 1601-3. From this time a tragic darkness enters Shakespeare's plays.
6) **Henry Wriothesley:** Neville had known Henry Wriothesley, the Earl of Southampton, since he was a boy and they were imprisoned together in the Tower. They were close friends. Southampton dedicated a document about Richard III to Neville (British Library, Additional MS 29307). Shakespeare dedicated poems to him. In 1613 John Chamberlain wrote that Wriothesley was Neville's "great patron" (McClure, 1939, Vol 1, 401).
7) **James I** was in Oxford when Neville was awarded his MA in 1605. On that occasion Matthew Gwynne presented his *Tres Sibyllae*, a Latin poem which referred to the prophecy that Banquo's descendants would inherit an endless empire (a possible source for *Macbeth*, 1606). Neville had visited Glamis castle in 1583. James I consulted Neville about his own writing.
8) **The Strachey Letter** was a source for *The Tempest*. A private manuscript, it was circulated within the Virginia Company, of which Neville was a member.
9) **John Fletcher** dedicated a play (*A King and No King*) to Neville before he co-wrote the last plays with Shakespeare.
10) **Ben Jonson** wrote a poem addressed to Neville and *The Staple of News*, a play about the First Folio, which hints that Neville was the author (James, 2008, 268). At the time the First Folio was printed Jonson was living at Gresham College, which was founded by Neville's great uncle (James, 2005, 210).

Brenda James has discovered much more evidence of Neville's authorship and I have built on this by identifying his early works from the mid 1580s in my previous book *Enter Pursued by a Bear*.

# Introduction

> My labour may showe mine vttermost goodwill, of the more learned I require their further enlargement, and of fault-finders dispensation till they be more fullie informed.
>
> Raphaell Holinshed[1]

In 2005 Brenda James published her discovery that Henry Neville was the secret writer behind the nom-de-plume "William Shakespeare" (James & Rubinstein, 2005).

In her first book James revealed that there were documents that had belonged to Neville in the Worsley collection of manuscripts at the Lincolnshire Archives. Amongst these were two copies of *Leicester's Commonwealth*, a political treatise published in 1584. At first I did not realise the full significance of these but in the summer of 2008 I travelled to Lincoln and, together with Brenda and her husband, Howard, examined them over three days. It was on the second day that it began to dawn on me what I was looking at: nothing less than the document that triggered Shakespeare's history plays. Not only was this an autograph manuscript but a lost key to unlock the political motivation behind the series of plays stretching from *Edward III* through to *Henry VIII*. We can also include the Roman plays and the long poem, *The Rape of Lucrece*, because these too are political. Henry Neville was a politician: a Member of Parliament, Ambassador to France, political prisoner, and a candidate for Secretary of State. I realised with growing excitement that here was a document of enormous significance, annotated by the playwright up to eight years before he became 'Shakespeare'. I felt shock and disbelief that gradually gave way to a sense of awe. I was astonished that I had been given the opportunity to examine these documents in detail and as I did so they gradually gave up the secrets that are the substance of this book.

After my first visit to see the Worsley manuscripts I went to look at an original printed copy of *Leicester's Commonwealth* in York Minster Library. This small book, measuring just three by four inches (so small it was obviously easy to hide and smuggle) is housed in the old Archbishop's palace where, 101 years before it was published, Richard III had invested his son as Prince of Wales. This made me realise that Henry Neville was

---

1    From the Preface to the Reader of the 3rd Volume of Chronicles, 1577.

closer in time to Richard III than we are to Queen Victoria.

This book is especially about three copies of *Leicester's Commonwealth* which were owned by Henry Neville. Two are in the Worsley Manuscript collection (MSS 36 & 47) at the Lincolnshire Archives and one in the Northumberland Manuscript bundle of papers at Alnwick Castle, Northumberland. All three are handwritten copies. The latter is charred and incomplete after being in a fire on 18th March 1780. Fortunately the Worsley Manuscripts are in perfect condition. I explore the relationship between the Northumberland and Worsley Manuscripts in chapter 6.

Later I went to Lancaster University to see the annotated copy of Halle's *Chronicle* which was discovered in 1940 and which Alan Keen and Roger Lubbock were convinced was annotated by William Shakespeare (see chapter 4 and appendix 3). I was then able to compare the annotations in the margins of this document with those in Worsley MSS 47, Neville's letters and diplomatic papers at the British Library and the three volumes of Winwood's *Memorials*, which contain many of his diplomatic letters of 1599-1613, at the John Rylands Library, Manchester. I have also looked at the Tower Notebook (Worsley MSS 40) which was also discovered by Brenda James in the Lincoln Archives. This text "copied and collected out of the Recordes in the Tower Anno 1602" was written mostly by a scribe[2] but annotated by Henry Neville, during his imprisonment.

The only surviving manuscript believed to be by Shakespeare is the three pages written by "Hand D" in *Sir Thomas More*, a play by Anthony Munday (with help from Henry Chettle, Thomas Dekker, Thomas Heywood and Shakespeare) which is preserved in MS Harley 7368, at the British Library. Hand D has been identified as Shakespeare's. In chapters 3, 4 and 8, I will show that there is evidence for this being written by Henry Neville. Given the importance of the Hand D section of *Sir Thomas More*, what would scholars have made of a 132 page manuscript? This is what James had discovered in the Worsley 47 Manuscript of *Leicester's Commonwealth* and I have had the privilege of examining it in detail. It is the longest extant hand written document by Henry Neville, the hidden poet who disguised himself as William Shakespeare. Researching in Oxford I found two more annotated documents. The first

---

2   The scribe was possibly Neville's secretary, John Packer, as each section is signed off with a double P. He is mentioned in Neville's 1601 letter, see appendix 8.

was a small volume of political pamphlets from 1588-9 (4° L. 90. Art) in the Duke Humfrey Library (part of the Bodleian). This very room was established by the brother of Henry V whose murder we witness in Shakespeare's *Henry VI* part 2. The second was a volume on astronomy given to Merton College Library by Neville himself. I report on what I found in chapter 9.

Some readers may be puzzled by my inclusion of a number of apocryphal plays as by Shakespeare. In my previous book, *Enter Pursued by a Bear* (Casson, 2009), I offered evidence for Neville's hand in *Mucedorus* 1584-5, *Locrine* 1586-89, *Arden of Faversham* 1586-90, *Edmund Ironside* 1587-8, *The Troublesome Raigne of John* 1588-9, *Thomas of Woodstock* 1592-3, *A Yorkshire Tragedy* 1605 and the lost *Cardenio* 1613 (rediscovered by Lewis Theobald and published as *Double Falshood* in 1728). These are indeed relevant to this book as it was whilst examining *Mucedorus* that I first found evidence of the influence of *Leicester's Commonwealth* (see Appendix 7). I showed in my earlier book how traces of *Leicester's Commonwealth* could also be found in *Arden of Faversham* and *A Yorkshire Tragedy*. As will become apparent in this volume, I furthermore show its hidden influence in other plays and reveal a hitherto unrecognised early comedy by the bard: *Look About You* (see chapter 7).

The title *Much Ado About Noting* glances towards Shakespeare's comedy. As long ago as 1858 Richard Grant White noted that, in Elizabethan speech, 'nothing' and 'noting' sounded much the same. White argued that the plot of *Much Ado* "depends on 'noting' – watching, observing", indeed looking (Humphreys, 1981, 4). The annotations on the Worsley and Northumberland manuscripts and the Halle *Chronicle* are the 'much ado' of this book on noting. To see what they contain I have had to note carefully and look again and again at the documents. Such looking led me to my discoveries and to *Look About You*. Somehow this play has been overlooked and it is time to take proper note of its enormous significance: indeed to make Much Ado about *Look About You*!

**Permissions**
The illustrations from the Worsley Manuscripts are published with the permission of the Eighth Earl of Yarborough and Lincolnshire Archives.
Images from the annotated Halle's *Chronicle* are reproduced by kind permission of the Trustees of the Second Baron Hesketh's Will Trust.

Images from the Northumberland Manuscript are reproduced by kind permission from His Grace, The Duke of Northumberland, from the Archives of The Duke of Northumberland at Alnwick Castle: DNP MS 525.

The portrait of Henry Neville is © English Heritage, 'Private Collection'.

MS Harley 7368, Folio 9 (part of the Hand D section in *Sir Thomas More*) and Cotton Manuscripts, Caligula EX folio 21V, (Henry Neville's letter, 19th February, 1601) are © The British Library Board.

Images from the politike pamphlets in chapter 9 (4° L. 90. Art) are reproduced with permission from The Bodleian Library, University of Oxford.

**Acknowledgements**

I am very grateful to Brenda James for her support in agreeing that I should concentrate my research on the Worsley Manuscripts of *Leicester's Commonwealth*. Without her I simply would not have written this book. I am also grateful to Dr. Dwight Peck upon whose study of *Leicester's Commonwealth* I have relied and who has helped me during the writing of this book. My thanks are due also to the staff of the Lincolnshire Archives who look after Worsley MSS 36, 47 and 40, and to Anne Cole for her help in reading the annotations and transcribing Neville's letter of 1601 (see appendix 8).

I am grateful to Helen Clish, Rare Book Curator, and Emily Wood, senior library assistant, at Lancaster University, for access to the annotated Halle's *Chronicle* and to the Hesketh Collection. Thanks also are due to Joanna Parker, the librarian of Worcester College, for her help in checking Leicester's connections with Gloucester Hall, Oxford (see chapter 3). As ever I am grateful to the many librarians who have helped me in my searches including Dr Arnold Hunt and Michael Boggan of the Manuscripts Department of the British Library; Peter Jarvis and Amar Nazir, at John Rylands Library at the University of Manchester; Clive Hurst, keeper of the manuscripts, at the Bodley Library; Julian Reid and Julia Walworth at Merton College Library, Oxford; Marilyn Dearden of Oldham Inter-Library Loans and the Uppermill Librarians. I am grateful to Professor Anthony Jackson for arranging access to the Literature on Line (LION) database at Manchester University.

Thanks are also due to Adrian Rodgers and Arash Hesami who helped with the photographs of the manuscripts and computer glitches. Mark Beddow helped source the Wilfred Owen quotation. Andy Smith and Di Adderley helped by reading the text, advising and spotting errors.

# Chapter 1

## *Leicester's Commonwealth*

"I will unclasp a secret book, and to your quick-conceiving discontents
I'll read you matter **deep and dangerous**."
*Henry IV* part 1 (1.3.186)

"there do ensue daily more **deep, dangerous,** and desperate practices…"
*Leicester's Commonwealth* (Peck, 79/*56*[3])

*Leicester's Commonwealth* appeared, imported from France, in September 1584. It was almost immediately banned, though a number of copies escaped the official dragnet. Elizabeth I issued a proclamation against it in October. To own it was punishable by imprisonment. What was this dangerous book about? Essentially it was a political tract with a number of interwoven themes. The most obvious of these was an attack on the character and behaviour of Robert Dudley, Earl of Leicester, the Queen's favourite. However there were other themes likely to arouse the Queen's displeasure, chief amongst which was the succession to the throne, should Elizabeth die without having a child. The Government (at the Queen's behest) had already ruled that discussion of the succession was treason. *Leicester's Commonwealth* not only did this but also looked at the succession over the centuries, reviewing the Wars of the Roses and the questionable claims to the throne of successive monarchs and those in the current generation. It also addressed the issue of religious toleration, the positions of Roman Catholics and Puritans, and the situation in other countries.

*Leicester's Commonwealth* is dramatic writing, being a discussion between three characters: a gentleman, a lawyer and a scholar, reported in letterform by the scholar. Despite the ban it was very popular, being hand copied and shared between people, including courtiers. It was popular because it combined the topical themes with humour and scandal, and addressed the anxiety that the Queen's childless reign might end suddenly in a dynastic struggle that could lead to civil war. Banned documents can, by the very act of banning, become more attractive to the public. The government secret

---

[3] I have used both Peck's (1985) published text and the internet download. I have therefore referred to the page numbers as Peck (65/*48*), putting the book page number first, followed by the internet text page number in italics (see appendix 1).

service tried to discover its authors but despite educated guesses, they were never sure. They failed to suppress it. It was followed by a French edition and by an *Addition of the Translator* (1585), which was even more vicious in its anti-Leicester scandal-mongering. A copy of this Addition is to be found in the Worsley Manuscript 36 (see Peck 229/*154*). *Leicester's Commonwealth* was re-printed in 1641 so we know it continued to be of interest for over 50 years despite Leicester's death in 1588, just four years after it was published.

*Leicester's Commonwealth* was not just nasty invective or political diatribe. It was carefully argued, historically researched, illustrated with glimpses of court life, illuminated, indeed "sexed up", by reported opinions, characters, stories. Whilst perhaps tedious for a modern reader unfamiliar with the urgent issues of the day, it is comparable to a combination of our popular newspapers and satirical magazines in mixing political writing about the central issue of the day with gossip and scandal.

Above all it asked forbidden questions. Who was going to succeed Elizabeth I? What were the lessons of history? *Leicester's Commonwealth* set the current controversies in their historical context, thereby aiming to illustrate the dangers the nation faced. It came to the conclusion that Mary Queen of Scots and her son James were the rightful heirs to Elizabeth and in this it was prophetic: James did succeed in 1603. Just three years after *Leicester's Commonwealth* was published, Mary, however, was executed, leaving the way open for James. Elizabeth lived far longer than the writers had feared.

*Leicester's Commonwealth* therefore appears within a momentous period: it expresses anxiety about the safety of the realm, the dangers of tyrannical government, of civil war and a coup-d'état. Within this period there were several conspiracies against the crown: the Throckmorton Plot (1583), the Parry Plot (1585) and the Babington Plot (1586). The last of these was stage-managed by Walsingham in a carefully choreographed sting to trap Mary Queen of Scots into expressing treason in coded letters: she fell into the trap and paid with her life. Henry Neville came of age during this time: he became the M.P. for New Windsor in 1584. His father and father-in-law were close to the government as senior courtiers and diplomats. I have previously traced the links between members of the Neville family and all three of the above plots (Casson 2009).

## Henry Neville and Leicester's Commonwealth

In 1583 Neville returned from a four-year grand tour of Europe. He was immediately invited to join a diplomatic mission to Scotland with Walsingham and the young Earl of Essex. This was the occasion on which he visited Glamis castle (later the setting for *Macbeth*). He also took on the ironworks producing cannon that he had inherited from Thomas Gresham (through his mother, Elizabeth Gresham). This industrial activity brought him into conflict with Ambrose Dudley, the Earl of Warwick and Leicester's elder brother, in 1583. As specifically mentioned in *Leicester's Commonwealth* Ambrose was Master of the Queen's Ordinance, responsible for her "armor, artillery, and munition" from 1560 (Peck, 105/72). Elizabeth sent him to discipline Neville "on his export of ordinance" (James & Rubinstein, 2005, 90). They argued and Ambrose complained to the Queen about Neville's attitude. Another man in the Ordinance office was Philip Sidney, the poet, who is thought to have been in post by the autumn of 1583 and who was made joint Master of Ordinance in 1585. Sidney, who was Leicester's nephew, read *Leicester's Commonwealth* during the winter of 1584-5 and wrote a reply. A copy of Sidney's letter arguing against Elizabeth's marriage to the Duke of Angou is in the Northumberland Manuscript bundle, which scholars have agreed once belonged to Henry Neville. There was a close relationship between the Neville and Sidney families. The two fathers were good friends and Neville travelled round Europe (1578-83) with Robert Sidney (Philip's brother). Philip Sidney is mentioned by name in *Leicester's Commonwealth* (Peck, 81/57).

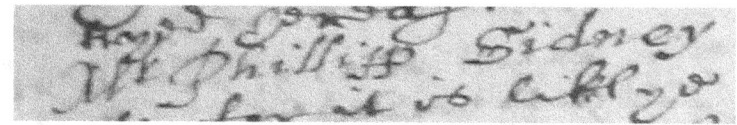

Worsley MSS 47, 10V

Elizabeth's edict against *Leicester's Commonwealth* prohibited ownership, distribution and printing. It did not explicitly forbid owning a hand written copy. Perhaps that is why Neville owned three such copies but no printed original (these are the Worsley Manuscripts 36 and 47 and the Northumberland manuscript copy). In a letter dated 27/6/1599 Neville, writing about the divisions between Catholic exiles since the death of Mary Queen of Scots, added these had intensified, "especially of late, since the title of the Infanta of Spaine hath bin sett on foote, according to the Books written by Parsons under one Doleman's Name" (Winwood, 1727, Vol 1,

51). The Jesuit Robert Parsons was later suspected of being one of the authors of *Leicester's Commonwealth*. He had written *De persecutione Anglicana* attacking Leicester in 1582. He wrote *A Conference about the Next Succession to the Crown of England* in 1595 under the name R. Doleman.

**The Nevilles in *Leicester's Commonwealth***
*Leicester's Commonwealth* is concerned with the succession to the throne. Neville's family had been intimately involved in this question. Neville's father had been a witness of Henry VIII's will, which is explicitly mentioned in *Leicester's Commonwealth*. In 1572 Neville's father-in-law, Sir Henry Killigrew, had been on a top-secret mission for the Queen and Leicester to covertly suggest to the Scottish ruling elite that they arrange for the assassination of Mary Queen of Scots. Henry Neville, the sixth Baron of Abergavenny (Neville's uncle), was one of peers who tried Mary Queen of Scots in 1586.
There are several Nevilles mentioned in the text: the first to appear is identified as Westmoreland: this was Charles Neville, (1543-1601), the sixth Earl of Westmoreland who, after the unsuccessful Northern Rebellion of 1569, lived in exile (Peck, footnote 11). Richard Neville, the Kingmaker, is prominent. One passage tells how:

"two Nevilles took upon them to join with Richard of York to put down their most benign prince King Henry VI, and after again in the other side to put down King Edward IV, it was not upon want of advancement, they being Earls both of Salisbury and Warwick and lords of many notable places besides" (Peck 135-6/*91*).

The wife of Richard III is mentioned (but not named): she was of course Anne Neville. Sir Henry Neville, Neville's father, is described as "walking upon the terrace at Windsor" talking with a friend.
Neville's in-laws, the Killigrews, were supporters of the Earl. William and his brother Henry Killigrew are mentioned in *Leicester's Commonwealth*. Neville married Anne Killigrew (Henry's daughter) in December 1584. Sir Robert Jermin is mentioned in a marginal annotation. His son married William Killigrew's daughter (Peck, footnote 168).
As far as we know, when *Leicester's Commonwealth* appeared, Neville had not written anything, yet within 6 years the first history plays were on stage. It is the central idea of this book that *Leicester's Commonwealth* stimulated Neville to create his plays and focussed his political thinking.

**Theatre and *Leicester's Commonwealth***

This document of political dynamite was bound to stimulate writers. Philip Sidney responded immediately, though his reply was never published. John Lyly's play *Endimion*, written 1585-8 (published in 1591), is "a tale of the Man in the Moon". Some scholars have suggested Endimion stood for Leicester, who was in love with Elizabeth I (= the moon = Cynthia). Another woman in love with Endimion is Tellus. This name might be a barely disguised and somewhat earthy anagram of Lletus (Lettice, the widow of the Earl of Essex who married Leicester, much to the Queen's displeasure). Sir **Toph**as, a bragging soldier, could then be Sir Chris**toph**er **Hat**ton. All these figures are in *Leicester's Commonwealth* and since the tract was published before the play it is possible that it influenced Lyly. Indeed Endimion dreams of a book in which he sees, "many wolves barking at thee Cynthia…ingratitude… Treachery… Envy…". This does sound rather like *Leicester's Commonwealth*. Wolves, ingratitude, treachery and envy are all mentioned in the tract. In the play Tellus speaks of "**tattling tongues**" (4.1). In *Leicester's Commonwealth* we find, "the tempest of men's **tongues**, which **tattled** busily at that time…" (Peck, 75/*54*). Other scholars have suggested Endimion was the Earl of Oxford, who was Lyly's patron (Bevington, 1968, 178).

Endimion and Diana (the chaste moon goddess also used as a symbol for Elizabeth I) are referred to in *Arden of Faversham*:

> There is no nectar but in Mosbie's lips.
> Had chaste Diana kissed him, she like me
> Would grow love sick, and from her watery bower
> Fling down Endymion and snatch him up:
> Then blame not me that slay a silly man
> Not half so lovely as Endymion.     (5.1.154)

I have suggested a date of 1586-90 for *Arden of Faversham*, which I have identified as an early play by Neville (Casson, 2009). If written before Leicester's death in 1588, this passage might be seen, rather daringly, to suggest that Elizabeth could cast off Leicester for another, more attractive, favourite (and at the time Leicester was aging and had lost much of his influence in an unsuccessful campaign in the Netherlands). The play also contains an unmistakeable reference to the 'murder' of Leicester's first wife as told in *Leicester's Commonwealth* (see chapter 7).

Cynthia and Endimion were referred to, ten years later, in Anthony Munday's *The Downfall of Robert the Earl of Huntington* (line 1203-4, written 1598, published in 1601). The Earl of Leicester appears and is compared with a bear. The Queen says, "Were this bear loose he would tear our mawes!" Salisbury replies, "But we can **muzzle** him, and bind his **pawes**" (Munday, 1965, lines 1912-14). The bear's **paws** are mentioned twice in the text of *Leicester's Commonwealth* and the Gentleman warns:

"You know the bear's love, which is all for his own paunch, and so this Bearwhelp turneth all to his own commodity, and for greediness thereof will overturn all if he be not stopped or **muzzled** in time" (Peck, 73/*53*). Later he advises that the Bear be "fast chained to a stake, with **muzzle**-cord," (Peck, 193/*127*).

I have already traced the links between these bear images, *Mucedorus* and Shakespeare's history plays, all of which predate *The Downfall of Robert the Earl of Huntington* (Casson, 2009: see Appendix 7 in this volume). I shall look further at Munday's play in chapter 7.

Was the greatest playwright of the period inspired by *Leicester's Commonwealth*? In the next chapter I explore the evidence for such influence in Shakespeare's works.

# Chapter 2

## *Leicester's Commonwealth* as a Shakespeare source

"the purpose of playing, whose end, both at the first and now, was, and is, to hold, as 'twere, the mirror up to nature; to show virtue her own feature, scorn her own image, and the very age and body of the time, his form and pressure."

*Hamlet* (3.2.22)

**History as Metaphor of the Present**

History was used by playwrights from *Gorboduc* (1561) onwards as a safely distanced metaphor through which to examine current political concerns. To complain that Shakespeare is not always historically accurate is to fail to recognise that the purpose of a history play is not to teach, or produce an accurate account, but to use history as a metaphor for the present: to sculpt the material into a shape that mirrors the current situation seen from a once removed position. The playwright and performers are then protected by being able to claim they are only telling an old story (as the actors did when questioned about the performances of *Richard II* on the eve of the Essex rebellion).

One of the avowed intents of *Leicester's Commonwealth* was to warn of the terrible dangers of civil war and draw the reader's attention to parallels between the current situation in 1584 and the Wars of the Roses. It aimed to educate but not for academic reasons: it was above all a political warning. The scholar asks the Lawyer to tell him:

"the ground of these controversies so long now quiet between York and Lancaster, seeing they are now like to be raised again…" (Peck, 148/*99*).

Wilfred Owen knew the catastrophic horror of war. In the preface to his war poems he wrote, "All a poet can do today is warn" (Stallworthy, 1994, 98). Just so, Shakespeare's motivation was not simply to dramatise past events but to draw the audience's attention to the parallel dangers of the present situation. Like *Leicester's Commonwealth* he did so by telling stories, shocking the audience with scandal and murder, amusing them with comic elements, entertaining whilst engaging them in dynastic and constitutional debate.

If *Leicester's Commonwealth* was a source that prompted Shakespeare-Neville to write his plays, which works did it trigger? I believe we can find within it the seeds of the following canonical works:

*Edward III*
*King John*
*Richard II*
*Henry IV*
*Henry V*
*Henry VI*
*Richard III*
*Henry VIII*
*The Rape of Lucrece*
*Julius Caesar*
*Thomas of Woodstock*: I also notice that Thomas of Woodstock is mentioned so the play of that name can also be added to the list (Peck, 160/*106*). I have previously written about this play being an early work by Neville (Casson, 2009, 170 - 190).

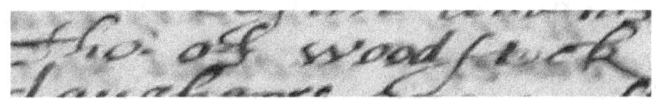

Worsley MSS 47, 48

*Timon of Athens*: Timon is mentioned in the *Addition of the Translator*, (an addendum to the French translation of *Leicester's Commonwealth*) a copy of which is to be found in Worsley MSS 36 (see also Peck, 239/*160*).

In other words the entire history cycle may be traced to the ideas and concerns of *Leicester's Commonwealth*. We may also now appreciate the contemporary political dimensions of *The Rape of Lucrece* and *Julius Caesar*. Examining Worsley MSS 36 and 47, Brenda James proposed that, "these two copies of *Leicester's Commonwealth* were also used by Neville as a source for his history plays" (James & Rubinstein, 2005, 90).

**History as Metaphor in Shakespeare**
The writers of *Leicester's Commonwealth* use history as metaphor for the present time. For example, the Earl of Leicester is described with reference to mythical and historical figures we later find in Shakespeare: "This then

is the Hector, this is the Ajax, appointed for the enterprise when the time shall come. This must be (forsooth) another Richard of Warwick, to gain the crown for Henry IX of the house of York, as the other Richard did put down Henry VI of the house of Lancaster and placed Edward IV, from whom Huntington deriveth his title…" (Peck, 104/*72*).

Worsley MSS 47, 21V

The Earl of Huntington, Henry Hastings, was Leicester's brother-in-law. He was "President of the Council of the North from 1572 until his death in 1595" (Peck, 205/*135*, footnote 95). In *Leicester's Commonwealth* he is seen as having a claim to the throne after Elizabeth's death and he is being promoted as such by the Earl of Leicester. But the authors warn that Leicester's motives may well be suspect, even treacherous. Leicester's relationship with Huntington is seen to echo that between Richard of York and the Duke of Somerset; Richard III and the Duke of Buckingham; Richard Neville, the Earl of Warwick and Edward IV; the Percies and Henry IV (Peck, 131/*89*). Shakespeare dramatises all these relationships in *Henry VI* parts 1 & 2, *Richard III* and *Henry IV* part 1. In *Henry V* a Huntingdon appears as a non-speaking role (5.2.85). This would have been John Holland, son of the Earl of Huntingdon who was executed after an abortive plot to assassinate Henry IV (Craik, 2005, 351). In *Henry V* Huntingdon is paired with the Earl of Warwick, Richard Beauchamp. His daughter, Anne, married Richard Neville who then succeeded to the title and appears as the 'King-Maker' in the *Henry VI* trilogy.

In writing about the immediate aftermath of the Earl of Essex's death the authors of *Leicester's Commonwealth* describe Leicester's "**hasty** snatching up of the widow"…(Peck, 76/*54*). This recalls Richard III's famous seduction of Anne Neville (whose husband he had just killed) in Shakespeare's play. Furthermore Richard later uses the word '**hasty**' when persuading Edward IV's widowed Queen to support his bid to get Elizabeth, their daughter, as his bride (4.4.237). Richard's attempt to marry Elizabeth is mentioned in *Leicester's Commonwealth* (Peck, 133/*90*). This links back to Huntington, whose surname was Hastings, and who is referred to as the "**Hasty** King" in *Leicester's Commonwealth* (Peck 132/*89*, footnote 179) whilst Leicester is called "the **Hasty** Earl" (Peck, 133/*90*).

The name Hastings is used 45 times by Shakespeare: in *Henry VI* part 3, *Richard III* and *Henry IV* part 2. In *Richard III* Hastings is trapped by Richard's duplicity and Catesby eventually presents his decapitated head, calling him a "dangerous and unsuspected" traitor (3.5.20). In *Henry IV* part 2, Westmoreland (Ralph Neville) arrests another Hastings for "high treason", calling him a traitor (4.2.107).

Another incident in *Richard III* is to be found in *Leicester's Commonwealth*:

"Richard of Gloucester had never been able to have usurped as he did if he had not first persuaded King Edward IV to hate his own brother the Duke of Clarence, which Duke stood in the way between Richard and the thing which he most of all things coveted, that is, the possibility to the crown." (Peck, 169/*112*: for a further look at this passage see chapter 5).

In Shakespeare's play we witness how Gloucester manipulates the King into distrusting his brother Clarence, and sanctioning his murder. The murder of the princes in the Tower is also mentioned in *Leicester's Commonwealth* (Peck, 178/*117*).

One incident in *Leicester's Commonwealth* seems to be replayed in *Henry VI* part 2. Supplicants from N. Wales, representatives of the community, came to London to protest to the Queen about Leicester's tyranny. For their "most humble supplication" they were "all taken and cast into prison", publicly humiliated, punished, fined and so ruined (Peck, 120/*82*). In *Henry VI* part 2 a group of petitioners, hoping to speak to Duke Humphrey, the popular Lord Protector, mistakenly offer their petitions to the tyrannical Duke of Suffolk, who, as Leicester was rumoured to be, is the secret lover of the Queen in the play. One of the petitions accuses Suffolk of "**enclosing** the commons", just as Leicester is accused of grabbing land in N. Wales. When Suffolk threatens him, the man replies, "I am but a **poor** petitioner of our whole township" (1.3.25), in other words a representative like the supplicants from Wales. One marginal annotation in the Worsley Manuscript 47 of *Leicester's Commonwealth* reads: "**poore** men resistnige warwicks **inclosure** at North hall were hanged by Leicester comaund" (27V, see appendix 1). Suffolk is then distracted by evidence of treason he can use against his enemy, the Duke of York, (Richard, who married Cecily Neville) and through the Queen's intervention the petitioners are able to escape. Thus we see a Neville ancestor is an enemy of a figure standing in for Leicester. Neville, as we saw in chapter 1, was in dispute with Leicester's brother Ambrose, in 1583, the year before *Leicester's Commonwealth* was published.

The above annotation in Worsley MSS 47 about hanging poor men offers us a window into the subtle influence of *Leicester's Commonwealth* on Shakespeare. The annotation in the printed version is, "Poore men resisting VVarwikes inclosure at North hal were hanged for his **pleasure** by Leycesters authoritie". The Worsley MSS 47 annotator has changed this last word to '**comaund**'. Shakespeare uses '**pleasure**' near '**command**' twice in early works: *Henry VI* part 2 (1.2.45: see below) and *The Two Gentlemen of Verona* (4.3.10). Shakespeare never uses the words the other way round, nor does he use 'authority' near 'pleasure'.

There is another incident in *Henry VI* part 2 which is prefigured in *Leicester's Commonwealth*: Duke Humphrey's ambitious wife, Eleanor, tells her husband about a dream in which she "sat in seat of majesty... in that chair where kings and queens are crowned" (1.2.36). He replies:

> Presumptuous **dame**, ill-nurtured Eleanor,
> Art thou not second woman in the realm,
> And the protector's wife, beloved of him?
> Hast thou not worldly **pleasure** at **command**,
> Above the reach or compass of thy thought?     (1.2.45)

This recalls the incident in *Leicester's Commonwealth* when Anne West said publicly that her sister, **Dame** Lettice, would one day sit on the throne (Peck 128/87). The accompanying marginal annotation in the Worsley manuscripts 36 and 47 is: "An **audatious** & most **undutifull** speach". Shakespeare uses '**undutiful**' in *Henry VI* part 3 (5.5.33) and '**audacious**' 7 times, two of which refer to speech: "audacious eloquence" in *A Midsummer Night's Dream* (5.1.103) and "audacious prate" in *Henry VI* part 1 (4.1.124). I will examine the annotations of the Worsley manuscripts in chapters 3 and 6.

Duke Humphrey, the Lord Protector, is directly analogous to Leicester because Elizabeth I had named Leicester "Protector of the Realm" when she was dangerously ill with smallpox. This then throws light on the following passage from *The First Part of the Contention* (an early version of *Henry VI* part 2) when Suffolk says:

> If our king Henry had shooke hands with death,
> Duke Humphrey then would look to be our King.  (1108)

*Leicester's Commonwealth* expresses the fear that Leicester might seize the throne if Elizabeth died and Leicester is described as a "**crafty fox**" (Peck, 127/*86*). Talking about Humphrey, Suffolk uses this very image in *Henry VI* part 2:

> Madam, 'tis true; and were't not madness, then,
> To make the **fox** surveyor of the fold?
> Who being accused a **crafty** murderer…  (3.1.252)

Leicester is accused in *Leicester's Commonwealth* of being a murderer, even of plotting the Queen's death. In *The First Part of the Contention* and *Henry VI* part 2, outrage is expressed at Suffolk having negotiated away lands in France. A similar outrage to that expressed in *Leicester's Commonwealth* at Leicester, for his peace deal with the French, whereby he arranged for Calais to be handed over. One marginal annotation suggests he received a "bribe for the betraynig of Callis" (Worsley MSS 47, 24), and in the text it is stated that "this man's father before him sold Boulogne to the French by like treachery" (Peck, 111/*76*).

A key theme in *Leicester's Commonwealth* and in early Shakespeare is the danger posed by the monarch's favourites:

"we have examples of sundry princes in all ages and countries whose exorbitant favor to some wicked subject that abused the same hath been the cause of great danger and ruin, the sins of the favorite being returned and revenged upon the favorer" (Peck, 188/*123*).

One of the examples given is of the murder of Humphrey, Duke of Gloucester, by the Duke of Suffolk in Henry VI's reign when,

"Queen Margaret's too much favor and credit (by him not controlled) towards the Marquess of Suffolk that after was made Duke by whose instinct and wicked counsel she made away first the noble Duke of Gloucester" (Peck, 188/*124*).

Margaret and Suffolk are viewed as wicked and dangerous to the King and country: portraits we later see in Shakespeare's *Henry VI* part 2. They are blamed for "all the calamity and extreme desolation which after ensued both to the king, queen, and their only child, with **the utter extirpation of their family**" (Peck, 188/*123-4*; for the significance of my emphasis here see the section on *The Rape of Lucrece* below). We see the annihilation of this royal family in Shakespeare's play where we also witness Suffolk's death as told in *Leicester's Commonwealth*:

"Suffolk… being encountered and taken upon the sea in his passage, he was beheaded in the ship and so received some part of condign punishment for his most wicked, loose, and licentious life." (Peck, 189/*124*).

We can now see that Suffolk, the Queen's secret lover, is analogous to Leicester. It might be objected that Suffolk and Duke Humphrey cannot both equate to Leicester. Shakespeare however did not just look at people as good or bad: he teased out what was good in the bad and flawed in the good. He was also not simply writing an allegory about Leicester but responding to the political issues highlighted in *Leicester's Commonwealth* which had broader implications than the personality of one man.

A central issue of the 'sexed up' *Leicester's Commonwealth* is, as one of the printed marginal annotations emphasises, "The intolerable licentiousnes of Lei(cester's) carnalitie." Shakespeare also focuses on the licentiousness of leaders: Edward III, Edward IV, Richard III, Aaron and Tamora in *Titus Andronicus*, Claudius in *Hamlet*, Anthony and Cleopatra, and Tarquin in *The Rape of Lucrece*. He also burlesques the lecherous Falstaff in *The Merry Wives of Windsor*, tumbling him into a laundry basket. In *Leicester's Commonwealth* the Earl is depicted as seeking to satisfy his lust "in the very laundry itself" (Peck, 89/*62*). Richard I (the Lionheart), seduces Lady Fauconbridge before *The Troublesome Raigne of John King of England* and *King John* begin, with the result that a bastard, Philip, is born to dominate these plays. Fauconbridge was a Neville family name. Philip is knighted and renamed Plantagenet, (thus demonstrating Neville's ancestral connections with the Plantagenet kings). Furthermore in *The Troublesome Raigne* when Philip confronts his mother, she refers to the rape of Lucrece: "The Roman Dame that shed her blood to wash away her shame" (1.405). When he later revised the play Shakespeare-Neville cut this reference but simultaneously revealed the political significance of the Lucrece story by having the King of France accuse King John of committing "a rape upon the maiden virtue of the crown" (2.1.97). John's tyrannous usurpation is used as a metaphoric warning in *Leicester's Commonwealth* (see below).

## *The Rape of Lucrece*

In *Leicester's Commonwealth* there is an implicit reference to the aftermath of the rape of Lucrece. In complaining about Leicester's intolerable sexual appetite "upon men's wives" the writers refer back to historic examples of how previous times have punished such behaviour: "offences…were extremely punished in princes themselves, and that not only in the person delinquent alone, but also by **extirpation of the whole family** for his sake, as appeareth in the example **of the Tarquinians** among the Romans" (Peck, 87/*61*).

The underlying political meaning of *The Rape of Lucrece* is revealed in the final section of Shakespeare's opening argument:

"They came, the one accompanied with Junius Brutus, the other with Publius Valerius; and finding Lucrece attired in mourning habit, demanded the cause of her sorrow. She, first taking an oath of them for her revenge, revealed the actor, and whole manner of his dealing, and withal suddenly stabbed herself. Which done, with one consent they all vowed to **root out the whole hated[4] family of the Tarquins**; and bearing the dead body to Rome, Brutus acquainted the people with the doer and manner of the vile deed, with a bitter invective against the tyranny of the king: wherewith the people were so moved, that with one consent and a general acclamation the Tarquins were all exiled, and the state government changed from kings to consuls."

This last sentence hints at a political, even anti-monarchy, stance. Indeed the issue of electing kings is touched on in *Edmund Ironside*, *The Troublesome Raigne*, *Titus Andronicus*, *Henry VI* part 1, *Julius Caesar* and *Pericles* (see below).

In *Julius Caesar* Cassius refers back to Lucius Junius Brutus who expelled the Tarquins after the rape of Lucrece, when he is trying to enlist Brutus in the conspiracy against Caesar (1.2.158) and later Brutus himself says:

> My ancestors did from the streets of Rome

---

4     The addition here of the word '**hated**' also may derive from *Leicester's Commonwealth* as the Earl is described as '**hated**', one marginal annotation saying he was "extremly **hated**".

>    The Tarquin drive, when he was call'd a king.    (2.1. 53)

We can therefore see that the rape of Lucrece is directly linked with politics and the possibility of a coup d'état. As Tarquin enters Lucrece's bedroom his eyes' "high treason" misleads "his heart, which gives the **watch-word** his hand full soon to draw the cloud that hides the **silver moon**"…(369). Shakespeare and his contemporaries referred to Elizabeth I as Cynthia/Diana, the moon. The reference here to the moon suggests a possible identification of Lucrece with Elizabeth I. Is rapacious Tarquin then modelled on the image of Leicester? In *Leicester's Commonwealth* a coded '**watchword**' is revealed whereby the conspirators would identify their allies when it was time for the coup d'état. According to a marginal annotations it was "**Are you settled**?" Preparing to murder King Duncan, Macbeth declares,

>    **I am settled**, and bend up
> Each corporal agent to this terrible feat.    (1.7.80)

Macbeth moves towards his regicide "with **Tarquin's** ravishing strides" (2.1.56).

In *The Rape of Lucrece* we read:

>    Were Tarquin Night, as he is but Night's child,
>    The **silver-shining queen** he would disdain;
>    Her twinkling **handmaids** too, by him defiled…    (785)

Again, the "**silver-shining queen**" = the moon = Elizabeth I. Tarquin's interest in handmaids may be explained with reference to *Leicester's Commonwealth* in which the Earl is accused of being a sexual predator and offering "the waiting gentlewomen of her Majesty's Great Chamber… three hundred pounds for a night" (Peck, 88/*62*). Just after the Scholar's mention of the Tarquinians in *Leicester's Commonwealth*, the Gentleman says of Leicester:

"No man's wife can be free from him, whom his fiery lust liketh to abuse, nor husbands able to resist nor save from his violence if they show dislike or will not to yield their consent to his doings" (Peck 89/*62*).

Shakespeare's play *Edward III* dramatises the lustful attempt on a wife's virtue by the King. In doing so the playwright refers directly to the rape of Lucrece (2.2.193) contrasting the heroic refusal of a "true English lady" with the fate of Tarquin's victim. This heroic wife is the Countess of Salisbury. In the play she is the daughter of the Earl of Warwick. She names her cousin as Montague, he calls her 'aunt'. These unhistorical names all point to the Neville family: "a century later… Alice Montague married Richard Neville; their son Richard, by marrying Anne Beauchamp, secured the title of the Earl of Warwick, and appears as 'king-maker' in" *Henry VI parts 2 & 3* (Melchiori, 2001, 57).

Lucrece has a long tirade against Night, **Opportunity** and **Time**. In *Leicester's Commonwealth*, in a discussion of treason, the words, " **time**, ability, or **opportunity**" (Peck, 68/*50*) occur and later: "ability, **time**, will and **opportunity**" (Peck, 70/*51*).

Leicester's grandfather Edmund is described as a '**copesman**' (Peck, 111/*76*). I had previously noted that the word '**copesmate**' was used in *The Rape of Lucrece* and *The Tragedy of Arden of Faversham*, the latter containing at least one reference to *Leicester's Commonwealth* (Casson, 2009, see also chapter 7).

The Tarquins and the rape of Lucrece are referred to in the following works:
*Leicester's Commonwealth* written 1583-84 (published anonymously 1584)
*The Troublesome Raigne of John* 1587-9 (published anonymously 1591)
*Titus Andronicus* 1592-3 (published anonymously 1594)
*Edward III* 1592-3 (published anonymously 1596)
*The Rape of Lucrece* 1593 (published as by 'William Shakespeare' 1594)
*Julius Caesar* 1599 (published in the First Folio, 1623)

### *Titus Andronicus*
Dated about 1592-3 *Titus Andronicus* predates *The Rape of Lucrece* but is clearly linked to it, as not only is Lavinia raped, but also Lucrece and Tarquin are mentioned in the play and the name Lucius is to be found in both, as a surviving avenger.
There are discernable links between *Leicester's Commonwealth* and *Titus Andronicus*. When Titus sends letters complaining of his sufferings, Saturninus, the tyrannical ruler of Rome, complains that these are "libelling against the senate and blazoning our injustice everywhere" (4.4.17). The

Queen's Proclamation against *Leicester's Commonwealth* (which is in the form of a letter) labelled it a libel.

It has been suggested that Queen Tamora's lover, Aaron, the Moor, might represent Leicester (who was nicknamed "the gypsy" because of his dark looks). In *Leicester's Commonwealth* the Gentleman speaks of how dangerous it was for courtiers who witness Leicester's "errors or misdeeds... for if it had been but only suspected that they had seen such a thing, it would have been as dangerous unto them as it was to **Acteon** to have seen **Diana** and her maidens naked; whose case is so common now in England as nothing more, and so do the examples of divers well declare, whose unfortunate knowledge of too many secrets brought them quickly to unfortunate ends" (Peck, 100/*69*).

In one speech Tamora says:

> Had I the power that some say **Dian** had,
> Thy temples should be planted presently
> With horns, as was **Actaeon**'s; and the hounds
> Should drive upon thy new-transformed limbs,
> Unmannerly intruder as thou art! (2.2.61)

Whilst this image might be considered a commonplace, I note that a number of words are used in both *Leicester's Commonwealth* and *Titus Andronicus* such as 'commonwealth', 'opportunity', 'tyrant', 'election', 'title', 'pretend' 'faction', 'dangerous', 'discontent', 'detested', 'ingratitude', 'bear-whelp', 'conspirator', 'competitor', 'controlment', 'banquet' and 'trenches'. 'Bear-whelp' occurs twice in *Leicester's Commonwealth* including a specific identification of "my Lord of Leicester (whom you call the Bearwhelp)" (Peck, 2006, 61). Richard III, (who married Anne Neville), calls himself, "an unlicked bear-whelp" in *Henry VI* part 3 (3.2.161). I also note "stop the mouths" is found in *Leicester's Commonwealth* (Peck, 87/61) and "stop their mouths" twice in *Titus Andronicus* (5.2.161,167) in the same scene as 'banquet' and 'trenches'. Shakespeare only uses 'tattle' once: in *Titus Andronicus* (4.2.170); the word 'tattled' is used in *Leicester's Commonwealth* (Peck, 75/54). Whilst this list is not exhaustive it is perhaps long enough to suggest *Leicester's Commonwealth* may have been a source for *Titus Andronicus*. Bate (2006, 21) wondered whether *Titus Andronicus* "may be shot through with an unexpected vein of republicanism." Hadfield (2005) confirmed this and demonstrated the continuity between *The Rape* of *Lucrece* and *Titus Andronicus* in which he saw Shakespeare exploring republican politics. This critical exploration continues in *Julius Caesar*.

## *Julius Caesar*

The play *Julius Caesar* can now be seen to be a warning to both Elizabeth I and Robert Devereux, the Earl of Essex, (the favourite who followed in Leicester's footsteps, who was indeed his step son). To the Queen it could be seen as a warning not to trust a man who was a friend, honourable but dangerously close; to the Earl it was a warning that assassination would lead to civil war. However worthy the aim, the end would not justify the means. In referring to Julius Caesar, *Leicester's Commonwealth* specifically states he was warned of his impending assassination:

"We know that the forenamed Emperor Caesar had not only the warning given him of the inclination and intent of Brutus to usurpation, but even the very day when he was going towards the place of his appointed destiny, there was given up into his hands a detection of the whole treason with request to read the same presently, which he upon **confidence** omitted to do" (Peck, 180/*119*).

These warnings are of course in Shakespeare's play when Calphurnia, the Soothsayer and Artemidorus attempt to warn Caesar of the conspiracy against him. When Caesar boldly brushes off Calphurnia's concern, she replies, "Your wisdom is consumed in **confidence**" (2.2.49). One of the annotations in the margin of the Worsley MSS 47 copy of *Leicester's Commonwealth* reads, "To much **confidence** verie perilous in a Prnice. This was the distruction of Julius Cesar by Marc: Brutus" (58). This refers to the following passage in the text:

"It may be that her Majesty is brought into the same opinion of my Lord of Huntingdon's fidelity as Julius Caesar was of Marcus Brutus, his dearest obliged friend, of whose ambitious practices and aspiring when Caesar was advertised by his careful friends, he answered that he well knew Brutus to be ambitious; but I am sure (quoth he) that my Brutus will never attempt anything for the Empire while Caesar liveth, and after my death let him shift for the same among others as he can. But what ensued? Surely I am loth to tell the event, for omination's sake, but yet all the world knoweth that ere many months passed this most noble and clement emperor was pitifully murdered by the same Brutus and his partners in the public Senate when least of all he expected such treason. **So dangerous a thing it is to be secure** in a matter of so great sequel, or to trust them with a man's life who may pretend preferment or interest by his death" (Peck, 179/*118*).

In *Julius Caesar* we find "**security** gives way to conspiracy" (2.3.7)[5]. The ironic aspect of the warning the play offered was that, "ere many months passed" after the first performances of *Julius Caesar*, the Essex Rebellion led not to Elizabeth's but to Devereux's death and to Henry Neville's imprisonment in the Tower. We can clearly see the warning of the danger of civil war in the play and the tract: the authors of *Leicester's Commonwealth* explicitly link the Roman experience of civil war with the threat to the security and peace of the contemporary English state, as they tell of the:

"Romans who received notable damages and destruction also in the end by their divisions and factions among themselves, and specially from them of their own cities and countries who upon factions lived abroad with foreigners and thereby were always as firebrands to carry home the flame of war upon their country." (Peck, 183/*121*)

This passage effectively describes Shakespeare's plays, *Titus Andronicus, Coriolanus, Anthony and Cleopatra* and *Julius Caesar*.
In *Julius Caesar* I find the following significant words that occur in *Leicester's Commonwealth*: 'ambition', 'tyrant', 'ingratitude', 'commonwealth', 'conference', 'ancestors', 'dangerous', 'monstrous', 'imminent', 'faction', 'conspirator', 'testament'. This list is shorter than that of *Titus Andronicus* but nevertheless points to a possible relationship between the texts. In the next chapter I will present further links between Shakespeare's *Julius Caesar* and *Leicester's Commonwealth*.
One detail omitted from *Julius Caesar* is that Brutus was rumoured to be Caesar's illegitimate son. In *Henry VI* part 2 Suffolk, going to his death, says, "Brutus' bastard hand stabbed Julius Caesar" (4.1.137). The illegitimate Henry Neville created two great roles for bastards, in *King John* and *King Lear*, both of which have connections with *Leicester's Commonwealth* (see below and chapter 3).

### *King John* and *The Troublesome Raigne*
The story of *King John* and that of *The Troublesome Raigne of John King*

---

[5] See chapter 7 for a further connection between this quotation, *Leicester's Commonwealth* and Shakespeare-Neville.

*of England* is to be found in *Leicester's Commonwealth*.
"Arthur… was declared by King Richard his uncle… lawful heir apparent to the crown of England… albeit after King Richard's death his other uncle John most tyrannously took both his kingdom and his life" (Peck, 160/*107*).

The plays are about the dangers and damage done to the country when the wrong person inherits or usurps the crown and therefore dramatise the forbidden topic of the succession, a core concern of *Leicester's Commonwealth*. Whilst fighting for John's right to succeed his brother, Richard I, Eleanor (the Queen mother) reveals she has a will that expresses Richard's wishes for the succession. In *The Troublesome Raigne* Arthur and his mother Constance repudiate this testament, suggesting it is a forgery by Elinor and not valid. We find just such an argument over Henry VIII's will in *Leicester's Commonwealth*. Indeed one of the signatories of that disputed testament was none other than Sir Henry Neville (Neville's father). This reference to Henry VIII's will is in a discussion about foreign birth being a bar to succession. The authors state that "Arthur… was declared … lawful heir apparent… though he were born in Bretaigne out of English allegiance" (Peck, 160/*107*).
This link between *The Troublesome Raigne* and *Leicester's Commonwealth* may even help in dating the play if John stands in for Leicester and Arthur for young James of Scotland, whose "foreign birth" was a topic discussed in *Leicester's Commonwealth*. Arthur's life is threatened by the tyrannical King John. In *Leicester's Commonwealth* the threat to James' life is made explicit:

"I think the youth of Scotland be of much more importance for their purpose to be made away, both for that he may have issue and is like in time to be of more ability for defense of his own inheritance, as also for that he being once dispatched his mother should soon ensue by one sleight or other" (Peck, 178/*118*).
In *King John* Eleanor says the will "**bars** the title of" Arthur. In *The Troublesome Raigne* Elinor says the will "**barres** the way…" In *Leicester's Commonwealth* the writers use the word '**bars**' in discussing the impediments to the succession of the Queen of Scots and her son, of which Henry VIII's will was one (Peck 154/*103*). As the threat of Leicester usurping the throne ceased after his death in 1588 the play may well have been written 1587-8 (it was published 1591).

*Leicester's Commonwealth* warns of the Earl's skills (aided by several doctors) as a poisoner. This could explain the young Shakespeare's interest in poisons, which is dramatically realised when a monk poisons King John (seen on stage in *The Troublesome Raigne*, but only reported in the revised *King John*).

In *Leicester's Commonwealth* an attempt to hide the birth of an illegitimate child of Lady Sheffield is described:

"the good wife of the castle also (whereby Leicester's appointed gossips might without other suspicion have access to the place) should feign herself to be with child, and after long and sore travail (God wot) to be delivered of a cushion (as she was indeed), and a little after a fair coffin was buried with a **bundle of clouts in show of a child**"… (Peck, 90/*63*).

In *King John* the grief stricken Constance says:

> If I were mad, I should forget my son,
> Or madly think **a babe of clouts** were he.   (3.3.56)

In the annotations of the Worsley MSS 47 copy of *Leicester's Commonwealth* there is special attention paid to the illegitimate son of Lady Sheffield (see chapter 3).

## *Hamlet*

In *Leicester's Commonwealth*, when the Earl of Essex is said to have been poisoned (he may have died of dysentery) a woman, Alice Draycot, is poisoned by drinking from his cup. Essex says to her, "Ah poor Alice, the cup was not prepared for thee, albeit it were thy hard destiny to taste thereof" (Peck, 83/*59*). This recalls Gertrude's death in *Hamlet*, a play which other scholars have suggested has some relationship with Essex's death. Leicester was believed to have poisoned Essex and indeed married his widow, just as Claudius does (James & Rubinstein, 2005, 150). Now we know that Neville was a supporter of the Earl of Essex (the old Earl's son and Leicester's step son) and was sent to the Tower after the Essex rebellion we can see the connection between *Hamlet* and the two Earls of Essex (James, 2008, 84, 338, 345).

## Metaphors and Imagery

In reading *Leicester's Commonwealth* at the very start of his career, Shakespeare-Neville found a document that used metaphors and imagery that he himself was later to use in his writings. Many nature images are used and these are often comparable to the bard's. We find tree imagery used in *Leicester's Commonwealth*:

"when they have **cropped** all they can from the **tree** left them by their father Edmund (I mean the race of King Henry VII), then will they pluck up the stem itself by the **roots** as unprofitable and pitch in his place another trunk (that is, the line of Huntingdon) that may begin to feed anew with fresh **fruits** again and so for a time content their appetites" (Peck, 114/78).

Shakespeare uses many tree images. In *Henry VI* part 3 (1589-91) Margaret cries, "How sweet a plant have you untimely **cropped**" (5.5.62) when her son is stabbed to death in front of her. In *Edward III* (1592-3) the young Black Prince presents:

>This sacrifice, this first **fruit** of my sword,
>**Cropped** and **cut** down even at the gate of death… (3.5.84)

In *Locrine*, which I have identified as an early play by the bard, dating it to 1586-89, the young King brags that he:

>rippeth up the **roots** with razours keen:
>So Locrine with his mighty curtleaxe
>Hath **cropped off the heads** of all thy Huns… (4.2.21)

In *Edmund Ironside*, another early play (1588), Canutus says:

>A traitor may be likened to a **tree**,
>Which being shred and topped when it is green,
>Doth for one twig which from the same was cut
>Yield twenty arms, yea twenty arms for one,
>But being hacked and mangled with an axe,
>The **root** dies and piecemeal rots away.
>Even so with traitors. **Cut me off their heads**,
>Still more out of the self-same stock will sprout… (2.3.41)

In *Richard II* (1595) a Gardener instructs two servants:

> Go thou, and like an executioner,
> **Cut off the heads** of too fast growing sprays,
> That look too lofty in our **commonwealth**:
> All must be even in our government.
> You thus employ'd, I will go **root away**
> The noisome weeds…         (3.4.33)

In *Henry VI* part 3 (1589-91) King Edward says:

> Brave followers, yonder stands the thorny **wood**,
> Which, by the heavens' assistance and your strength,
> Must by the **roots** be **hewn** up yet ere night.   (5.4.67)

Lucius, using another implicit tree image, says in *Titus Andronicus*:

> And with our swords, upon a pile of **wood**,
> Let's **hew** his limbs till they be **clean** consumed.   (1.1.132)

In *The Troublesome Raigne* Essex plans, "To **roote** and **cleane extirpate** tirant John" (11.42, Sider 134). We have already seen the word '**extirpation**' is used in *Leicester's Commonwealth* (Peck, 87/*61*). James (2008, 247) pointed out that Shakespeare and Neville (in his letters) both use the word '**clean**' in this sense of 'absolutely'.

In *Richard II* the Gardener, using the garden as a metaphor for the kingdom, tells us that:

>               Bolingbroke
> Hath seized the wasteful king. O, what pity is it
> That he had not so **trimm'd** and dress'd his land
> As we this garden! We at time of year
> Do wound the bark, the skin of our **fruit-trees**,
> Lest, being over-proud in sap and blood,
> With too much riches it confound itself:
> Had he done so to great and growing men,
> They might have lived to bear and he to taste
> Their **fruits** of duty: superfluous branches

> We **lop away**, that bearing boughs may live:
> Had he done so, himself had borne the crown,
> Which waste of idle hours hath quite thrown down. (3.4.54)

In *Leicester's Commonwealth* we find: "Consider the **fruit** of the garden, and thereby you may judge the gardener's diligence" (Peck, 115/*79*). Neville, a forester, knew about trees. In a letter dated 19/11/1599 Neville wrote "**cutt off the Roote** and Foundation of all true Friendship" (Winwood, 1725, Vol 1, 130).

On the very next page there is a river simile: "For as a great and violent **river**, the **more** it is **stopped** or contraried, the **more** it riseth and **swelleth** big and in the end dejecteth with **more** force the thing that made resistance…" (Peck, 117/*80*). We can compare this to two images in *Venus and Adonis*:

> Rain added to a **river** that is rank
> Perforce will force it overflow the bank. (71)

> An oven that is **stopp'd**, or **river** stay'd,
> Burneth **more** hotly, **swelleth** with **more** rage:
> So of concealed sorrow may be said… (331)

The repeated 'more' is used often by Shakespeare.
The bard uses falconry as a source of metaphors. In *Leicester's Commonwealth* I find: "the great falcons of the field (I mean the favourites of the time) fail whereon to feed…" (Peck, 72/*52*). In *Henry VI* part 2 the king uses this metaphor for ambitious men:

> But what a point, my lord, your **falcon** made,
> And what a pitch she flew above the rest!
> To see how God in all his creatures works!
> Yea, man and birds are fain of climbing high. (2.1.5)

In *The Taming of The Shrew* Petruchio starves Kate in order to tame her:

> My **falcon** now is sharp and passing empty;
> And till she stoop she must not be full-gorged,
> For then she never looks upon her lure. (4.1.177)

The well-fed falcons of *Leicester's Commonwealth* are out of control and a danger to "the peace and unity of the state" (Peck, 72/*52*).

The writers of *Leicester's Commonwealth* use war imagery to describe how Leicester has gathered and reinforced his power: "His cunning in plotting and fortifying the same, both by **force and fraud**, by **mines** and **countermines**, by **trenches, bulwarks**…" (Peck, 123/*84*). In *Henry VI* part 3 Queen Elizabeth uses the words, "**force and fraud**" (4.4.33) in describing the danger she faces in the civil war. In *Henry V* Fluellen speaks of '**mines**' and '**countermines**' (3.2.57,62). Shakespeare also uses '**trenches**' and '**bulwarks**' in metaphors. The second sonnet opens with:

> When forty winters shall besiege thy brow
> And dig deep **trenches** in thy beauty's field…

In *Titus Andronicus* I find:

> Witness these **trenches** made by grief and care…   (5.2.23)

In the copy of Halle's *Chronicle* believed to have been annotated by Shakespeare, the word '**trenches**' occurs in one annotation (f.xxv[a], Keen & Lubbock, 1954, 143, see chapter 4).
In *Richard III* Richmond says:
> The prayers of holy saints and wronged souls,
> Like high-rear'd **bulwarks**, stand before our faces…   (5.4.220)

Perhaps the clearest example of the metaphors transferred from *Leicester's Commonwealth* into Shakespeare, apart from the bear and boar imagery I have previously written about (Casson, 2009, see Appendix 7), is when Leicester is likened to Judas who, "with a courteous kiss", betrayed Jesus (Peck, 172/*114*). This image is repeated again in the 1585 *Addition of the Translator* where Leicester is described as "with all kind deceits, dissembling, lying, and flattering, showing so good a countenance to Monsieur as **Judas** did when he **kissed his master**…" (Peck, 232/*156*).
 In *Henry VI* part 3, Gloucester, kissing the baby Prince Edward, has an aside, "so **Judas kiss'd his master**," (5.7.33). This echo of the *Addition* to *Leicester's Commonwealth* in *Henry VI* part 3 might be considered coincidence, an accident of language, were it not for the fact that on the

very next page of the *Addition* we find Leicester compared with **Catiline**. In *Edward III* I find:

> England was wont to harbour **malcontents**,
> **Bloodthirsty** and seditious **Catilines**… (3.1.13)

In *Leicester's Commonwealth* the Earl is called a '**malcontent**' (Peck, 76/*55*) and "Captain **Catiline**" (Peck, 185/*122*). In *The True Tragedy of Richard Duke of York* (an early version of *Henry VI* part 3) we find Gloucester, saying, "I can… set the **aspiring Catilin** to school" (3.2.193). The word '**aspiring**' is used in *Leicester's Commonwealth*. In the later Folio version of *Henry VI* part 3 this line is changed to: "I can… set the murderous Machiavel to school" (3.2.193). Machiavel is also referred to in *Leicester's Commonwealth*. In *Edmund Ironside* Alfric accuses Edricus (who may be a Leicester figure) of being "like **Judas** to betray his lord into the hands of **bloodthirsty** Danes" (5.1.10). In *Leicester's Commonwealth* we find Judas betraying Jesus to those "whom he well knew to **thirst** after his **blood**" (Peck, 172/*114*). In *Henry VI* part 1 Warwick (Richard Neville) calls for peace between court factions "except ye **thirst** for **blood**" (3.1.117). Earlier in this scene the King had warned that "Civil **dissension** … gnaws the bowels of the **commonwealth**" (3.1.72). In *Leicester's Commonwealth* Sir Christopher Hatton is quoted as warning of "what **dissension**, what **bloodshed** had ensued" if Elizabeth were to be assassinated (Peck 140/*94*).

In *Leicester's Commonwealth* wolves are a metaphor for rebels. A printed marginal note states: "The comparison of vvolues & Rebels." The annotator of Worsley MSS 47 renders this as, "wolves & Rebells howe alike".

Worsley MSS 47, 58V

In *Leicester's Commonwealth* the image of wolves is introduced thus:

"…these men deal as **wolves** by nature in other countries are wont to do, which going together in great numbers to assail **a flock of sheep** by night" (Peck, 181/*119*).

In 2006 Michael Egan showed that the play *Thomas of Woodstock* was indeed by Shakespeare and I then demonstrated the links between it and Neville (Casson, 2009). In the play Woodstock's wife has a dream:

> Methoughts as you were ranging through the woods
> An angry lion with a herd of **wolves**
> Had in an instant round encompassed you;
> When to your rescue, against the course of kind,
> **A flock of** silly **sheep** made head against them,
> Bleating for help, against whom the forest King
> Roused up his strength, and slew both you and them. (4.2.20)

Thomas interprets the dream:

> Where I compared the state (as now it stands,
> Meaning King Richard and his harmful flatterers)
> Unto a savage herd of ravening **wolves**,
> The commons to **a flock of** silly **sheep**
> Who, whilst their slothful shepherd careless stood,
> Those forest thieves broke in, and **sucked their blood**. (4.2.31)

In *Julius Caesar* Cassius says:

> And why should Caesar be a tyrant then?
> Poor man, I know he would not be a **wolf**
> But that he sees the Romans are but **sheep**. (1.3.103)

In *Henry VI* part 3 a Neville is named before wolves are mentioned.

> Stern **Falconbridge** commands the narrow seas;
> The duke is made protector of the realm;
> And yet shalt thou be safe? Such safety finds
> The trembling **lamb** environed with **wolves**. (1.1.241)

This Falconbridge is Thomas, Bastard of Fauconberg, an illegitimate son of

William Neville, Lord Fauconberg and Earl of Kent.
**Alliteration**
The writers of *Leicester's Commonwealth* often use alliteration. For example:

1) "of Court, Council and country without controlment,"(Peck, 73/*53*);
2) "the tempest of men's tongues, which tattled busily at that time…" (Peck, 75/*54*);
3) "plot, practice, and pretend" (Peck, 126/*85*);
4) "daily more deep, dangerous, and desperate…" (Peck, 79/*56*).

We can hear echoes of these in Shakespeare:

1) "The body of the **country**, city, **court**" (*As You Like It*, 2.1.59);
2) "you must be tittle-**tattling** before all our guests? **'tis** well they are whispering: clamour your **tongues**" (*Winter's Tale*, 4.4.245);
3) "To thy suggestion, **plot**, and damned **practise**" (*King Lear*, 2.1.72);
4) "I will unclasp a secret book, And to your quick-conceiving discontents I'll read you matter **deep** and **dangerous**" (*Henry IV* part 1, 1.3.186).

Whilst these may be just coincidence the last one is especially suggestive of *Leicester's Commonwealth*.

**Political Thinking: *Leicester's Commonwealth* and Shakespeare**
*Leicester's Commonwealth* expresses real fears of the dangerous influence of over-powerful favourites, tyranny, usurpation and civil war. It recalls that Henry VII and Henry VIII both withdrew their favour "from certain subjects of high estate" (Peck, 74/*53*). Shakespeare's plays show the fall of many such men from royal favour. From the early histories to *Henry VIII* we witness their falls from grace, imprisonment, trials, executions and murders. *Leicester's Commonwealth* ends with the hope that Leicester will be brought to trial. The over riding concern however is the succession to the throne. *Leicester's Commonwealth* traces the origin of the contention between the houses of York and Lancaster to "the issue of Edward III", namely the descendants of John of Gaunt (Peck 148/*99*). In his history plays Shakespeare brings together elements found in *Leicester's Commonwealth* with members of the Neville family (who could claim descent from John of Gaunt and Edward III). When we recognise *Leicester's Commonwealth* as a Shakespeare source and Neville as the hidden writer this synthesis makes complete sense.

In response to the central question of "Who will be the next monarch?" the authors of *Leicester's Commonwealth* mainly stick with the hereditary principle and try to work out who is the most qualified person by lineal descent. However, commenting on the administration of justice, the Gentleman says:

"Truly, it should not, for to that end were princes first **elected**, and upon that consideration do subjects pay them both tribute and obedience: to be defended by them from injuries and oppressions, and to see laws executed and justice exercised upon and towards all men with indifferency." (Peck, 190/*125*)

Worsley MSS 47, 63[6]

From the very earliest history plays a central theme is how the King gains the throne, by hereditary right, conquest, usurpation or the people's choice. Indeed the words 'elected' and 'election' are used:

At the start of *Edmund Ironside* the Archbishop of Canterbury states:

> The clergy and the rest
> That have for public profit of the realm
> For peace, for quiet and utility
> **Elected** prince Canutus for our king…           (1.1.27)

However this is a disputed election, like that at the start of *Titus Andronicus*, and the threat of civil war is never far away. In *The Troublesome Raigne* the Bastard tells the beleaguered John, "the nobles have **elected** Lewes King" (10.75, Sider, 112). King John then criticises the nobles because they have chosen to "**elect** a forren king" (10.130, Sider, 125). These words do not

---

[6]   The writer makes two errors in copying, deleting "doe" and repeating 'Princes'.

appear in the revised *King John*.

*Titus Andronicus* begins with an election of the Roman emperor: in the first scene the word '**election**' is used three times (1.1.16, 22, 185). The disaster is that Titus, a soldier rather than a politician, refuses the people's choice and suggests they '**elect**' Saturnine (1.1.232). Hamlet also talks about the '**election**' of the monarch, using the word twice (5.2.65, 360). Coriolanus is reluctantly involved in an '**election**' (2.3.215, 224). In *Pericles* when the King is absent for years the Lords offer the crown to Helicanus if the King cannot be found. One says:

> If in his grave he rest, we'll find him there;
> And be resolved he lives to govern us,
> Or dead, give's cause to mourn his funeral,
> And leave us to our free **election**.   (2.4.30-34)

In other words Shakespeare follows through the constitutional concerns in *Leicester's Commonwealth* but goes further, and begins to explore the possible consequences of electing a King. This is not of course an election in modern terms with universal suffrage. However it does introduce the idea of choice rather than divine right or the hereditary principle. This interest in the election of those who have power in the realm is further evident in the annotated Halle's *Chronicle* where the annotator has highlighted one item (with #) in a list of charges against Richard II:

Halle's *Chronicle*, f.viii

# 19 Item at the sommons of the Parliament when knightes and burgesses should be **electe** that the **election** had bene full proceded, he put out diuers persons **elected**, & put in other in their places to serue his wyll and appetite.

Furthermore the annotator of Halle's *Chronicle* made a note, "5 article they complayne ageyinste Knightes of th(e) parliament **electyd**" (Henry IV fxxii[b], Keen & Lubbock, 1954, 130). Thus the highlight # and this annotation both draw attention to the issue of **elections** being contested. I will examine the relationship between the annotated Halle's *Chronicle* and the Worsley MSS 47 annotated copy of *Leicester's Commonwealth* in chapter 4 and appendix 3.

When we realise Shakespeare is Neville, a member of parliament and a politician, we are more able to appreciate the political ideas implicit in the plays. Recognising *Leicester's Commonwealth* as a source for Shakespeare-Neville's works illuminates the bard's political motivation: he is not just creating an illustrated history of England but a vivid political debate about the state of the nation. Hadfield (2005, 53) confirmed this: "Shakespeare… more than any of his contemporary playwrights, was especially interested in how political institutions functioned, who they represented, and how individuals came to occupy offices of state."

James suggested that Neville, having studied *Leicester's Commonwealth*, (as well as Halle and Holinshed), was determined to prevent civil war "ever breaking out again. With theatres being the only thing approaching mass media at the time, they were an obvious way to influence the population to reject any arguments over dynasties that might break out in a repeat of the bad old days" (James & Rubinstein, 2005, 90).

# Chapter 3

## The Annotations of Worsley MSS 47

"paper writ o'both sides the leaf, margin and all…"

*Love's Labour's Lost* (5.2.8)

**The date of the annotations**

The 1584 printed version of *Leicester's Commonwealth* has annotations, or marginal subheadings, pertaining to the text. These differ from the annotations in the reprinted 1641 edition, which modernises the spelling and cuts a few of these marginalia. The Worsley Manuscripts 36 and 47 are clearly based on the 1584 version. Indeed the Worsley MSS 47 *Leicester's Commonwealth* is followed by a text dated 15th August 1613 so it must predate the 1641 version. It would make little sense to go to the trouble of copying and annotating *Leicester's Commonwealth* after Leicester's death in 1588, therefore these copies were probably made between 1584 - 1588. Given the political sensitivity and topicality they are more likely to have been made earlier in this period. I therefore suggest they were made between autumn 1584 and summer 1586. The manuscripts do not use the title '*Leicester's Commonwealth*'; instead they use the full title beginning "*The Copy of a letter written by a Master of Arts of Cambridge to his friend in London.*" The title '*Leicester's Commonwealth*' seems to have been applied as shorthand for this from about September 1586 when Hugh Davies referred to it as "the Earl of Leicester his Common Wealth" (Peck, 1985, 5). On the front page of the Northumberland Manuscript, which belonged to Neville and has been dated to 1596, it is listed as *Leycesters Common Wealth*.

Northumberland Manuscript

One of the annotations in Worsley MSS 47 (about Robert, or Robin, Dudley, an illegitimate son of Leicester and Lady Douglass Sheffield, see below) provides good evidence for dating the Worsley annotations to 1584-6.

I have designated the two annotators of the Worsley Manuscripts 36 and 47, A & B, respectively. The vast majority of the annotations of the Northumberland Manuscript copy of *Leicester's Commonwealth* are lost, either through fire damage or through the trimming of the edges of the pages: occasionally it is possible to make out single last letters that the trimmer left on the edge of the text. Of those that do survive a number are fragmentary, illegible or in poor condition (see appendix 2). I designate this annotator as C. I explore the relationship between A, B, and C in chapter 6.

**Who were A & B?**
It may be that these writers were scribes working to their employers' instructions. However there is some evidence that suggests they were themselves Nevilles. One of the printed annotations states:

"The vvords of Sir Thomas Layton brother in Lawe to my Lord."

A identifies this Lord:

"The words of S$^r$ Tho: Leighton Leyc: brother in law to S$^r$ Hen: Nevill"

B makes this:

"The words of S$^r$ Tho: Layton brother in law to my Lord of Leyc: to S$^r$ Henr: Nevill."

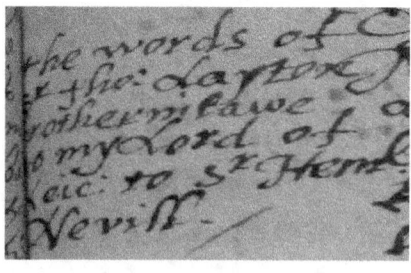

Worsley MSS 47, 32

This would be Neville's father who was also called Sir Henry Neville. In Worsley MSS 47, B's document, after the copy of *Leicester's Commonwealth*, there is a record of a discussion between the Archbishop of Canterbury and King James about the divorce of Frances Howard and Robert Devereux, the young 3rd Earl of Essex, dated 15/7/1613. In a letter written just one month earlier, on 18/6/1613, Neville mentioned this divorce (Winwood, 1725, Vol 3, 463). Indeed there is another extant letter written on 16/7/1613[7], the day after he wrote the notes in Worsley MSS 47 on the Essex divorce. Furthermore we can compare the way Annotator B writes the name Henr: Nevill (see above) with his signature with on a letter from 1601. We can see that the double 'll' is similar to the way 'Nevill' is written in Worsley MSS47.

Neville signature, 1601

I therefore agree with Brenda James who first suggested Annotator B was none other than Henry Neville (James & Rubinstein, 2005, 89).

**Annotator A: Worsley MSS 36**
Annotator A is careful, neat, copies accurately and spells in a modern way. S/he notes women's roles and William Killigrew. I hypothesise that A was Anne (née Killigrew), Neville's wife. William was her uncle. William Killigrew's son, Robert, was a friend of Henry and Anne Neville and lived with them at Lothbury. He owned a copy of Shakespeare's second sonnet, now in the British Library, Sloane MSS 1792 (James, 2008, 266). Robert's son, Thomas Killigrew, became a playwright. In 1669 a royal warrant gave the King's players, the company established by Thomas Killigrew and Sir William Davenant, the exclusive right to perform twenty of Shakespeare's plays (Halliday, 1964, 266). James (2008, 177-187) has shown that there are good reasons to believe Davenant was the illegitimate son of Henry Neville.

There is clearly a relationship between annotators A & B. Their annotations are similar and often it seems there is a conversation going on between them as they copy together. I shall further examine Annotator A's work and the relationship between A and B in chapter 6.

---

7   In Stowe 174, folio 116, British Library

**Annotator B: Worsley MSS 47**
Annotator B is much more independently minded, is in a hurry, makes mistakes, abbreviates, omits things, adds his own notes. He has a particular excitement about the Wars of the Roses, changing his style into an italic hand for emphasis (and incidentally making it easier to read than the secretary script). B focuses on what interests him rather than just copying. He shows a capacity for independent analysis, adding his own glosses on passages, whereas A faithfully copies with only occasional extra notes or changes.

Armstrong (1979, 155) stated that evidence showed "Shakespeare wrote at great speed". The errors and abbreviations of Annotator B suggest he wrote at speed. This then is consistent with B being the young Henry Neville (who only started to use the pseudonym 'William Shakespeare' in 1593).

What is especially remarkable is that when Annotator B departs from the words used in the 1584 printed marginalia (and those of Annotator A) he uses words that Shakespeare later uses. These are not common words: having searched the Literature on Line data base (LION), I am able to state that, whilst some are used by other writers of the period, they are generally used more often by Shakespeare than by other writers. For this I researched the use of the words between 1584 (the earliest date the manuscripts could have been annotated) and the next use of the word on LION up until 1625. Not only does Shakespeare use the vocabulary of Annotator B but these words are used in a cascade of inter-linked passages and associations which I will now trace, taking into this analysis the early works which I have previously identified as by the young Neville (Casson, 2009) and diplomatic letters written by Neville between 1599-1600. In some cases B is not inventing these words, just picking them out from the text of *Leicester's Commonwealth* and noting them in his independent version of the marginalia.

**Words used by B and Shakespeare**
In the 1584 printed marginalia there is one note: "Nevv mẽ most contẽptuous" which Annotator A copies as: "New men most contemptuous." Annotator B however varies this to: "newe men most **contumelious**".

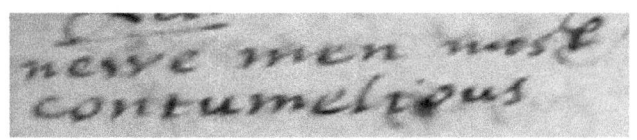

Worlsey MSS47, 55V

Robert Wilson used 'contumelious' in his play *The Three Lords and Three Ladies of London* which was published in 1590. Shakespeare used this rare word more times than any other writer of the period. It is used in *Edmund Ironside* (a play dated by Sams to 1588) when the Archbishop of York tells the Archbishop of Canterbury to "leave thy **contumelious** threats" (3.1.20). James (2008, 247) noted that Neville used '**contumely**' in his letters (e.g. 4/6/1606: Winwood, 1725, Vol 2, 217), and that this word was used by Hamlet (3.1.71). '**Contumelious**' is also to be found in *Henry VI* part 1 (1.4.38); *Henry VI* part 2 (3.2.204) and in *Timon of Athens* (5.5.173). In *Henry VI* part 2 Queen Margaret is speaking to the Earl of Warwick, Richard Neville.

The very next annotation by B. is:

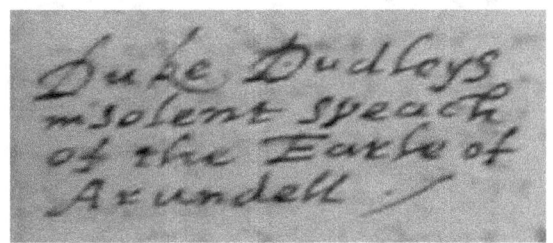

Worsley MSS 47, 55V

"Duke Dudleys **insolent** speach of the Earle of Arundell" whereas the printed annotation is "D. Dudleys **ieste** (= jest) at the Erl. of Arũdel." The word '**insolent**' occurs in *Henry VI* part 2 (3.1.7) in the scene previous to '**contumelious**'; and in *King John* (2.1.122). In the latter case Queen Eleanor is retorting to Constance's taunt about King John, calling him, "Thy usurping son". This is the fourth use of this word 'usurp/ing/er/ing' in four lines. Annotator B. has a note "Knige John an **vsurper**" whereas in the printed annotation the note is "King Iohn a Tyraunt."

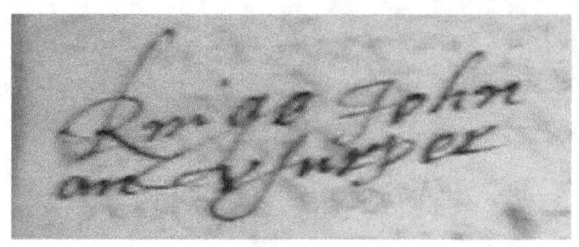

Worsley MSS47, 48V

The words 'usurpe', 'usurpation' and 'usurper' are to be found in *The Troublesome Raigne*, the last being spoken by King John himself. 'Usurper' is also used in *Henry VI* part 2 three times (1.3.33; 1.3.186; 4.4.29). Within the first of these scenes the name 'Nevil' occurs (1.3.73). The word 'usurper' is used six times by Shakespeare. One of these uses is in *Henry V*, in a long speech by the Archbishop of Canterbury about the laws of succession. In it he speaks of, "**The law Salique** that they have **in France**" (1.2.11). Annotator B is the only annotator who notes "**The Lawe Salique in ffraunce**".

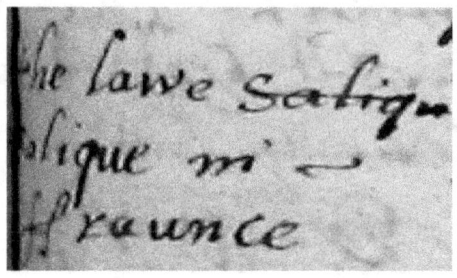

Worsley MSS 47, 39

The phrase used in the main text of *Leicester's Commonwealth* is "**the Law Salick in Fraunce**" (original spelling). B and Shakespeare spell this as 'Salique'. In the First Folio it is spelt 'Salike' and 'Salique'. (The Annotator of Halle's *Chronicles* is also interested in the Salique law: see chapter 4.) Furthermore in *Henry V* the Archbishop uses the words, "There is no **bar** to make against your highness' **claim** to France" (1.2.35). In his annotations B uses the word '**barr**' eight times in relation to succession to the throne and '**clayme**' twice (and '**claymeth**' once). The word '**barres**' is only used once in the printed annotations, '**claime**' four times. These words then are brought together when King Henry asks:

> My learned lord, we pray you to proceed
> And justly and religiously unfold
> Why **the law Salike** that they have **in France**
> Or should, or should not, **bar** us in our **claim**…   (1.2.9)

The Archbishop of Canterbury concludes a long speech with:

> Howbeit they would hold up this **Salique law**
> To **bar** your highness **claiming** from the female,
> And rather choose to hide them in a net
> Than amply to **imbar** their crooked titles
> **Usurp'd** from you and your progenitors.   (1.2.91)

The only annotation in the printed version of *Leicester's Commonwealth* that uses the word '**barres**' reads: "**Barres** pretĕded against the **claime** of Scotland and Suffolk." Annotator B renders this as: "**Barrs** p$^{re}$tended by the **conspirators**". Shakespeare used the word '**conspirators**' in just one play, *Julius Caesar* (3.2.225; 5.1.50; 5.5.70). Annotators A & B specifically note the fate of Julius Caesar. Annotator B however adds another name: "This was the destruction of Julius Cesar by **Marc: Brutus**".

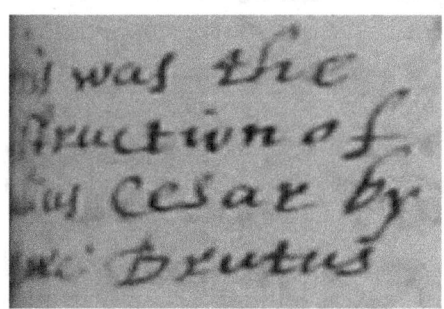

Worsley MSS47, 58[8]

Is this the seed-germ of Shakespeare's play? According to the LION database, Shakespeare is the only writer of the period (apart from the

---

8    (As are a number of annotations, this is partially lost down inside the binding, but can be read by sight, although photographing it is difficult).

authors of *Leicester's Commonwealth*) to use the name Marcus Brutus, which he does three times in *Julius Caesar*. Furthermore B's version of the printed annotation, "A thing worthye to be noted in ambitious men." is "A **worthie** ~ **noate** of an **ambitious man**".

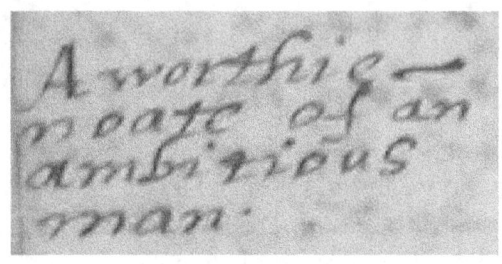

Worsley MSS 47, 35V

In *Julius Caesar* I find: "**worthy note**" (1.2.180) in a play in which Antony repeatedly states:

> Yet Brutus says he was **ambitious**;
> And Brutus is an honourable **man**.   (3.2.94)

I also noticed the phrase "**itching** humour of ambition" in *Leicester's Commonwealth*. In *Julius Caesar* Brutus accuses Cassius of having an "**itching** palm" (4.3.10). The plays *Julius Caesar* and *Henry V* were both written in about 1599. Perhaps Neville re-read his copy of *Leicester's Commonwealth* that year. I have certainly found some of the vocabulary of these annotations in Neville's diplomatic letters of 1599. Why might Neville revisit *Leicester's Commonwealth* in 1599? Whereas the anxiety about Elizabeth's health and succession had been acute in 1584 it was even greater 15 years later. Indeed within two years the Essex rebellion was an attempted coup d'état by the Queen's favourite. In chapter 2 I suggested the Shakespeare play might be seen as a warning to Essex not to precipitate civil war.

In *Julius Caesar* Cassius says:

> if you know
> That I do fawn on men and hug them hard
> And after scandal them, or if you know
> That I profess myself in **banqueting**
> To all the rout, then hold me **dangerous**.   (1.2.74)

In *Leicester's Commonwealth* the Earl is described as making friends with courtiers and nobles only to betray them later. Two adjacent annotations by B about Leicester's behaviour are:

"by **banquetnig** her Matie"

"Leic: chaungnig lands with her Matie whereby he notablye **indaungereth** the crowne"

Worsley MSS 47, 25

Annotator A uses neither '**banqueting**' nor '**indaungereth**' nor are they used in the printed marginalia (though 'banquets' and 'endangered' do occur in the printed text). In *Troilus and Cressida* I find '**banqueting**' (5.1.45) before a battle and '**dangerous**' three times (2.2.65; 4.5.104; 5.2.38). In *Thomas of Woodstock* (which Egan, 2006, identified as by Shakespeare and I have shown was by Neville, Casson, 2009) there is another dangerous banquet at which Thomas is arrested:

> There is no time, I fear, for **banqueting**.
> My lord, I wish your grace be provident,
> I fear your person is betrayed, my lord.
> The house is round beset with armed soldiers.        (4.2.157)

The word '**dangerous**' is used five times in *Thomas of Woodstock*. The context of B's annotations about '**banqueting**' and '**indaungereth**' is about Leicester's flattery and manipulation of Elizabeth. B spells 'daunger' with a 'u', as he does 'straunger'. Neville in his 1599 letters

used these very spellings (Winwood, 1725, Vol 1, 86, 98).
Shakespeare uses '**endanger**' in one of his earliest plays, *The Two Gentlemen of Verona*. Thurio says:

> I hold him but a fool that will **endanger**
> His body for a girl that loves him not. (5.4.132)

Thurio is a cowardly suitor who abandons a woman, who does not love him, in the forest. This recalls Amadine who is abandoned by Segasto, the coward who ran away from the bear in the forest in *Mucedorus*. Amadine, promises her rescuer:

> Well, shepherd, for thy worthy valour tried,
> **Endangering** thy self to set me free,
> Unrecompensed, sure, thou shalt not be. (1.3.59)

In my previous book (Casson, 2009), arguing that this was Neville's first comedy, I explored the links between *Mucedorus* and *Leicester's Commonwealth* as the hero rescues Amadine (Elizabeth I) from a dangerous bear (Leicester). I dated the first version of *Mucedorus* to 1584/5, the very time these annotations were made (see Appendix 7). Indeed one of B's unique annotations is the word 'Beares'.

Worsley MSS 47, 6V

In *Henry IV* part 1, Hotspur, facing a civil war battle without the support of his sick father, complains:

> nor did he think it meet
> To lay so **dangerous** and dear a trust
> On any soul removed but on his own.
> Yet doth he give us bold advertisement,
> That with our small **conjunction** we should on,
> To see how fortune is disposed to us… (4.1.33)

The greatest danger *Leicester's Commonwealth* pointed to was civil war and it did so not only by looking back to classical examples, such as the aftermath of the assassination of Julius Caesar, but especially to the Wars of the Roses. The story of the dynastic struggles during that civil war is told in *Leicester's Commonwealth*. The account begins with the image of Roses. The printed annotation is: "The read rose and the whyte." A. does not copy this. B. copies it as "The redd Rose and the white."

Worsley MSS 47, 40V

This is exactly the phrase Shakespeare uses in *Henry VI* part 1 when he dramatises the image by bringing the contenders of the original quarrel together in a rose garden. Warwick (Richard Neville) prophecies:

>             this brawl to-day,
> Grown to this faction in the Temple-garden,
> Shall send between **the red rose and the white**
> A thousand souls to death and deadly night.          (2.4.124)

In *Henry VI* part 3 we find:

> **The red rose and the white** are on his face,
> The fatal colours of our striving **houses**:          (2.5.97)

According to LION, no other poet or playwright of the period uses the words, "**The red rose and the white**." In *Richard III* the colours are reversed but the phrase is the same:

> We will unite **the white rose and the red**:
> Smile heaven upon this fair **conjunction**,
> That long have frown'd upon their enmity!          (5.5.19)

One printed *Leicester's Commonwealth* marginal note is: "The happy **cōiũnctiō** of the tvvoe **houses**." A copies this as: "The happy **coniunction** of the ii **howses**".

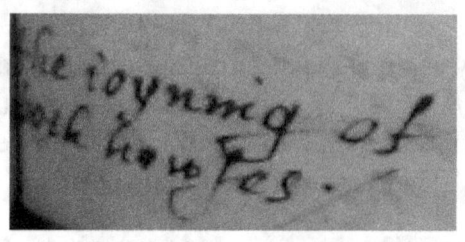

Worsley MSS 47, 41

B renders this as: "The **ioynnig** of **both howses**". Shakespeare uses "**both your houses**" three times in *Romeo and Juliet*, a play which shows the disastrous consequences of division between 'houses'. Elsewhere Annotator B uses **conjunction** about a marriage. The printed annotation reads: "Leycester conuinceth himselfe of impudencie." A copies this exactly. B however writes: "his impudent **Coniunction** w$^{th}$ Dame Letteice". Shakespeare not only uses the word '**conjunction**' more times than any other writer of the period but also brings together the idea of marriage and peace: in *Henry V* the French King says of Henry's marriage to Katherine:

> this dear **conjunction**
> Plant neighbourhood and Christian-like accord
> In their sweet bosoms, that never war advance
> His bleeding sword 'twixt England and fair France. (5.2.346)

In *King John* Queen Elinor says:

> Son, list to this **conjunction**, make this match;
> Give with our niece a dowry large enough:
> For by this knot thou shalt so surely tie
> Thy now unsured **assurance** to the crown…        (2.1.469)

In *Leicester's Commonwealth* B notes, "two poyntes of **assurance** wch a prince hath from his subiectes". The printed annotation is, "A point of necessarie policie for a Prince." Neville uses '**assurance**' several times in a letter of 15/5/1599 (Winwood, 1725, Vol 1, 21, 22, 23). Shakespeare uses '**assurance**' 28 times. The word '**assurance**' is also used in *Edmund Ironside* (3.2.84) and twice in *Mucedorus* (5.1.121). In *Henry VIII* Queen Katherine says:

> I am a most poor woman, and a stranger,
> Born out of your dominions; having here
> No judge indifferent, nor no more **assurance**
> Of equal friendship and proceeding. Alas, sir,
> In what have I offended you? what cause
> Hath my behavior given to your **displeasure**…?   (2.4.13)

B has an annotation: "Parties **chased from** court vpon Leicesters **displeasure**". The printed annotation is: "Leycesters anger & insolẽcie."

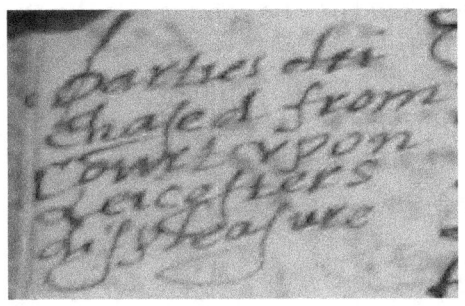

Worsley MSS 47, 18V

Neville uses '**displeasure**' in a letter dated 27/4/1600 (Winwood, 1725, Vol 1, 178). Shakespeare uses 'displeasure' 42 times, and "chased…from" three times. In *Henry V*, *The Comedy of Errors*, *Edward III* and *Merchant of Venice* both 'displeasure' and 'chased' occur. In *The Comedy of Errors* these words occur within the same speech by Adriana (5.1.142,153) They also occur in *Locrine*, which I have identified as an early work by Neville (Casson, 2009). In *Henry VI* part 1, Joan uses the words, "**chased… from**" (1.2.115). 34 lines earlier she says she must "free my **country** from **calamity**" (1.2.81).

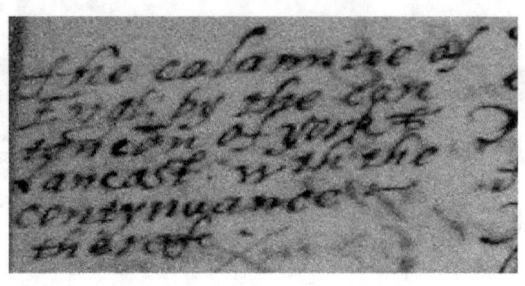

Worsley MSS 47, 40V

One of B's annotations reads, "The **calamitie** of Engl: by the **contencõn** of York & Lancast: w[th] the **continuance** ~ thereof." The printed version is: "The miserie of England by the **cõtentiõ** betvv York and Lãcaster." What is immediately apparent is that B is using alliteration: "**calamity, contention, continuance**". In *Coriolanus* we find such alliteration with '**calamity**' when Volumnia says:

> The **country**, our dear nurse, or else thy person,
> Our **comfort** in the **country**. We must find
> An evident **calamity**...       (5.3.111)

The main text of *Leicester's Commonwealth* at this point reads, "our **country**'s **calamity** by that **contention**" (Peck, 144/*96*) so we can see that B picked up this alliteration from the text - not from the printed annotation - but varied it with an additional word, '**continuance**'. Neville used '**continuance**' in a letter dated 15/5/1599 and twice in a letter of 26/5/1599 (Winwood, 1725, Vol 1, 21, 36); he used the word '**contention**' in a letter dated 27/6/1599 (Winwood, 1725, Vol 1, 51). B and Shakespeare use 'calamity' in relation to a country: England, France and Italy. Shakespeare uses 'calamity' 10 times; 'continuance' 10 times; 'contention' 9 times: the majority of these words are used in early plays. 'Contention' was also used in the title of the quarto *Henry VI* part 2 which was printed as *The First Part of the Contention Betwixt the Two Famous Houses of York and Lancaster*. B's annotation included the words "the contencõn betweene York & Lancast:". Again the word order matches: it is not "Lancaster and York".

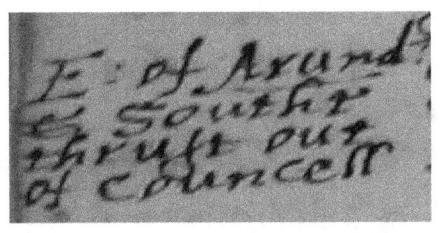

Worsley MSS 47, 24V

Similar to "Parties **chased from court**", B has another annotation: "E of Arund: & Southt **thrust out of** councell". The printed marginal note, of which this is a variant, states: "Arundel and Southamptõ put out of the Councell by D. Dudley." Shakespeare uses "**thrust out**" four times. The earliest of these is when Warwick (Richard Neville) in *Henry VI* part 3 says:

> And when the king comes, offer no violence,
> Unless he seek to **thrust** you **out** perforce.           (1.1.33)

Annotator B uses 'tiranie' instead of the printed 'Tyraunt' in an early marginal note. In the 1609 edition of the sonnets this very same spelling is used in sonnet 115: "times tiranie". Shakespeare used 'tyranny' 37 times including in *Henry VI* part 2, where he also uses 'thrust' and names the Nevils:

> The princely Warwick, and the **Nevils** all,
> Whose dreadful swords were never drawn in vain,
> As hating thee, are rising up in arms:
> And now the house of York, **thrust from** the crown
> By shameful murder of a guiltless king
> And lofty proud encroaching **tyranny**...           (4.1.91)

Furthermore B's full annotation is: "**The tiranie of the** Engli: state". The printed annotation is: "The Tyraunt of Englishe state." B therefore has put a second definite article into the phrase. The phrase "**the tyranny of the**..." is to be found in the Argument that introduces *The Rape of Lucrece*.

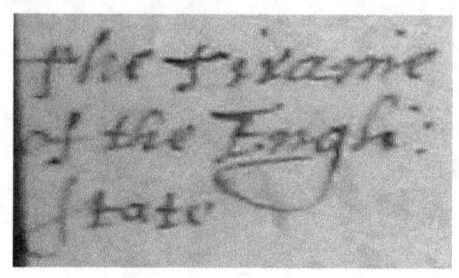

Worsley MSS 47, 6

B also notes "A **tiranous reuenge vpon** a tirante" instead of the printed version: "A most terrible reuenge takẽ vpũ a Tyrant." In *Titus Andronicus* I find the words, "**revenge upon** the…**tyrant**" (1.1.140).

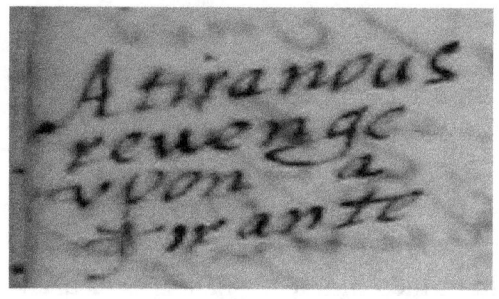

Worsley MSS47, 29V

Shakespeare uses 'tyrannous' 13 times. In Sonnet 131, in the 1609 edition, it is spelt 'tiranous'. In *Pericles* he uses the word near 'tyrant':

> I knew him **tyrannous**; and **tyrant**s' fears
> Decrease not… (1.2.82)

Shakespeare is the only writer of the period to bring these two words together. He also used '**tyrannous**' in *Edward III* (3.3.48). Neville uses the word '**tirannous**' (spelt with an 'i', as in B's annotation) in a letter dated 20/3/1600 (Winwood, 1725, Vol 1, 161).

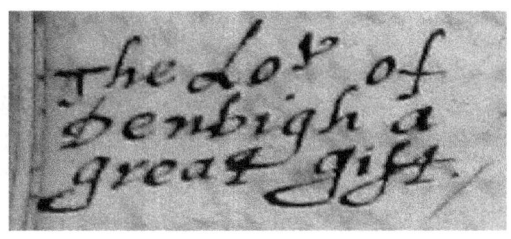

Worsley MSS 47, 27V

B has one note, "The Lo^rd of Denbigh a **great gift**" and adds, lower down the page, "his oppresion there":

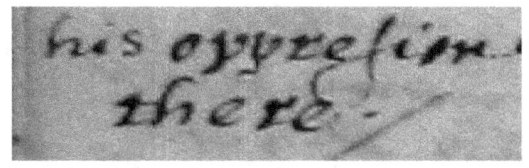

Worsley MSS 47, 27V

The printed version is, "The Lord Shippe of Dẽbighe and Leyces. oppressiõ used therĩ". Shakespeare uses "**great gift**" in Sonnet 87: the spelling in the 1609 edition is "So thy **great guift**, upon misprision growing…" Is there an echo of 'oppression' in 'misprision'? Neville used the words, "**great Guifts**", in a letter dated 13/7/1599 (Winwood, 1725, Vol 1, 65). In *Titus Andronicus* Demetrius says:

> But me more good to see so **great** a lord
> Basely insinuate and send us **gifts**. (4.2.22)

I have suggested that *Mucedorus* and *Locrine* are early works by Neville so it is interesting to find these words in those plays. In *Mucedorus* I find:

> This **gift**, assure thy self, contents me more
> Than **greatest** bounty of a mighty prince… (1.3.18)

In *Locrine*:

> A **grateful gift** given by a gracious King:
> Lo, here the **gift** of fell **ambition**,

> Of **usurpation** and of **treachery**! (4.3.89)

Given that Leicester is accused of **ambition**, **usurpation** and **treachery**, the proximity of such charges with these words is significant. Indeed I have found '**grateful**' three times in *Leicester's Commonwealth*, used in the same way as in *Locrine* (which I dated to 1586-9), '**ambition**' 14 times, '**usurpation**' four times and '**treachery**' six times. Furthermore the next three lines in *Locrine* are:

> Lo, here the harms that wait upon all those
> That do intrude themselves in other's lands,
> Which are not under their dominion. (4.3.91)

This warning, whilst ostensibly given to a foreign invader, could equally apply to a man accused, as in *Leicester's Commonwealth*, of grabbing other people's land.

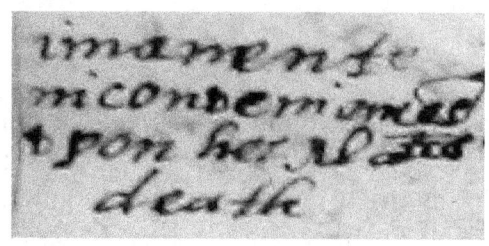

Worsley MSS47, 37V

B has an annotation: "imanente inconueniences upon her Ma[ties] death." The printed version is simply "Great inconueniences". The only time the bard uses 'inconueniences' is in *Henry V* (5.2.66) written in 1599; the word is also to be found in Neville's letter of 1/8/1599 (Winwood, 1725, Vol 1, 82). In *The Troublesome Raigne* I have found "imminent mishaps" (3.479, Sider, 1979, 58). Shakespeare uses 'imminent' near 'death' twice. In *Henry VI* part 2 the Earl of Salisbury (Richard Neville, the 5[th] Earl) says, "You have defended me from **imminent death**" (5.3.19). Hamlet speaks of, "The **imminent death** of twenty thousand men…" (4.4.60). Furthermore I find in *Edmund Ironside*:

Alfred: Here danger **imminent** doth compass us;
    There friends and friendly counsel shall defend us;

>           Therefore rejoice we are escaped the Danes,
>           Whose greedy maws devours the Saxons' blood
>           Like hungry lions, void of any good.
> Emma: Good boy, in whom thy father's feature lives,
>           Though **death** hath seized him in his wasteful arms. (4.2.15)

This passage contains elements of the Shakespearean death image cluster identified by Spurgeon (1958), confirming Sams' thesis that *Edmund Ironside* is an early Shakespeare play. Othello speaks of "the **imminent deadly** breach" (1.3.137).

B has a note "The **base & abiect** behavio[r] of D: Du: in his **downefall** and **adversitie**".

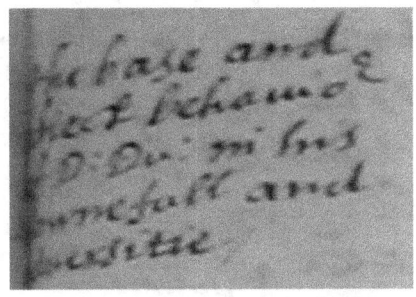

Worsley MSS 47, 56

This is his version of the printed marginalia "The most abiect behavior of Duke Dudley in aduerse fortune." B's annotation in effect contains two hendiadys using words later found in Shakespeare's plays of the 1590s. B uses "**downefall and adversitie**". Shakespeare uses '**downfall**' 7 times, all in early works of the 1590s. He also uses '**adversity**' 7 times. In *Henry VI* part 3 we find both '**downfall**' (3.3.104; 5.6.65) and '**adversity**' (3.1.24). In *Edmund Ironside* we find '**downfall**' (5.1.114) and in *Edward III* '**adversity**' (4.4.117); in *Locrine*: "**downfall** and decay" (5.2.8).

In *Henry IV* part 2 the Earl of Westmoreland, (Ralph Neville) says, "rebellion came like itself, in **base** and **abject** routs…" (4.1.33). In *Edmund Ironside* written much closer to the date of the Worsley Manuscript annotations both words are used several times, twice near each other and once in the same line:

> I was as mean as any **basely** born.
> Fie, say not so, it will discredit thee.
> Tut, no man hears me. Aye, but think not so,
> For it will make thy peacock's plumes fall down
> If one such **abject** thought possess thy mind.     (1.2.3)

and

> Which thoughts **abase** my state most **abjectly**.     (1.2.7)

Just 9 lines later the word 'furnished' occurs (1.3.2), see below.
The 'baseness' of Leicester's ancestry is described in *Leicester's Commonwealth* as "base lineage" (Peck, 174/*115*). In the Quarto of *The First Part of the Contention* (the earliest version of *Henry VI* part 2, lines 1981 – 2095) there is a scene that includes the words 'subiect', '**abiect**', '**basely**', '**maintenance**', '**base**', 'vsurped', 'beares' and 'Neuels' (Neville's): all of which are in B's annotations and three of which are spelt in the same way.

Worsley MSS 47, 22

One of B's annotations is: "the sworde a straunge **mayntenaunc of** the title of a kingdome". The printed version is: "The svvord of greate force to iustifie the title of a kingdom." In *Henry IV* part 1 the King, speaking of his son, John of Lancaster, says he saw him, "hold Lord Percy at the point with lustier **maintenance** than I did look for of such an ungrown warrior" (5.4.20). In other words John was holding the rebel Percy at bay with his sword in a battle for the title of a kingdom. Just before the King says this, John leaves the stage with his supporter, the Earl of Westmoreland, who was none other than Ralph Neville, 6[th] Baron of Raby and 1[st] Earl of Westmoreland, who married Joan Beaufort, daughter of John of Gaunt, Duke of Lancaster. Grandfather of Edward IV and Richard III, Gaunt was also Henry Neville's ancestor. (By extraordinary coincidence Joan is buried with her mother, Kathryn Swynford, in Lincoln Cathedral, less than half a mile from the archives that currently hold the Worsley Manuscripts and John of Gaunt's will.) Neville uses the word '**maintenance**' several times in his letters of May-June 1599 (Winwood, 1725, Vol 1, 24, 49, 51, 53). In one letter, of 22/10/1599, he writes "the **maintenance of** her state" (Winwood, 1725, Vol 1, 123) which echoes the wording of B's annotation. In *The Two Gentlemen of Verona* Antonio says:

> I am resolved that thou shalt spend some time
> With Valentinus in the emperor's court:
> What **maintenance** he from his friends receives,
> Like exhibition thou shalt have from me.
> To-morrow be in readiness to go:
> Excuse it not, for I am **peremptory**.            (1.3.66)

One of the printed marginalia is "Leycester **peremptorie** dealing." B copies this as "Le: **pemtorie** dealings". Shakespeare uses this word in *Henry VI* part 3. Edward IV describes the Earl of Warwick, Richard Neville, as '**peremptory**' (4.8.59). In a letter dated 8/12/1604 Neville uses '**peremptory**' near the words "**abundance** will ever **furnish** them better" (Winwood, 1725, Vol 2, 38). One of B's annotations reads, "Leic: **furnished w**$^{th}$ money **in aboundance**"; the printed version is "Ley. furniture in money." In a letter dated 2/11/1600 Neville uses the words "**furnished with**" (Winwood, 1725, Vol 1, 271). In another letter dated 7/8/1599 Neville writes that the Queen "dis**furnished** herself to **furnish** them" (i.e. the French). Within ten lines he uses the word '**abondance**' (Winwood, 1725, Vol 1, 84-5). Shakespeare used "**furnished with**" three times and '**abundance**' 13 times, three of which are "**in abundance**".

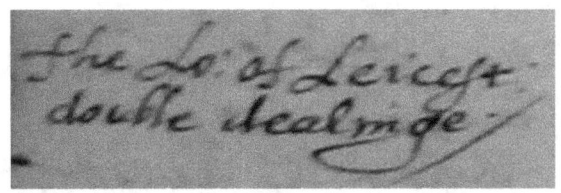

MSS47, 51V

B annotates: "the Lo: of Leicest: **double dealnige**." This is his alliterative version of the printed marginal note: "My L. of Leycester agayne playeth double." Shakespeare uses "**double-dealing**" in *Twelfth Night* (5.1.27).⁹ Neville, in a letter dated 27/6/1599 writes that the exiles Charles Paget and Tresham "will not **dare to double**" with the government if allowed to return (Winwood, 1725, Vol 1, 52). Again, Neville uses alliteration in another letter of 1/11/1599: "**dealing** thus to **delude** us…" (Winwood, 1725, Vol 1, 126). B uses the word '**deludenige**' (of Sʳ Christo: Hatton) in one annotation (instead of the word 'deceiving' in the printed version).

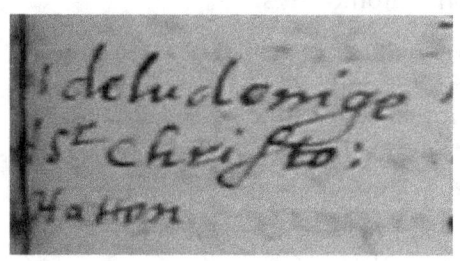

Worsley MSS 47, 56

Shakespeare uses the word '**deluding**' twice, in *The Taming of The Shrew* (4.3.31) and *Othello* (1.1.138).

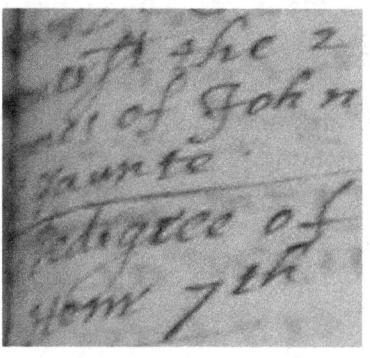

Worsley MSS 47, 43

B's annotation: "the 2 Sonnes of **John of Gaunte** The **pedigree** of K. Henr: 7ᵗʰ" is echoed in two Shakespeare plays: "he from **John of Gaunt** doth bring his **pedigree**" in *Henry VI* part 1 (2.5.76) and "**John of Gaunt**… a **pedigree**" in *Henry VI* part 3 (3.3.81-92). In Worsley MSS 47, B, now

---

9     In Holinshed 1587 *Chronicles* (1976, 184) there is "double dealing" in the reign of Henry II.

annotating independently of the printed text and A, follows on with a list of the descendants of Edward III: "the yssue of **K: Edw 3** Rich 2":

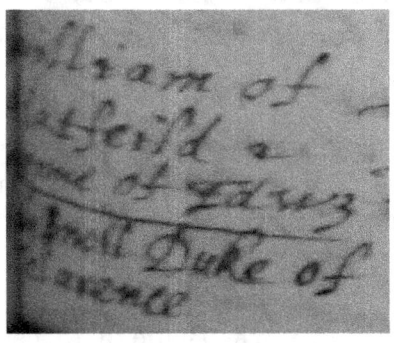

Worsley MSS 47, 43

**William of Hatfeild a sonne of Edw 3**
**Lyonell Duke of Clarence**
and at the top of the next page
**Edmund of Langley the first duke of Yorke**

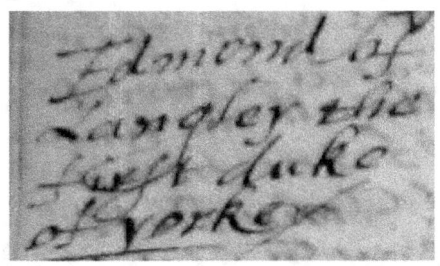

Worsley MSS 47, 43V

In *Henry VI* part 2 Richard Duke of York also lists the descendants of Edward III:

> **Edward the Third**, my lords, had seven sons:
> The first, Edward the Black Prince, Prince of Wales;
> The second, **William** of **Hatfield**, and the third,
> **Lionel Duke of Clarence**: next to whom
> Was John of Gaunt, the Duke of Lancaster;
> The fifth was **Edmund Langley**, **Duke of York**…   (2.2.10)

These names with their titles are all listed in the same order as in B's annotation. Later in the scene we hear, "But **William of Hatfield** died without an heir" (2.2.33). The speaker is Richard Neville, Duke of Salisbury. Also present is his son, Richard Neville, Earl of Warwick. Underlining their identity Warwick says to York, "The **Nevilles** are thy subjects to command" (2.2.9). Richard of York had married Cecily Neville. "**Lionel Duke of Clarence**" is mentioned four times in *Henry VI* parts 1 & 2. Langley is mentioned three times by Shakespeare, twice as "**Edmund Langley, Duke of York**".

One of B's annotations reads: "The Battle of Tadcaster on Palme Sundaye Barnett and **Tewxburie**" whereas the printed version is: "The battaile by Tadcaster on palme Sõdaye, An. 1460."

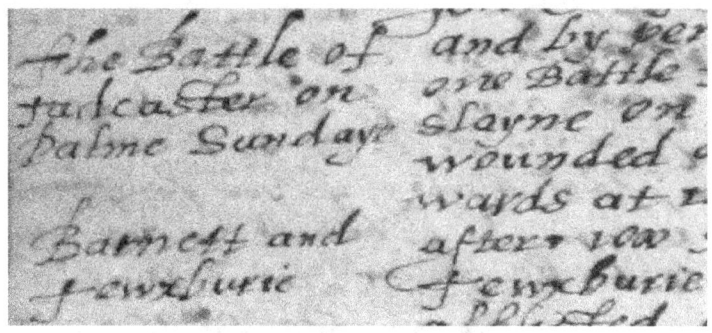

Worsley MSS 47: 40V

B repeats the spelling '**Tewxburie**' in his version of the text. The battle of Tadcaster is otherwise called the battle of Towton (Peck, 1985, 214 footnote 203), which Shakespeare dramatises in *Henry VI* part 3, Act 2, scene 3. B notes the battle place names of Barnet and Tewkesbury. We find these in *Henry VI* part 3. The First Folio spelling of these is:

> That they doe hold their course toward Tewksbury.
> We hauing now the best at Barnet field...      (5.3.19)

In the 1595 quarto version of *Henry VI* part 3 (*The True Tragedy of Richard Duke of York*) one of these place names is spelt differently: **Tewxburie**. (Barnet is not mentioned.) Thus the early version of *The True Tragedy* matches Annotator B's spelling. Furthermore B notes, "Henr: the 7th his **descent**."

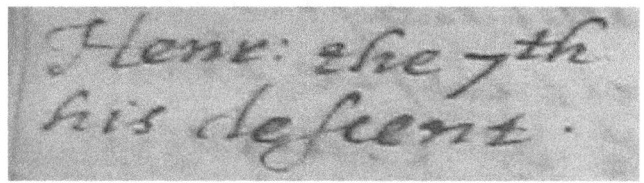

Worsley MSS 47, 41V

In *The True Tragedy* I find "Henries lineallie **discent**" whereas the Folio version is "Henry lineally descends" (3.3.87). Again B is closer to the quarto word. In *Leicester's Commonwealth* we read that, "my Lord of Leicester is very well known to have no title to the crown himself, either by **descent** in blood, alliance, or otherways" (Peck, 127/*86*). In a passage in *The Troublesome Raigne of John King of England* that links the succession to the throne, a testament and usurpation, I find the word '**discent**' used three times. Neville's father was a signatory to the contested will of Henry VIII which attempted to control the succession to his throne. B has a unique annotation, "K: H: 8th s testamte".

Worsley MSS 47, 45V

The Bastard Fauconbridge in *The Troublesome Raigne* uses the word '**discent**' when talking about his own inheritance. The illegitimate Neville would have had anxieties about threats to his inheritance: indeed he had a legal dispute with his step mother after his father's death. Shakespeare used the word '**descent**' 17 times in canonical works. Neville used the word '**descents**' in relation to royal lineage in a letter of 1/11/1600 (Winwood, 1725, Vol 2, 35).

Another unique annotation by B is, "Eccliasti: livings".

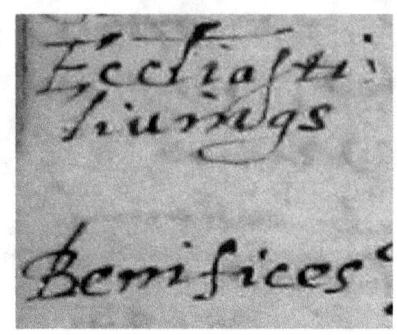

Worsley MSS 47, 23V

The printed marginalia simply states, "Cleargie". The very next annotation is "Benefices". Neville uses 'Ecclesiasticall' in a letter dated 5/10/99 and 'Benefices' in another of 27/4/1600 (Winwood, 1725, Vol 1, 117, 178). Shakespeare uses the word 'Benefice' in *Romeo and Juliet* (1.4.81). Also to be found in *Romeo and Juliet* are the words "**a pitiful case**" (4.5.93). B has an annotation "The matter of Snowden **a pittifull case**" whereas the printed marginal note is "The case of Snovvden forest most pittifull".

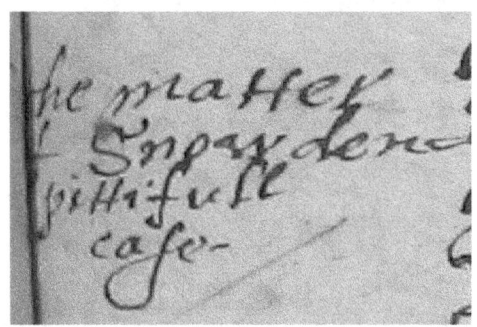

Worsley MSS 47, 28

Another unique annotation by B is, "copercinerie betweene daugh-ters" (though some of this is almost invisible down inside the binding). The printed marginal note states only "Diuision among daughters." 'Coparcenary' is a legal term for a shared inheritance (OED).

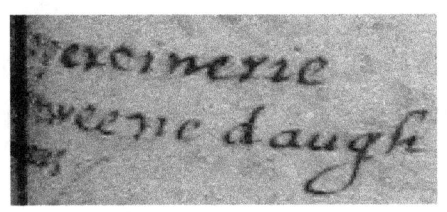

Worsley MSS 47, 47

The context in *Leicester's Commonwealth* concerns the inheritance of the crown, contrasting normal civil laws of inheritance with the special legal status of the monarchy:

"it is a general and common rule that if a man die seized of land in fee simple, having daughters and no son, his lands shalbe divided by equal portions amongst his daughters, which holdeth not with the crown, but rather the eldest daughter inheriteth the whole as if she were the issue male." (Peck, 158/*105*).

Whilst 'coparcenary' is the correct legal term for this, the word is used neither in *Leicester's Commonwealth* nor by Shakespeare. However when I consulted Sokol & Sokol's comprehensive *Shakespeare's Legal Language*, I found they referred four times to 'co-parceny'. Two of these passages make the very same point as *Leicester's Commonwealth*: namely that the crown was excluded from this legal option. The final discussion relates to King Lear's division of the kingdom between his daughters (Sokol & Sokol, 2004, 416). The editors refer to the senile Brain Annesley and his daughter Cordell. Given Neville's friendship with Southampton he would have known the Earl's father's wife, Cordell and her struggle on behalf of her father (James & Rubinstein, 2005, 175). Neville was a JP (1583) and an MP (1584) and so knew the law. Indeed his first recorded act in Parliament, in 1588, was to introduce a bill ensuring the inheritance settlement (jointure) for his wife, Anne (James & Rubinstein, 2005, 89). He was interested then in the inheritance rights of women.

One annotation by B reads: "The **discon**: in Oxford by the wickednes of theire cha: **the state of the** vniuersit". "The discon:" is clearly short for "The discontent". The printed version is: "The disorders of Oxeforde by the vvickednes of their Chãcellour." Shakespeare uses 'discontent' 19 times and 'disorders' 3 times. B's choice of word is again in the direction of Shakespeare's preferred usage. B.'s annotation uses the words 'discontent' and "the state of the university". These words are in *King John*: 'discontent' occurs twice (3.4.179 and 4.2.53). The bastard Faulconbridge says, "**The** lineal **state** and glory **of the** land" (5.7.102). The name Faulconbridge is of course a hidden Neville, as I showed in my previous book (Casson, 2009). I have come to believe that *The Troublesome Raigne of John King of England* was Shakespeare-Neville's first version of *King John*. It is therefore interesting to note that the words 'discontent' and 'discontentment' occur in that play (8.206; 10.213). 'Discontentment' occurs five times in *Leicester's Commonwealth* (e.g. Peck, 132/*89*). Neville used 'discontent' and 'discontentment' repeatedly in his letters (Winwood, 1725, Vol 1, 80 and 123) and in a letter, dated 27/1/1600, he wrote "**the state of the** Complaint" and in another of 24/4/1600, "**The** present **state of** France…" (Winwood, 1725, Vol 1, 152, 175-6).

B mentions Oxford three times whereas there is only one annotation about Oxford in the printed edition and it is referred to twice in the annotations of Worsley MSS 36. His special interest is understandable as Neville had attended Merton College, Oxford from 1574-77.

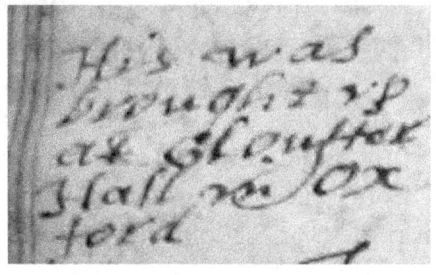

Worsley MSS 47, 13V

One of B's annotations about Oxford reads: "His was brought vp at Gloucester Hall in Oxford". This is explained by another annotation: "Sheffeild now Emba: in ffraunce and **Robte Dudley** in Gloucester Hall".

Worsley MSS 47, 10V

Lady Douglass Howard (as Lady Sheffield) is mentioned in *Leicester's Commonwealth*. She became "Embassadesse in Fraunce". "In 1573 Leicester married Lady Douglass, widow of John Sheffield, in a secret ceremony, which he later repudiated." Lady Douglass had a son called Robert (or Robin) Dudley. "In 1578 Leicester married Lettice Knollys, widow of Walter Devereux, and ever after referred to Robert as 'my base son.'"[10] Robert was born in 1574 so he was ten years old when *Leicester's Commonwealth* appeared. The text of *Leicester's Commonwealth*, which B copies says, "one boy called Robin Sheffield now living, some time brought up at Newington..." Robert for a time was at the home of Leicester's cousin John Dudley, who lived at Stoke Newington (Haynes, 1987, 59). In referring to Gloucester Hall, B is thus offering new information on Robert. Gloucester Hall was founded in 1560 (it is now Worcester College). Leicester's first wife Amy lay in state in Gloucester Hall in September 1560 (Haynes, 1987, 33). Her funeral took place there on September 20th (Foster, 1981, 120). Leicester became chancellor of Oxford University from 1564. In Leicester's household account book there is a record of payments to Doctor Dallapere in October 1584: this was John Delabere. Leicester had arranged for him to be elected Principal of Gloucester Hall in 1581. In January 1585 there were further payments to "Mr. Doctor Dellapere for v horsehire and their meate for Mr. Robert Dudley when he came from Oxford to Whitney" (Adams, 1995, Vol 6, 188, 216). Thus at precisely the time I am suggesting the Worsley MSS 47 annotations were made, 1584-6, Robert was indeed at Gloucester Hall. He eventually matriculated at Christ Church on 17 May

10    From: http://www.shakespeare-whowashe.nl/nederlands_speakers.html accessed 12/1/09

1588, aged 14. B shows special interest in this boy labelled as 'base' by his father. From 1604 - 1606 Neville served on a Parliamentary committee concerned with illegitimate children (James, 2008, 347).

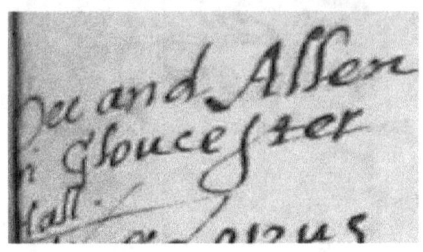

Worsley MSS 47, 27

B's third reference to Gloucester Hall, "Dee and Allen in Gloucester Hall" is of the utmost historical importance for it is documentary proof that Neville, and therefore Shakespeare, was aware of Dr. John Dee and took an interest in him. Dee was the leading mathematician of his day, a Renaissance man who combined practical science, such as navigation, with mystical Hermetic Neo-Platonism. John Dee has often been seen as the model for Prospero in *The Tempest*.

Dr. Thomas Allen, also a mathematician, went to Gloucester Hall in 1570 and lived there for the rest of his life (until 1632). His choice of Gloucester Hall was due to its being the habitation of great mediaeval mathematicians of the Benedictine Order (Foster, 1981, 127). Furthermore Foster (1981, 103) suggested Allen had been trained in mathematics at Merton College, which Neville attended c 1574 - 7. Given Neville's interest in mathematics this annotation about Dee and Allen is not surprising. Indeed Neville must have known Allen because his own tutor, Henry Savile, was a friend and colleague (Foster, 1981, 109, 112).

Dr. John Dee was out of England from 1583 - 1589 (Peck, footnote 138). Therefore B must be referring to a visit to Oxford by Dee before September 1583. Since Dee had been Leicester's tutor, and the Earl had become his main patron, he might well visit Leicester's young son at Gloucester Hall during a visit to Oxford. It is more likely however that Dee was simply visiting Allen, his fellow mathematician. In the spring of 1583 Neville had arrived back in England from his European travels with Savile (who surely would have gone back to Oxford on their return). In June 1583 the Prince Palatine, Count Albert Laski, was in Oxford and, in the company of Sir Philip Sidney, visited Allen (Foster, 1981, 111). The party later went to see

Dee at his home, Mortlake. Laski invited Dee to visit Poland and so they left England together in September 1583. It is possible that Neville was in Oxford during June 1583 or heard a report of the events there that summer from Savile. This annotation further suggests an early date for Worsley 47, with B recalling recent events.

Towards the very end of the text, A & B have an annotation "his oaths profaned".

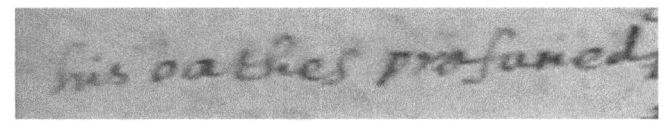

Worsley MSS 47, 65V

The making and breaking of 'oaths' was a preoccupation of early Shakespeare. In *Richard III* Queen Elizabeth says:

this is no **oath**:
The George, **profaned**, hath lost his holy honour... (4.4.289)

B is the only annotator who notes: "Doct Shawe" against a passage about Richard III (Peck, 146/*98*).

Worsley MSS 47, 41

In the First Folio edition (1623) of *Richard III* we find Richard saying:

Go, Lovel, with all speed to Doctor **Shaw**..."      (3.5.97)

Dr. Ralph Shaw delivered a sermon on June 22[nd] 1483 in which he said that Edward IV was illegitimate (Given-Wilson & Curteis, 1984, 3). Neville, being illegitimate himself, had reason to be interested in this detail.
One annotation not in the printed version that is in Worsley 47 is, "Inordinat affeccõn by the Prince to a peculier and wicked person."

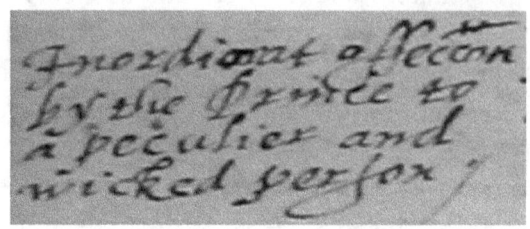

Worsley MSS 47, 61V

Shakespeare uses 'inordinate' 3 times, 'peculiar' 8 times, 'wicked' 60 times, 'affection' 78 times: all these words are in *The Rape of Lucrece*.
The penultimate annotation on the Worsley MSS 47 is: "His weaknes if her Ma^t: turne but her favor from him." In this B has chosen the word 'favour' instead of the word 'countenance' in the printed annotation which reads: "The vveaknes of Ley. yf her Ma. turne but her countenaunce from him."

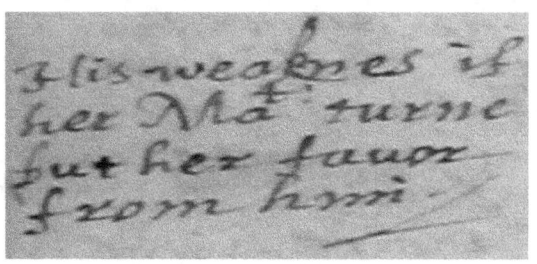

Worsley MSS 47, 65V

Shakespeare uses 'favour' 123 times and 'countenance' just 59 times: in other words Shakespeare had a preference for the word 'favour', displayed here by the annotator of Worsley MSS 47.

Shakespeare does not use two words used by B in annotations: 'aspirants' and 'claimeth', although he does use 'aspire' and 'claims'.

There is evidence that Worsley MSS 47 continued to be consulted by its owner: after James I came to the throne he added a note, squeezing this into a gap between two other, possibly earlier, annotations: "whose sonne James 6[th] most happily joined both kingdomes into one".

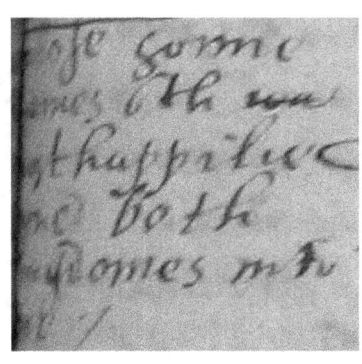

Worsley MSS 47, 44

Henry Neville was a political supporter of the unification of the two countries. Shakespeare's plays showed the danger of dividing kingdoms so we can be sure the playwright preferred unifying rather than dividing the nation. Given that this annotation must date after 1603 is there any evidence of Shakespeare-Neville referring to *Leicester's Commonwealth* after that date? Indeed, as I showed in my previous book, there is just such a reference in *A Yorkshire Tragedy* printed in 1608 (see Casson, 2009). The murderous Husband says to the nursing maid who tries to protect his son:

> I'll break your clamour with your neck downstairs:
> Tumble, tumble, headlong! (Throws her down.)
> So, the surest way to charm a woman's tongue
> Is break her neck: **a politician did it**. (5.10)

This last line is a direct reference to death of Leicester's wife, Amy Robsart, who was believed to have been murdered by pushing her downstairs.

**Textual details: forms of abbreviation**
There are two special types of abbreviation in the annotations: the tilde and miniature superscript letters. A tilde is a curved line ~ placed over a letter to show that the following letter or letters have been omitted, for example: 'occacõn', 'acceptacõn', and 'ambicõn', where the final 'i' is omitted. There are also miniature superscript letters: "Her Ma$^{ties}$" for "Her Majesty's", 'w$^{th}$' for 'with', "y$^e$ testam$^{te}$" for "the testament". Occasionally these two forms of abbreviation are used together as in 'p$^r$paracõn'. Whilst these might be seen as entirely conventional forms

of abbreviation it is interesting to note that, as Crystal (2008, 56) pointed out, both tildes and superscripts are to be found in the First Folio. Crystal also noticed that the superscript 'w[t]' for 'with' is to be found in the Hand D (Shakespearean) section of the manuscript of *Sir Thomas More*. Since the compositors of the Folio were quite possibly working from authorial manuscripts the occurrence of these devices in the Folio and in the MSS 47 manuscript copy of *Leicester's Commonwealth* demonstrates a continuity in style of abbreviation between these texts. In manuscript documents in the British Library I have found Neville using the same miniature superscript "her ma[ties]" for "Her Majesty's" (Cotton MSS, Caligula EX, f 21, 21V).

Neville letter, 1601, see appendix 8

**Annotator B's trade mark 'ni'**
Often Annotator B spells words that contain an 'in' as 'ni'. At first I thought this was simply a matter of B delaying the dot over the 'i' but eventually I realised this was a habitual characteristic of the writer. This is visible in many annotations, for example:

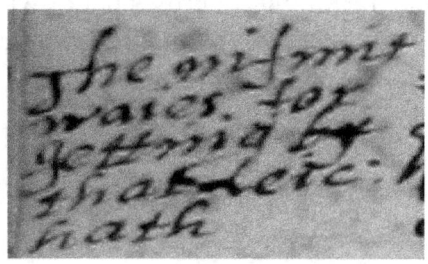

Worsley MSS 47, 23V

"The nifinit waies for gettnig [by] that Leic: hath". Looking at the placing of the dots over the 'i' we can see that in the case of the words 'waies' and 'Leic:' the dot is accurately placed. In 'nifinit' and 'gettnig' the placing of the dot makes it clear that B is spelling the 'in' as 'ni'. There are many examples of this in B's copy of the main text. For example, taking words at random on three consecutive pages, 53, 54, 55 (with other examples taken from elsewhere in the manuscript):

"sniguler nigratitude" (singular ingratitude):

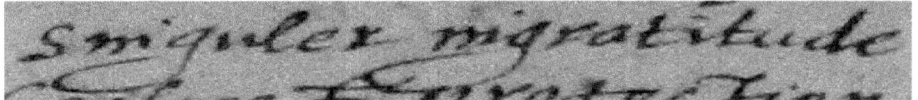

Worsley MSS 47, 53

'hopenige' (hoping):

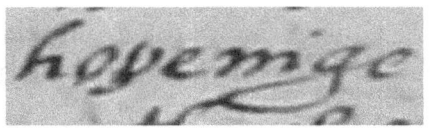

Worsley MSS 47, 54

'nidaunger' (endanger):

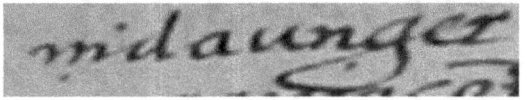

Worsley MSS 47, 54

"managnige & contriunige" (managing and contriving):

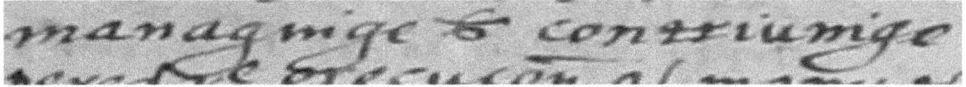

Worsley MSS 47, 54

"connnige ni this knid" (cunning in this kind):

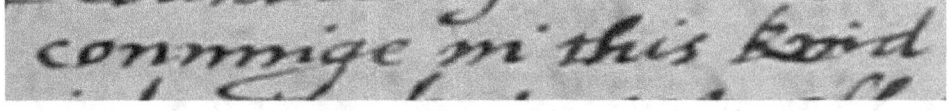

Worsley MSS 47, 54

'aganist' ('against'):

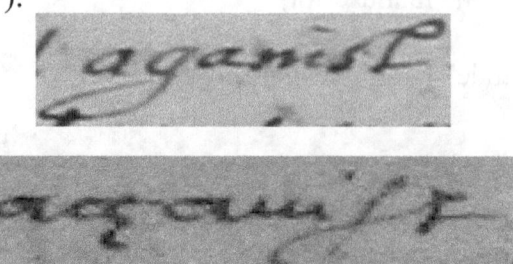

Worsley MSS 47, 55; 4

In Worsley MSS 47 'aganist' is more often spelt with the 'n' before the 'i', though occasionally it is spelt 'against'. (See appendix 1 for other examples.)

'Knig/e/s' (King):

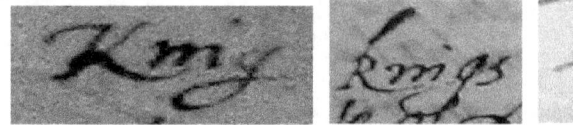

Worsley MSS 47, 53; 41V; 9V

Indeed two words are especially significant examples of the 'ni' habit, as in the following example: "aganist theire knige":

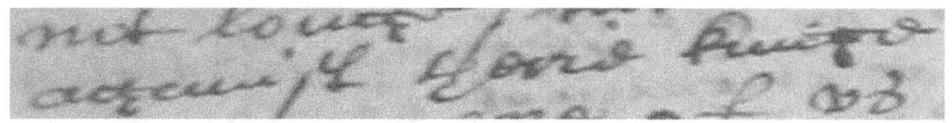

Worrsley MSS 47, 4V

In the Halle's *Chronicle* annotations, believed by Keen and Lubbock (1954) to be by Shakespeare (see chapter 4), the words 'king' and 'against' are used frequently, some of which are spelt in this way:

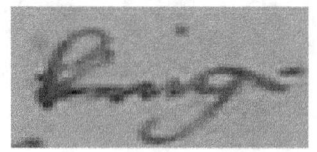 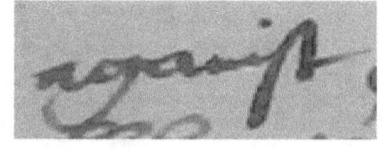

Halle *Chronicle* Henry IV, f.xxiv[b];   f.xxi[a]

I have also found examples of the 'ni' habit in the Hand D portion of the manuscript of the play *Sir Thomas More*, identified as that of Shakespeare (folios 8 - 9, Harley MS 7368, in the British Library). Indeed two of the words which especially illustrate this are 'knig' and 'aganist', (see Crystal, 2008, 36, or Farmer, 1910 and appendix 9).

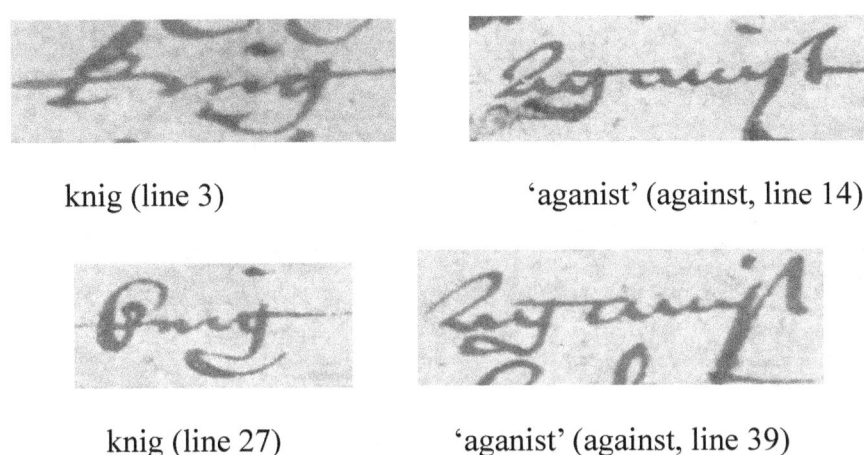

knig (line 3)  'aganist' (against, line 14)

knig (line 27)  'aganist' (against, line 39)

We can compare this with the word 'knig' in portions of the Worsley MSS 47 text in secretary script:

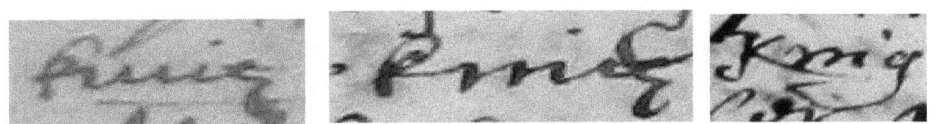

Worsley MSS 47, 7; 19; 31V

Furthermore we can compare these with a signed letter by Henry Neville from 1601:

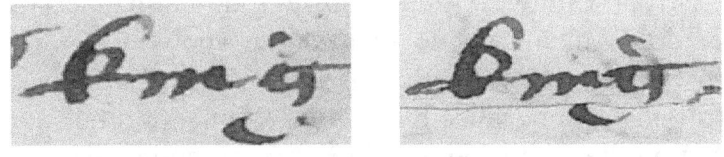

Neville letter, see appendix 8

Indeed other words in Neville's letter exhibit this 'ni' tendency such as 'ordniary' (ordinary), 'proceednig' (proceding), 'towchnig' (touching), 'behnid' (behind), 'thnike' (think) and 'ni' (in, twice):

Neville letter 1601

This habit persisted right to the end of his life. In a letter of 16[th] July 1613 Neville writes 'ni' instead of 'in' six times (Stowe, 174, folio 116, British Library). Indeed through this idiosyncratic spelling I have been able positively to identify an anonymous document in the Cotton Manuscript collection as by Neville (Caligula X, British Library, folios 3-5V) because it contains, "Touchnig the succession ni France my mounige ni this poyte…"(3); 'forbearnige' (4); 'concernige' and 'kniges' (4V); "knige hmiself" and 'hmi' (him) (5); 'miportnige' (importing) (5V).

On the first page of the Northumberland Manuscript, owned by Neville, there is a Latin verse:

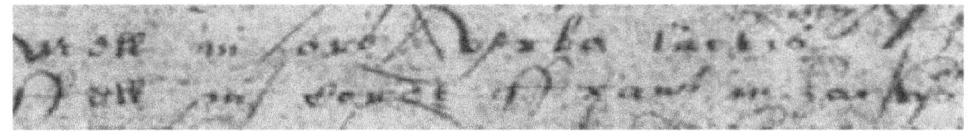

## Northumberland Manuscript

> Mell ni ore Verba lactis
> Ffell ni corde ffraus in factys

I translate this as:

> Honey in mouth, words of milk,
> Wicked in heart, false in deeds. [11]

Whilst the penultimate word is definitely 'in', the placing of the dot in the second word of each line clearly makes these 'ni'.

Furthermore other words in *Sir Thomas More* are spelt with the 'n' before the 'i'

*Sir Thomas More* "ni donig" (in doing: line 12)

We can see this spelling in Worsley MSS 47:

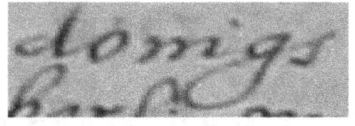

Worsley MSS 47, 59

There is also:

---

11   Compare Anne Neville's words in *Richard III*: "my woman's **heart** grossly grew captive to his **honey words**" (4.1.87).

'pvnice' (p[ro]vince, line 33)

It is also possible to make out the following on the earlier, damaged folios 8 and 8V. On folio 8 there is 'nifected' (infected); on folio 8V, 'ploddnig' (plodding), "knigs ni your desires" (kings in your desires), "ni ruff" (in ruff) and 'frenids' (friends). The last is also to be seen in Worsley 47 and folio 9 of *Sir Thomas More*.

 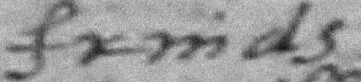 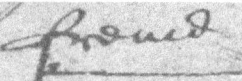

Worsley MSS 47, 59                          *Sir Thomas More* folio 9

In the penultimate Worsley MSS 47 annotation B writes 'hmi' instead of 'him': indeed he does this in three annotations (14V, 64V, 65V) and once writes 'hmiselfe' (26). The accurate placing of the dot over the 'i' in 'his' and 'if' show that the writer could place the dot accurately.

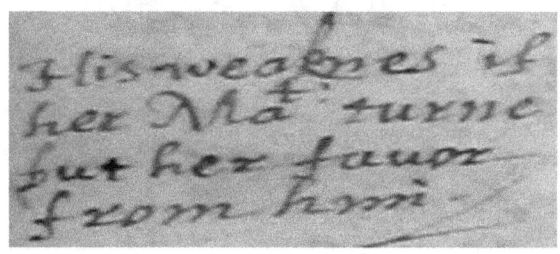

Worsley MSS 47, 65V

Furthermore this spelling 'hmi' is to be found in the main text and indeed other words such as 'smiple' (simple):

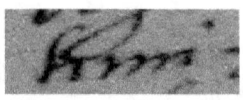 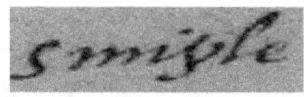

Worsley MSS 47, 53

71

In *Sir Thomas More* the word 'him' is spelt 'hmi' three times in three lines and 'hmisealfe' once. (*The Sir Thomas More* manuscript is in secretary script whereas the Worsley annotations are in italic but this spelling is still clearly 'hmi'.)

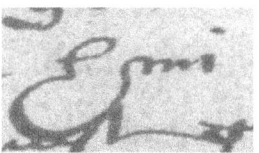 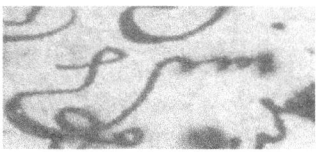

*Sir Thomas More*: hmi (him, lines 10 and 8)[12]

Furthermore we can compare these with examples of 'hmi' in secretary script sections of Worsley MSS 47 (which were written perhaps 7 years earlier):

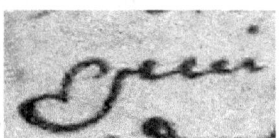 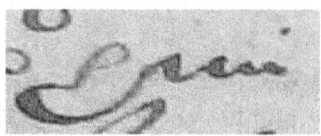

Worsley MSS 47, 2V: hmi; 6V

This opens the way for a palæographer to compare Neville's hand writing in his letters, Worsley MSS 47, Halle *Chronicle*, *Sir Thomas More* and Northumberland manuscripts.

**Conclusion**

Some of the similarities of vocabulary used in MSS 47 and by Shakespeare can be classed as weak (such as the occurrence of "thrust out"), others as stronger (such as "imminent… death" and 'contumelious') whilst Annotator B's reference to "The Law Salique in France" with the words 'claim' and 'bar' may be regarded as crucial. The unique reference to Dr. Shawe is indeed intriguing. Taken together they show a pattern of vocabulary and historical reference used by no other writer except Annotator B and Shakespeare. I have also shown that the vocabulary used by B in his annotations is not only used by Shakespeare but also by Neville in his letters. I therefore agree with James, in identifying B as Neville and indeed as Shakespeare.

---

12   All illustrations are from folio 9, Harley MS 7368. All line numbers are from Crystal, 2008, 37-8.

## Chapter 4

## The Annotator of Halle's *Chronicle* and
the Annotator of *Leicester's Commonwealth* Worsley MSS 47

> "... what obscured in this fair volume lies
> Find written in the margent ..."
> *Romeo and Juliet* (1.3.84)

In 1954 Keen and Lubbock published their book on the annotations found in the margins of a copy of Halle's *Chronicle*. These hand written notes were on the reigns of Richard II, Henry IV and Henry V: indeed they often matched Shakespeare's plays. (There are seven annotations at the start of the section on Henry VI but they stop abruptly on the second page.) Was this a unique example of Shakespeare's own handwriting as he researched his history plays? Lubbock and Keen claimed these annotations were by William Shakespeare from Stratford and created a complex web of associations to show how the young Shakespeare could have had access to this volume. They hypothesised that he was the same person as one William Shakeshafte who was mentioned in the will of Alexander Houghton in 1581, who lived at Lea Hall in Lancashire. There is, needless to say, no evidence whatsoever that this Shakeshafte was Shakespeare. Due to a printed label in the book that read **EEd**, Lubbock and Keen suggested the volume may have been in the library of Sir Robert Worsley, (1643-1675), because another book with a similar label, **App**, had been found containing his name. He was the grandson of Sir Richard Worsley and Frances, Henry Neville's daughter. They lived at **App**eldurcombe on the Isle of Wight. Brenda James was thus able to show that this volume of Halle's *Chronicle* had a direct connection with Neville (James & Rubinstein, 2005, 51). Indeed the current owner of the Worsley Manuscripts is Lord Yarborough one of whose forebears, the second Baron of Yarborough, had married "the nineteenth century heiress of the Isle of Wight Worsleys" (James & Rubinstein, 2005, 233, Plate 10). Through this marriage Appeldurcombe House came into the family.[13] The annotated Halle is now in the Lancaster University Library. James further suggested that **EEd** stood for Richard Eedes, an Oxford scholar

---

13   From: http://en.wikipedia.org/wiki/Earl_of_Yarborough accessed 31/3/09

who travelled to Scotland with Neville in 1583 and is mentioned in Francis Meres' list of playwrights (which included Shakespeare) in 1598 (James & Rubinstein, 2005, 235-6). The first owner of the Halle *Chronicle* was Sir Rychard Newport of High Ercall, Shropshire, who died in 1570. His daughter Magdalen was a patroness of literature, friend of John Donne and mother of the poet George Herbert (McLaren, 1949, 44). She had married Richard Herbert, who was related to the Earls of Pembroke and so to Mary Sidney, Countess of Pembroke. Neville knew Donne, the Sidneys and William Herbert, Earl of Pembroke, who was later to be a dedicatee of the First Folio (James & Rubinstein, 2005, 199-200). Whether Neville borrowed the book, or was given it, we will probably never know but he was within the social orbit of Magdalen Newport/Herbert.

**The date of the Halle annotations**
If the date for the annotations in the Worsley copies of *Leicester's Commonwealth* MSS 36 and 47 is 1584-6 they would probably predate the annotations in Halle's *Chronicle*. One of the Halle annotations, (on folio f.xxiii[b] of the Henry IV section[14]) is against a passage that includes the words "effusion of our Christian blood". This phrase is to be found in *Henry VI* part 1 when Gloucester speaks of stopping the "**effusion of our Christian blood**" (5.1.9). I found "much **effusion** of our English **blood**" in *The Troublesome Raigne of John King of England* (1.2.416) and a "great **effusion of blood**" in *Locrine* (2.2.88). I have also found two other rare words 'transfret' and 'celeritee' in Halle that are in *Locrine* which I have dated to 1586-9. It is therefore possible that Neville read Halle as early as 1586 but this would still post date the annotations of *Leicester's Commonwealth*. Keen and Lubbock (1954, 20) did not date the annotations but suggested they were written "several years earlier than any of his (Shakespeare's) writing that survives", by which they must mean before 1590 and the *Henry VI* plays. However since the reigns annotated in Halle are mainly those of Richard II, Henry IV and Henry V and the dates of Shakespeare's plays on those reigns are approximately 1595 – 99, even if we allow several years of research and writing, it is probable that Halle's *Chronicle* would not have been annotated before the early 1590s. This then could also explain the difference in the styles of handwriting. Neville, who James (2008, 234) has pointed out, was used to varying, even disguising,

---

14    I have retained Keen and Lubbock's system of numbering the folios.

his handwriting, was several years older by the time he came to annotate the Halle. Even if we allow for the possibility that the young bard was doing historical research some time before writing his history cycle this would only bring the date of the Halle annotations back as far as 1588. However the fact that the annotator does not proceed to annotate the reign of Henry VI suggests a later date as the trilogy on that reign had already been written by 1591. The annotations of Halle are more detailed and sophisticated than those of the Worsley MSS 47 copy of *Leicester's Commonwealth*, which also argues for a later date. The date of the Halle annotations probably lies between 1586-1596, though I suspect they were made in the latter part of this decade, probably 1594-8, and so about ten years after those in Worsley MSS 47.

**The vocabulary and themes of Worsley MSS 47 and Halle's *Chronicle***
There are many similarities between the annotations of Halle's *Chronicle* and those of Worsley MSS 47, which would make sense if they were written by the same person. Of course there is some overlap of subject matter and certain common words are bound to arise given that both documents are looking at the same period of history. A full list of the words found in common in the annotations is in appendix 3.
Of all the shared words and associated material the most remarkable is what first struck Keen's eye when he opened the ancient volume on June 22$^{nd}$ 1940. He saw the Latin words, "<u>In terram salicam mulieres ne succedant</u>" had been underlined. These very words are quoted by the Archbishop of Canterbury in *Henry V*. He helpfully translates this as, "No woman shall succeed in Salike land" (1.2.39 First Folio spelling). The Halle annotator had written in the margin "note the exposition".

Halle's Chronicle, Henry V, f.iv$^b$

The text referred to explains:

"which is to say, let not womē succede in the land *Salicque. This land Salicque the deceitful glosers name to be the realm of Fraunce. This lawe the logicall interpretours assigne to directe the croune and regalitie of the same region, as who would, say that to that preheminence no woman were liable to aspire, nor no heire female was worthy to inherite."

The asterix refers to a printed marginal note "* the lands Salique". Scholars agree that the Halle's *Chronicle* passage was the source used by Shakespeare for *Henry V*. We can now see a direct connection between these two annotated texts, of the Worsley MSS 47 copy of *Leicester's Commonwealth* and Halle's *Chronicle*. The unique annotation in Worsley MSS 47, as I explained in chapter 3, reads, "**The Lawe Salique in ffraunce**" and in *Henry V* the King says, "**the Law Salike,** that they have **in France**" (1.2.11, First Folio spelling). The phrase used in the main text of *Leicester's Commonwealth* is "**the Law Salick in Fraunce**" (original spelling).

This wording is not to be found in Halle's *Chronicle* which speaks of "Salike land", not "Lawe Salique", (though the word 'lawe' occurs in the next sentence). However the Worsley MSS 47 spelling in the text matches that of the printed marginal annotation in the Halle's *Chronicle*.

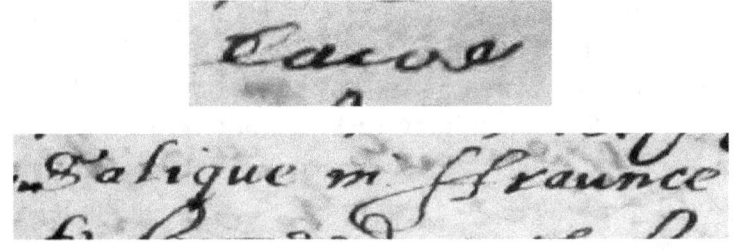

Worsley MSS 47, 39[15]

The First Folio mostly spells the word "**Salike**" but on the last occasion it is used by the Archbishop the word is spelt, '**Salique**'. Thus we can see that *Leicester's Commonwealth* sparked Neville's interest in this law, which he then researched in Halle and used in *Henry V*.
Both annotators are therefore concerned with the laws of succession and lines of generations. One of the annotations of Halle's *Chronicle* is "nota a pedegree":

---

15   This illustration is divided because the word 'lawe' is at the end of the previous line.

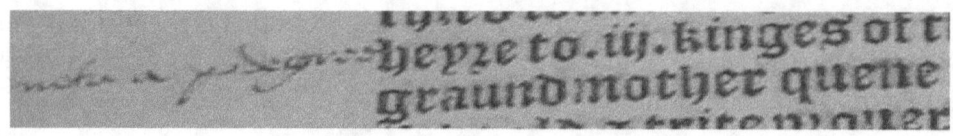

Halle *Chronicle*, Henry V, f.xlii[a]

In Worsley MSS 47 the annotator has written, "Pedigree of Henr 7[th]".

Worsley MSS 47, 43

*Edward III*, a play recently accepted into the Shakespeare canon, opens with the King asking Artois to "go forward with our **pedigree**". He then uses the words, "**died and left no issue**" (1.1.9). One Halle annotation reads, "three Kinges **dyeing withowt yssue**" (Henry V, f.v[b], Keen & Lubbock, 1954, 136). The annotator of Worsley MSS 47 has a note, "Arbella after maried to y[e] Earle of Hartfo grandchild & **dies without yssue**" (44). The printed annotation is just 'Arbella'. (See the Appendix 10 for further reflections on this annotation.) In *Henry VIII* we hear, "if the king should **without issue die**" (1.2.134).

In the *Leicester's Commonwealth* printed annotations (copied in both Worsley MSS 36 and 47) we find, "The **joyninge** of **bothe hovvses**". In the Worsley MSS 47 annotations this is repeated twice, referring to the Tudor resolution of "the controuersie betweene **Yorke and Lancaster**". In Halle's *Chronicle* there is an annotation which uses the words "heares males of **bothe (t)he howses yorke and lan=(c)ast**[re] were destroyed" (Keen & Lubbock, 1954, 128).

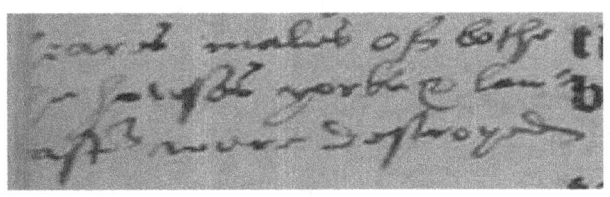

Halle's Chronicle, Henry IV, f.x[a]

This is a variation on Halle's actual text which reads, "bothe the lines" (Henry IV, fx[a]). Another printed annotation in *Leicester's Commonwealth*, copied by MSS 36 reads, "The happy **coniunction** of the ii **howses**".

At the end of *Richard III* Richmond says (in the First Folio version of the text):

> We will vnite the White Rose, and the Red.
> Smile Heauen vpon this faire **Coniunction**,
> That long haue frown'd vpon their Enmity...

(five lines cut)

> All this diuided **Yorke and Lancaster**,
> Diuided, in their dire Diuision.
> O now, let *Richmond* and *Elizabeth*,
> The true Succeeders of each Royall **House**,
> By Gods faire ordinance, **conioyne** together...        (5.7.19)

We can see the words '(con)**join**' and '**conjunction**' from *Leicester's Commonwealth* are used with the words 'house' and "Yorke and Lancaster". Three times Mercutio cries, "A plague o' **both** your **houses!**" when he is wounded in a brawl in *Romeo and Juliet* (3.1.92, 100, 108). We can now appreciate the political meaning of that play which is not just about star-crossed lovers but about the danger of civil war between two houses. Shakespeare-Neville is warning the country to stay united: this is the political motive behind his reading of *Leicester's Commonwealth*, his research in Halle and his writing of the plays.

This danger is the subject of another of the annotations in Worsley MSS 47: "**daungers of dissention in o**[r] **Realme**". Shakespeare uses "**dissension in our**" 8 lines before '**realm**' in *Henry VI* part 1 (4.1.139). The annotator of Halle notes '**discention**', '**civil discenscyon**' and again '**cyvyle dissention**' and uses the word '**realme**' (Keen & Lubbock, 1954, 133, 138, 144). In *Henry VI* part 1 the King says, "**Civil dissension** is a viperous worm that gnaws the **bowels** of **the commonwealth**." (3.1.72). In *Leicester's Commonwealth* the words '**dissension**' and '**bowels**' are used twice. Again we can see a weaving of these sources in the Shakespeare plays.

In *King John*, Cardinal Pandulph says, "a civil war set'st **oath** to **oath**" (3.1.264). The making and breaking of oaths is a major theme of early Shakespeare. In both Worsley MSS 36 and 47 there are annotations that are not in the printed text about "his **oathes profaned**" (66V/65V). In Halle's *Chronicle* the annotator wrote about oaths three times: "conspiracy by indenture and **othe**"[16], "An **othe taken** and **not regardyd**"[17] and "An **othe taken**" (Keen & Lubbock, 1954, Henry IV, f.xii$^b$, 129; f.xxx$^a$, 134; Henry V, f.xl$^b$, 147). In Shakespeare I have found the word '**oath**' used with '**profaned**' and '**take/ta'en/taking**'. The making and breaking of oaths is a theme in the following plays: the *Henry VI* trilogy, *Titus Andronicus*, *Edward III*, *The Two Gentlemen of Verona*, *Love's Labours Lost* and *King John*. I have also found this theme in the apocryphal plays I have previously shown are early works by the bard: *Locrine*, *Arden of Faversham*, *The Troublesome Raigne* and *Edmund Ironside* (Casson, 2009).

In Worsley MSS 47 there is an annotation: "**a pittifull case**". The Halle annotator also writes of "**a pitiuse case**" (Keen & Lubbock, 1954, Henry V, f.xxix$^a$, 145). I have already noted that in *Romeo and Juliet* the words "a pitiful case" occur (4.5.93). The annotation in the printed version of *Leicester's Commonwealth* reads, "The case of Snovvden forest most pittifull". Worsley MSS47 makes this into, "The matter of Snowden **a pittifull case**". Thus we can see that the Worsley MSS47 annotator has altered this note in a way that is compatible with the annotator of Halle and with Shakespeare. Furthermore the Halle annotator writes: "prisoners **pitifully** slayne" and "(A) noble and notable acte of **pytie**" (Henry V, f.xix$^a$; f.xxvi$^a$: Keen & Lubbock, 1954, 141, 144). Shakespeare uses 'pity', 'pitiful' and 'pitifully' in his works.

---

16    This is the same spelling that Neville uses in the 1602 Tower Notebook (on folio 89) "k. othe" (= king's oath), Worsley MSS 40.

17    The words "**not regarded**" are used in *Henry VI* part 2 and *Henry IV* part 1 but these are not of oaths.

## Historical Figures in Halle, Worsley MSS47 and Shakespeare

The following named or titled historical figures are mentioned in the annotations of both Halle and Worsley MSS 47 and by Shakespeare.

| Halle's *Chronicle* | Worsley MSS 47 | Shakespeare |
|---|---|---|
| The duke of Herford | Earle of Herford 44 | Earl of Hereford: in *Richard II, Richard III* and *Henry VIII* |
| Duke of Norfolk | Duke of Norffc. 54, 55 | *Henry VI* part 3, *Richard II, Richard III, Henry IV* part 2, and *Henry VIII* |
| John of gaunt | John of Gaunt Duke of Lanc: 42V John of Gaunte 42V, 43 | *Henry VI* parts 1,2,3, *Henry IV* parts 1 & 2, *Richard II* |
| Edmund duke (of) yorke | Edmund of Langley the First duke of Yorke 43V | *Henry VI* parts 1 & 2, *Richard II* |
| Arundell | Arund 24V Arundell 55V | *Troublesome Raigne, Thomas of Woodstock,* as Mowbray: *Richard II, Henry IV* part 2 |
| archebishop of cant' | Archb: of Canter: 10V Archb: of Caunterb: 30 | *Richard II, King John, Henry V, Henry VIII* |
| Henry duke of Lancaster | Hen: Duke of Lancaster 35V | *Henry VI* parts 2 & 3, *Richard II* |

| Kynge Richard (II) | Ric 2, 35V<br>Rich 2, 43 | *Richard II*, *Henry VI* part 1, *Henry IV* parts 1 & 2 |
|---|---|---|
| Kinge henry the iiiith | K.Hen: 35V<br>Henr: 4. 42V | *Richard III*,<br>*Henry IV* parts 1 & 2 |
| The Pearcyes<br>lord percey | The Peirceyes 35V | *Richard II*,<br>*Henry IV* parts 1 & 2 |
| earle of northumberland | the Duke of Northumberland 31, 34, 49V, 59 | *Henry VI* part 3,<br>*Richard III*, *Richard II*,<br>*Henry IV* parts 1 & 2,<br>*Henry VIII* |
| The duke of Clarence | Duke of Clarence 43, 43V, 44, 31V | *Henry VI* parts 1,2,3,<br>*Richard III*, *Henry V*,<br>*Henry IV* part 2 |
| duke of Bedford | Earl of Bedd: 21V | *Henry VI* parts 1 & 2,<br>*Henry V* |
| duke of glocester | Duke of Gloucester 44, 57, 35 | *Henry VI* parts 1,2,3,<br>*Richard III*, *Henry V*<br>*King Lear* |
| duke of yorke | duke of Yorke 43V, 59 | *Henry VI* parts 1,2,3,<br>*Richard III*, *Richard II*,<br>*Henry V* |
| Julius | Julius 58 | *Henry VI* parts 1 & 2,<br>*Richard III*, *Richard II*,<br>*Julius Ceasar*, *Hamlet*,<br>*Cymbeline*,<br>*Antony & Cleopatra* |

Some of these figures are the same person: Henry Bolingbroke was Duke of Hereford and Lancaster and became Henry IV. Others are titles held by different men in different generations and reigns. The name Arundell does not occur in canonical plays but is used in *The Troublesome Raigne* and *Thomas of Woodstock*, both of which I view as early works. Thomas Mowbray held the title and is in *Richard II* and *Henry IV* part 2. There are other historic figures common to Halle, Shakespeare and the *Leicester's Commonwealth* texts, but these annotated figures stand out (three of them give their names to the titles of Shakespeare plays) and mostly occur in the following history plays (I am ignoring those plays in which there is only one occurrence):

| | |
|---|---|
| *Richard II* | 12 |
| *Henry IV* part 1 | 5 |
| *Henry IV* part 2 | 7 |
| *Henry V* | 4 |
| *Henry VI* part 1 | 8 |
| *Henry VI* part 2 | 9 |
| *Henry VI* part 3 | 7 |
| *Richard III* | 6 |
| *Henry VIII* | 4 |

This scoring suggests the political importance placed on the reigns of *Richard II* and *Henry VI* as axiomatic of the concerns of Shakespeare. As these reigns were dogged by usurpation and civil war they are expressive of Neville's political concern for the state of the nation in the 1590s: what would happen when the childless reign of Elizabeth I drew to a close?

The Percy family clearly interested the annotators and Shakespeare. Henry Percy was the contemporary Earl of Northumberland. He married Katherine, eldest daughter and co-heir of John Neville, Baron Latimer.

One name that does not occur in the Halle annotations is Neville: it occurs twice in those of Worsley MSS 47. This is consistent with the earlier dating of the Worsley manuscripts: in the earliest Shakespeare plays the name Neville occurs repeatedly, indeed eight times in *Henry VI* part 2, whereas in later works Neville is more discrete or does not use the name at all, hiding the members of the Neville family behind their titles, such as the Earldoms of Salisbury, Westmoreland and Warwick. In one Halle annotation there is mention of "the earle of Westmoreland" (Henry V, f.ix[a], Keen and Lubbock, 1954, 137). He was Ralph Neville.

**The systematic annotator**
The Halle annotator lists 6 articles, numbering each with a number 1 - 6 (Henry IV f.xxii[a], Keen and Lubbock, 1954, 130). In the next section he lists three items with the words, "first…seconde…Thrydde" (Henry V, f.xvi[b], Keen and Lubbock, 1954, 140). In Worsley MSS 47 there are several annotations that are numerical lists:

"two excuses made by his frnds, 2, theire resons, 1, 2."
and
"argum[ts] of his meaning for himself before Huntingt: 1 argum[te], the nature of Ambicõn, 2 argum[te], his particular, disposicon, 1, 2."
and
"three barrs Against Marie Que: of Scotts and James 6[t] K: of Scotts, 1, fforraine birth, 2, K: H: 8[th] s testam[te], 3, Relligion."

I also note this numbering of points is to be seen in the Northumberland Manuscript:

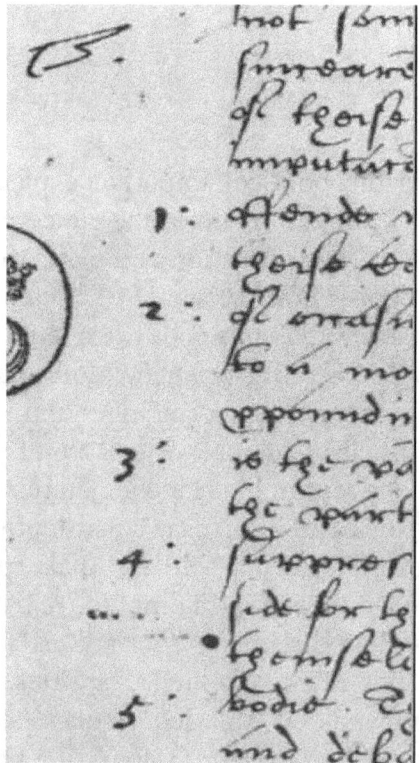

Northumberland MS: Folio 33

83

In annotations made in the margin of a letter from Robert Cecil, Neville lists five points: 1,2,3,4,5 (Yelverton, MS XXXIX, 38V, British Library). In another letter dated 15/6/99 Neville makes a list of four points to Cecil (Winwood, 1725, Vol 1, 47). On a printed leaflet about the wool trade Neville has left a note with 8 points highlighted (Cotton MSS, Caligula EX, 24, British Library). This last item is also remarkable for having a little drawing of a pointing hand in the margin, a device that is also used by the Halle annotator and at the top of the above illustration of the Northumberland Manuscript and again below.

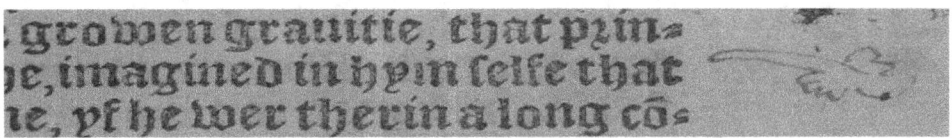

Halle's Chronicle

Northumberland MS: Folio 41

I have also found another pointing finger and other annotations by Neville in the margin of a letter from Robert Cecil (Folio 200, Cotton MSS, Caligula EIX, British Library).

**Spelling**
It would be unwise to make too much of the spellings of words in these documents because at the time there was no such thing as standard spelling. However if the same person was the author of both sets of annotations we would reasonably expect spellings to match some of the time. Where these match with the spelling in Neville's letters they become further evidence of a common author.

A printed marginalia of *Leicester's Commonwealth* states: "The comparison of vvolues & Rebels." B renders this as: "wolves and **Rebells**", with a double 'll'.

Worsley MSS 47, 58V

The annotator of Halle's *Chronicle* has a note "the **p(ra)ctize** of **Rebells**…" (Henry IV, f.xix[b], Keen & Lubbock, 1954, 130):

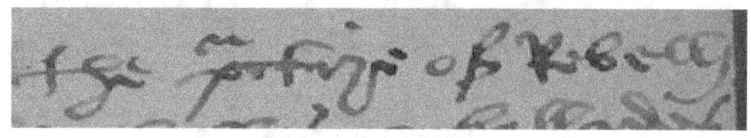

Halle's *Chronicle*, Henry IV, f.xix[b]

Furthermore in the scene believed to have been written by Shakespeare in *Sir Thomas More* the word '**rebell**' with a double 'll' is used four times, once in the plural.

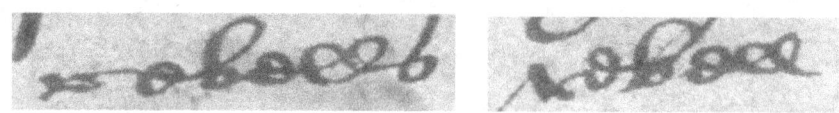

*Sir Thomas More* folio 9, lines 14 and 19

Neville uses this spelling of '**Rebells**' in diplomatic letters dated 8/8/99, 9/9/1600 and 28/12/1600 (Winwood, Vol 1, 89, 254, 287). He also spells '**practizes**' with a 'z' in three letters dated 26/5/99, 14/8/1599 and 25/1/1600 (Winwood, Vol 1, 34, 90, 147). Furthermore in a marginal annotation on a letter from Robert Cecil dated 12/5/1600, Neville notes "Irish **Rebells**" (Yelverton XXXIX, MS 48035, f.41V, British Library). In the First Folio, the word '**rebell**' is spelt with a double 'll' in *Henry VI* part 3 (1.1.50). Dover Wilson (1923, 133) found evidence in the spelling used in early quartos that Shakespeare habitually used a double final consonant.

The annotator of Hall's *Chronicle* spells '**howses**' with a 'w' three times.

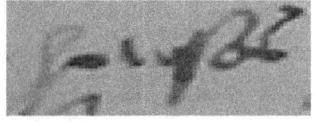

Halle's *Chronicle*, Henry IV, f.x[a]

Both Worsley MSS annotators A and B write of 'howses'.

Worsley MSS 47, 41V (Italic)

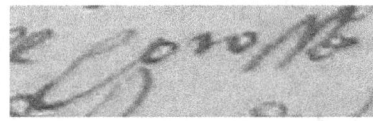

Worsley MSS 47, 7 (Secretary Script)

Neville uses this spelling in a letter dated 8/8/99 (Winwood, 1725, Vol 1, 89). Again in the manuscript of *Sir Thomas More* the spelling is '**howses**'.

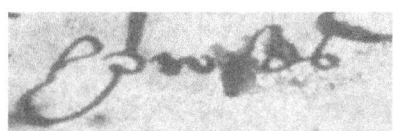

*Sir Thomas More* folio 9, line 25

The Worsley MSS 47 annotator often inserts a 'u' into words such as France, strange/stranger, change, danger, ancient, ancestors, Canterbury, tenant, whereas the MSS 36 annotator does not. So in MSS 47 I find: 'ffraunce', 'straunge/straungers', 'chaunge', 'indaungereth/daunger', 'aunciente', 'auncestors', 'Caunterb:', 'fflaunders', 'tenauntable'. There is also 'comaund' and 'mayntenaunce', words not used in MSS 36.

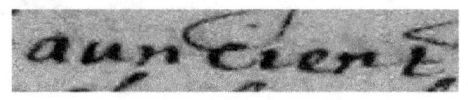

Worsley MSS 47, 47

In the Halle annotations I find: 'fraunce', 'straungers', 'daungerose', 'commaundement'. There are also 'avaunced', 'raunso(ming)', 'deliveraunce', 'defiaunce', 'aunswer', 'sufferaunce', 'chaunce'.

The 1591 Quarto version of *The Troublesome Raigne* has this characteristic spelling with 'au'. These match the MSS 47 words: 'Fraunce', 'auncient', 'auncestors', even including the rare 'tenaunte'.

Worsley MSS 47, 47

They also include words found in the Halle annotations: 'fraunce', 'chaunce', 'commaunded' and 'mischaunce'. There are also other 'au' such as 'slaunder' and 'demaund'. On folio 9 of *Sir Thomas More* there are 'comaund' and 'fraunc'. In the first quarto of *Titus Andronicus* there are 'command', 'demaund' and 'raunsome'.

Neville uses the following spellings in letters: 'straunge', 'commaundment', 15/5/1599; 'straungers' 1/9/1599; 'daunger' 7/8/99 (Winwood, 1725, Vol 1, 21, 86, 98). In a letter to Sir T. Edmonde, 16/7/1613, Neville wrote the word 'commaund' (Stowe, 174, f.116, British Library).

In Worsley MSS 47 Neville abbreviates words that start with 'per', 'pro', 'par' and writes:

'ptest' (protest):     'pmitted' (permitted):

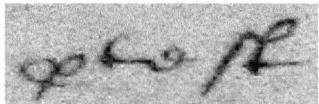 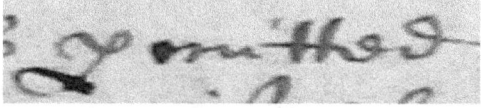

Worsley MSS 47, 2V; 6

'psonages' (personages):     'pceuve' (perceive):

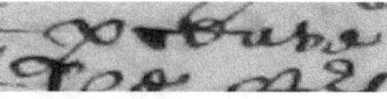

Worsley MSS 47, 16V; 19

'pte' (part):          "ni his psperitie" (in his prosperity):

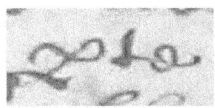

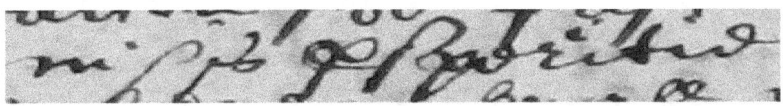

Worsley MSS 47, 16V; 19

"ni pnce" (in presence):        'psuade' (persuade):

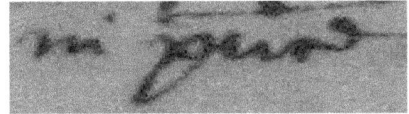 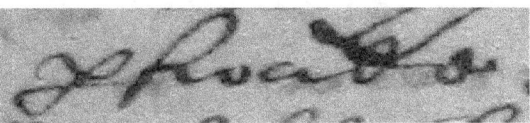

Worsley MSS 47, 32; 32V

'pfitt' (profit):          'pfitable' (profitable):

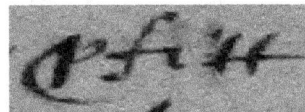 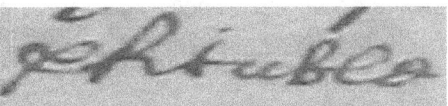

Worsley MSS 47, 53; 8V

"pticuler  pvicons" (particular provisions):

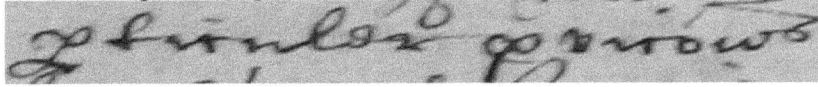

Worsley MSS 47, 23

"ni ppetuall" (in perpetual):      'phapps' (perhaps):

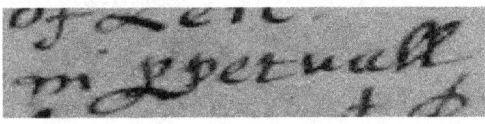 

Worsley MSS 47, 53; 9

The annotator of Halle's *Chronicle* likewise abbreviates words beginning with 'pre/pra/pri/pro/par/per': in these two examples this results in a double 'pp', just as in 'ppetuall' (in Worsley MSS 47, see above):

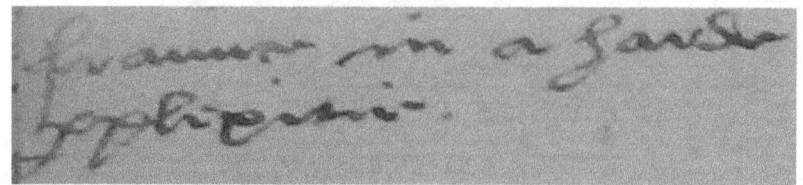

"fraunce in a harde pplexitie" Halle's *Chronicle* Henry V, f.xxiii<sup>a</sup>

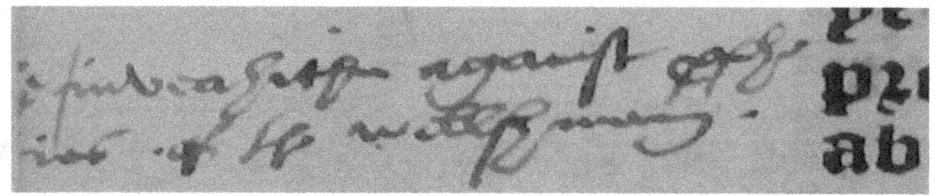

"(h)e inveahithe aganist pphe-(c)ies of the wellshmen"
Halle's *Chronicle* Henry IV, f.xxi<sup>a</sup>

In fact I have counted at least 37 examples of this habit amongst the Halle's *Chronicle* annotations. These are not noted by Keen and Lubbock who modernised the spelling and so missed the significance of these abbreviations. I first noticed the abbreviated 'pctize' (practice). The superscript tilde, shaped like an 'm', represents the missing letters. In secretary script the 'c' looks like an 'r'.

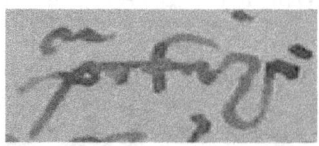

pctize (practice), Halle's *Chronicle* Henry IV, f.xix<sup>b</sup>

I then found p$^s$st (present)[18], repsent (represent), ppfecie (prophecy), pvocation (provocation), app$^s$hendyd (apprehended), re$^s$hendythe (reprehended), p'nce (prince), p'soner (prisoner), pliamẽt (parliament), pmised (promised), imp'soninge (imprisoning), apptaigninge (appertaining),

---

18   The superscript mark, here a small 's' as in 'p$^s$st', is not actually an 's' but a tilde, representing the abbreviated letters.

pclamation (proclamation), pvisyon (provision), ptector (protector), app°chnige (approaching), pcession (procession), pplexitie (perplexity), padvẽtur (peradventure), pthodawe (prothpdawe), p'ncipal (principal), pparation (preparation), pclaim (proclaim).

It is therefore startling to find that in the Hand D section of *Sir Thomas More* manuscript there are words beginning with 'pro/par' with only the initial 'p': 'pcure' (procure), 'pdon' (pardon), 'pclamation' (proclamation), 'pvnice' (province) and 'pceed' (proceed, deleted in the text, see chapter 8). These can be seen to mirror examples to be found in Worsley MSS 47.

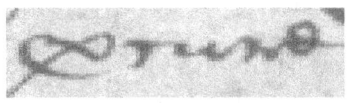

'pcure' (procure), *Sir Thomas More*

'pcure', (procure), Worsley MSS 47, 8V; 'pcured' 9; 'pcureth' 5V

'pdon' (pardon) *Sir Thomas More*

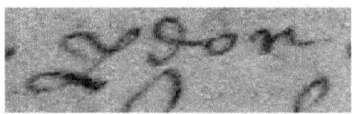

pdon' (pardon) Worsley MSS 47, 12V

Furthermore the handwriting of the abbreviated 'proclamation' in Worsley 47, the Halle and *Sir Thomas More* is similar:

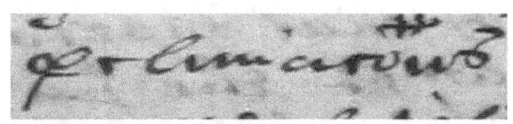

'pclimacõns' Worsley MSS 47, 45 (1584-6)

'pclamation' *Sir Thomas More* (1592-3)

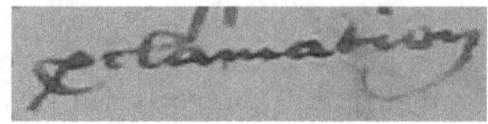

'pclamation' Halle's *Chronicle* Henry V f.ix$^b$ (1594-8)

Whilst the *Sir Thomas More* and Halle annotation are more alike, the 'pc' of the Worsley 47 and the Halle are closer.

It could be objected that this 'pro/par/per' abbreviation might be made by any writer. I therefore checked the entire text of *Sir Thomas More*, which is in several hands, to see if the other writers used such an abbreviation. The principal writer, Anthony Munday, never abbreviates nor do Chettle, Heywood or Dekker. Just one example occurs: Hand C, a copyist, writes 'pdon' (pardon). What is interesting about this is that, just nine lines earlier, the word 'deluded' occurs (see Gabrieli & Melchiori, 1990, 132). Shakespeare uses this word just once, in the early play *Henry VI* part 1 (5.4.76). We have seen the word '**deludenige**' in Worsley MSS 47, (56) and '**delude**' in a Neville letter of 1/11/1599 (in chapter 3). Hand C therefore may have been copying text written by the bard and accurately copied Neville's abbreviation of 'pdon'. This then provides possible evidence that Shakespeare-Neville wrote more of *Sir Thomas More* (as some editors have wondered) than just folios 8 and 9. Indeed as the scene is one in which one man is disguised, the situation points towards Neville. See chapter 8 for other examples in *Sir Thomas More* of handwriting comparable to Worsley MSS 47.

**Evidence for Neville in the Halle annotations**
One early annotation in Halle is "duke of Norfolk (dy)ed at venice" (Henry IV, f.iv$^a$, Keen and Lubbock, 1955, 127). This additional piece of information about Thomas de Mowbray is not only in the Halle text but also in *Richard II* (4.1.97). Neville and his father had both visited Venice. A hash mark, #, is placed in the margin next to a passage that includes mention of Windsor. In a later annotation he specifically notes "henry the

kynge of england his sonne borne at Windsor" (Keen and Lubbock, 1954, 148, Henry V, f.xlvi[b])[19]. Neville and his father were both wardens of the Windsor forest. Furthermore the annotator notes "a justinge at Oxford" (= jousting: Henry IV, f.xii[a], Keen and Lubbock, 1954, 129). Neville studied at Oxford. Paris is also noted several times (Henry V, f.xliii[b], f.xlviii[a], f.l[b], Keen and Lubbock, 1954, 147-9). Neville had travelled there as a young man and would later be ambassador in Paris. Thus we can see that these place names, Venice, Windsor, Oxford and Paris all have Neville connections which might explain why the annotator made a note of them.

**Edward Neville, the naughty boy**
On several pages of the annotated Halle there are squiggles and blots on the opposite page in a darker ink (Henry IV, f.xi[a/b]; f.xii[a/b]; f.xvi[a/b]; f.xvii[a/b]). They are all in the same area, about three inches up from the bottom of the page, as if the writer could not reach higher.

 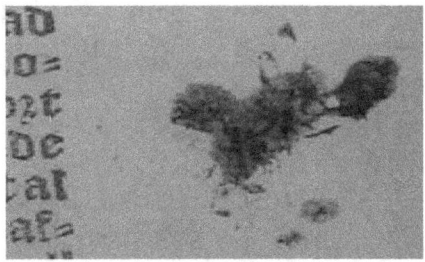

Halle's *Chronicle*: squiggles and blots

On one page this writer copies one of the annotations: the word 'execution'. This is clearly not by the original annotator: the handwriting and ink are different. The word 'execution' is also sloping upward to the right. Underneath is the name 'Edward' in a large childish hand.

---

19   The Halle annotator here spells 'son' with a double 'nn': 'sonne'. The Annotator of Worsley MSS47 likewise writes 'sonne' and this is the preferred spelling in the First Folio: 'sonne' occuring 555 times, 'son' just 68 times (Crystal, 2008, 62).

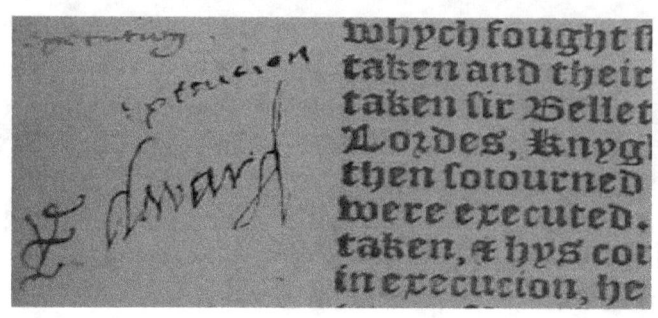

Halle's *Chronicle*, Henry IV, fxiv[a]

Keen and Lubbock (1954, 211) noticed this name and added that it was also "pricked out with a pin". I was unable to detect these perforations but the written name is bold indeed.

Neville had a son Edward, who was born in 1602, and who later became a fellow at King's College, Cambridge, dying in 1632 (James & Rubinstein, 2005, 336). I suggest that the Halle volume probably stayed in the family during this time and that we see here the youngest son naughtily scribbling in the margin, and proudly leaving us his name. These blotted marks however also have extraordinary implications. They must have been made between 1607-12 by a boy young enough to innocently, brazenly vandalise his father's book, old enough to read and write. Edward may have been the result of an extramarital affair by Anne during Neville's imprisonment in the Tower. During these years Neville wrote two plays about a husband's jealousy: *Othello* (written between 1601-4: about the time of Edward's birth or soon afterwards) and *The Winter's Tale* (1610 - 11). I have also traced the Shakespearean blot image cluster in *A Yorkshire Tragedy*, written in 1605, in which a husband believes his children are bastards (Casson, 2009). What is especially uncanny is that Edward copies just the one word, 'execution'. His great grandfather, also called Edward, was executed in the Tower of London, and this child annotator was conceived when Neville was incarcerated in the Tower.

**Conclusion**
Further analysis of the handwriting and other stylistic elements may be needed to confirm my view that the annotators of Halle and Worsley MSS 47 are the same person, namely Henry Neville and 'Shakespeare', though both texts were probably annotated before he started using

that nom-de-plume. The annotated Halle volume deserves to be better known and studied: I was astonished to learn that I may be the first person to examine it in the 60 years since Keen and Lubbock's book was published.

## Chapter 5

Neville's changes to vocabulary in his copy of *Leicester's Commonwealth*

> "my book wherein my soul recorded
> the history of all her secret thoughts"
> *Richard III* (3.5.26)

In this chapter I will trace some of the changes that Neville made as he copied the main text of *Leicester's Commonwealth* into the Worsley MSS 47 notebook. I will concentrate on that portion of the text that is in italic handwriting, from page 40V onwards. As the reader can see below, the italic is easier to read than the secretary script. Neville changes from secretary script for emphasis, to highlight names and when he seems more interested in the subject. He does this especially from the beginning of the section on the Wars of the Roses (see the top of page and marginal annotation for "the redd Rose and the white"), with secretary script at the top and bottom on this illustration.

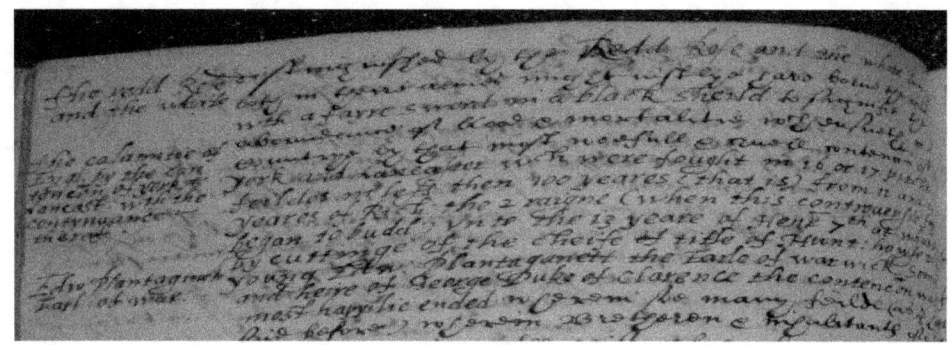

Worsley MSS 47, 40V

My case is that in making changes to the text, Neville was often unconsciously changing it in ways that point to his authorship of the works of Shakespeare. The first example of this I noticed was in a section on Richard III. In the printed version we find:

"Richard of Gloucester had never been able to have usurped as he did if he had not first persuaded King Edward IV to hate his own brother the Duke of Clarence, which Duke stood in the way between Richard and the thing which **he most** of all things **coveted**, that is, the possibility to the crown."

(Peck, 169/*112*)

Worsley MSS 47, 53

Neville copies this as, "he most desired" not 'coveted': Shakespeare never used "most coveted" but used "most desired" in *Cymbeline* (1.1.12). Shakespeare used 'desired' 33 times and 'coveted' just once. Is this merely a coincidence? Neville also writes "possibility of" instead of "possibility to". Shakespeare uses "possibility of" twice but never writes "possibility to". At the top left of this illustration is the word 'perpetual' (Neville spells this 'ppetual') which is used three times in *Leicester's Commonwealth*. This word is used by Clarence in *Richard III* when he describes a nightmare of his own death by drowning ("Unto the kingdom of **perpetual** night" 1.4.44). Thus we see the word being used in the very context it appears in *Leicester's Commonwealth*, so pointing to it being a source for Shakespeare.

I will now look at the next 26 pages of Worsley MSS 47 to note the changes Neville makes in copying the text. On page 40V, (see above illustration) Neville omits several lines of text, jumping from "most woeful and cruel contention" straight to "of York and Lancaster". Perhaps he is in a rush to get to his favourite subject but he misses out references to Marius and Sulla, and the Italian Guelphians and Ghibellines (Peck, 144/*97*). The omissions are telling: Shakespeare never refers to these names. Thomas Lodge however "based *The Wounds of Civil War* (c 1588) on Plutarch's and Appian's Roman histories of the rivalry between Marius and Sulla" (Bevington, 1968, 234).

In the printed text there is the phrase, "like to plunge us deeper than ever in civil discord" (Peck, 146/*98*). Neville copies this as, "like **to plague us** deper the ever in ciuell discord."

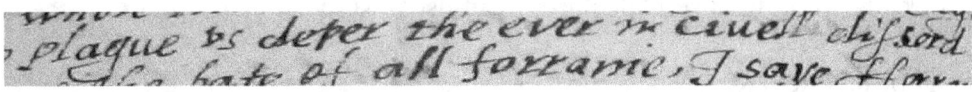

Worsley MSS 47, 41V

In *King Lear* Edgar uses the words, **"to plague us"** (5.3.170). Shakespeare never writes "to plunge us". Later Neville makes this substitution again, when the printed text says, "so plunged…in all vice" (Peck, 194/*127*) Neville writes, "soe plagued":

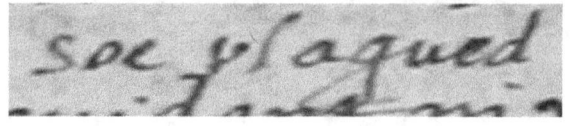

Worsley MSS 47, 65V

Shakespeare used 'plunge' 5 times, 'plunged' 3 times, 'plague' 90 times and 'plagued' 4 times.

In the printed text we read, "Edward V and his brother, who after were both murdered in the Tower," (Peck, 151/*101)*. Neville however names the brother as "Rich: d: of york".

MSS 47, 43V

In *Richard III* the young Prince Edward greets his brother, naming him, "Richard of York" (3.1.96). We later hear of their murder in the Tower.

In copying the text "as shalbe declared", Neville changes it to "as shalbe shewed".

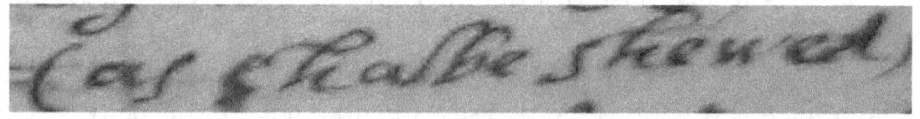

Worsley MSS 47, 44

Shakespeare never used "declared" but used "showed" ten times.

The printed text states:

"...as heir to any person. And this rule of our common law is gathered in these selfsame words of a statute made in the twenty-fifth year of King Edward III, which indeed is the only place of effect that can be alleged out of our law against the inheritance of strangers in such sense and cases as we now treat of." (Peck, 157/*105*)

Neville adds legal details from his own knowledge of the law:

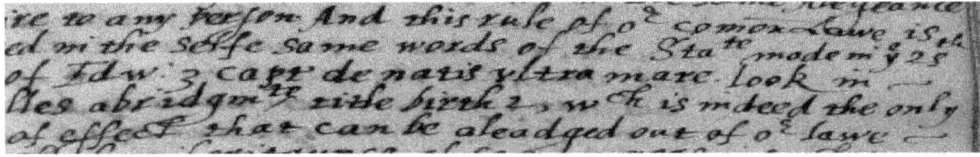

Worsley MSS 47, 47

The addition reads "capt de natis vltra mare. Look in ~ Rastalles abridgm^te title birth 2". John Rastell's *Graunde Abridgement* was a 16th Century legal encyclopaedia (Guy, 2009, 104). Shakespeare used the word 'abridgement' 4 times. In chapter 8 I identify Rastell and show the links between him and members of the Neville family.

I have already noted the unique annotation about the shared inheritance rights of sisters: "copercinerie betweene daugh" (in chapter 3). The printed text states that "lands shalbe divided by equal portions among his daughters" (Peck, 158/*105*). Neville copies this as, "land shalbe deuided by equall pro/porcõns amongst them".

Worsley MSS 47, 47

Shakespeare never used 'portions' but used 'proportions' six times, three times in *Henry V* alone which further argues, as I did in chapter 3, that Neville re-read his copy of *Leicester's Commonwealth* in 1599. Indeed it is telling here that Neville deliberately changes the word 'portions' by inserting 'pro'. Furthermore Shakespeare used "amongst them" six times but "among them" only twice, showing he has a preference for the former, as he does in his copying.

Neville's father was a witness to Henry VIII's will: the text of *Leicester's*

*Commonwealth* calls this an "alleged testament". Neville writes this as "**pretended** [will] testam^te " and scores out 'will'.

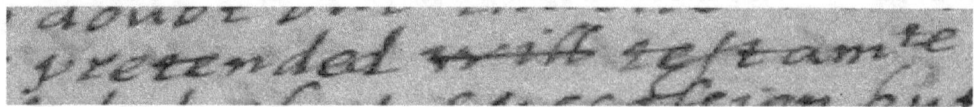

Worsley MSS 47, 49V

Shakespeare never used the word 'alledged' but does use 'pretended' twice in early works.

The text of *Leicester's Commonwealth* tells us of Henry VIII's "doubt and irresolution" (Peck, 164/*109*). Neville copies this as "doubte and suspicõn"

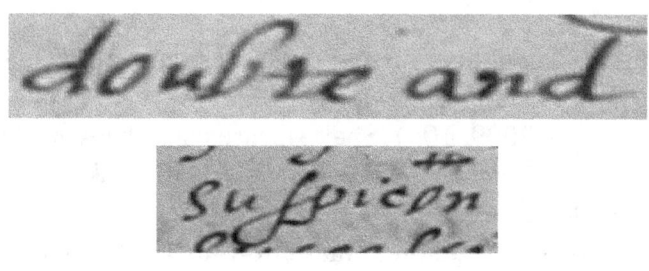

Worsley MSS 47, 50[20]

Shakespeare never used 'irresolution' but used 'suspicion' 34 times.

Within the same sentence as 'irresolution' the words, "all occasions of controversies" are varied by Neville to "all occasõns of contrarietie".

Worsley MSS 47, 50

Shakespeare used 'contrarieties' in *Henry VI* part 1 (2.3.58) and 'contrariety' in *Coriolanus* (4.6.76). In *Henry VI* part 1 the speaker used the words "riddling merchant" just two lines before 'contrarieties': in *Leicester's Commonwealth* the Dudleys are called "cunning merchants" in the previous

---

20   The illustrations here are divided because the words are separated by the first two being at the end of a line, the last at the start of the next line.

paragraph.

The Lawyer asks rhetorically, "why should the rest be damnified thereby?" (Peck, 169/*112*). Neville copies this as, "whie should yᵉ rest be defamed".

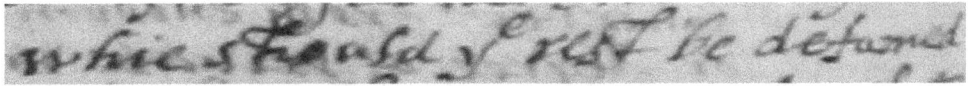

Worsley MSS 47, 52V

Shakespeare never used 'damnified' but does use 'defamed' in *Henry VI* part 2 (3.1.123).

The printed text has a preacher in Scotland "stepping to the pulpit" (Peck, 170/*113*). Neville has him "slippe into yᵉ pulpit".

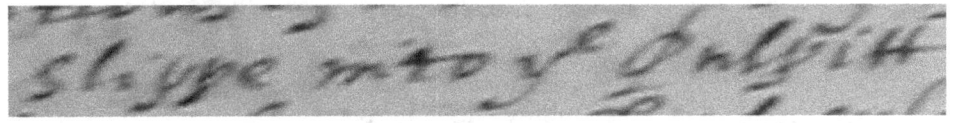

Worsley MSS47, 53V (Italic)

James (2008, 250) noted Shakespeare and Neville's frequent use of "let slip" (see also chapter 7). In the Hand D section of the *Sir Thomas More* manuscript, believed to be hand written by Shakespeare (see chapter 8) we find "to slipp him lyke a hound".

*Sir Thomas More*, folio 9 (Secretary Script)

From this pulpit are preached sermons, "with such bitterness of speech" (Peck 170/*113*). Neville copies this as "wᵗʰ such bitter speaches".

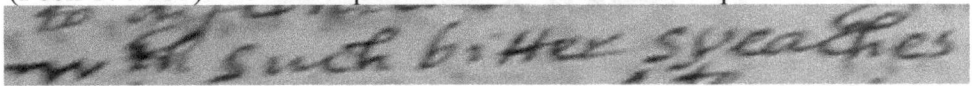

Worsley MSS 47, 53V

Whilst he does not use the phrase "bitter speeches", Shakespeare has 'bitter' "words/scoffs/invective/terms/taunts/names/threats/jest/tongues". He used the word 'bitter' 76 times. He used 'bitterness' just 11 times, none of which are directly about speech, thus again demonstrating that when the annotator of Worsley MSS 47 departs from the vocabulary of the printed text he does so according to Shakespeare's preferences. Furthermore on the very same page, whilst the Archbishop of St. Andrews has "much grief" in the printed text (Peck 171/*113*), Neville writes "w<sup>th</sup> **great grief**".

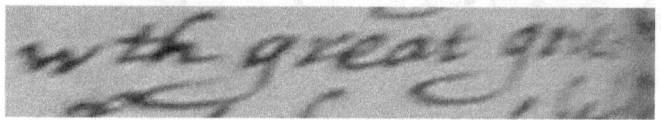

Worsley MSS 47, 53V

Indeed Neville does this a second time, copying "to her grief" (Peck, 177/*117*) as "to her **great greife**".

Worsley MSS 47, 57

Shakespeare used the words "**great grief**" three times, in *The Rape of Lucrece* (1117); *King John* (3.1.70) and *The Winter's Tale* (3.2.1). In *The Troublesome Raigne of John*, which I assert is an early version of *King John*, the words, "A **greater grief**", are spoken by Salisbury[21], the illegitimate son of Henry II (12.140, Sider, 1979, 157) and the dying King John says, "So **great a grief**" (13.54, Sider, 1979, 161). In a letter dated 26/5/1599 Neville writes of the news that, "the Emperour was sick unto Deathe and that he had… a **great** Dispit and **Grief**" (Winwood, 1725, Vol 1, 30).

Writing of plots against the young James of Scotland the word 'machination' is used (Peck, 171/*113*). Neville copies this as 'imagniacõn':

Worlsey, MSS 47, 54

<u>Shakespeare ne</u>ver used 'machination' but used 'imagination' 30 times.
21    The Earldom of Salisbury eventually came to the Neville family: Richard Neville was the 4<sup>th</sup> Earl.

When in the printed text Leicester is said to have 'cozened' the Queen (Peck, 173/*114*), Neville varies this word to 'deceaued'.

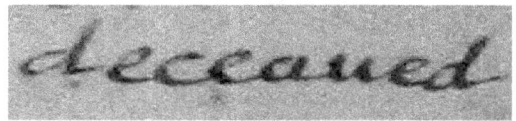

Worsley, MSS 47, 54V

Shakespeare used 'cozened' 7 times and 'deceived' 57 times. Again Neville's word preferences are Shakespeare's.

In the printed text there is a report of a "devilish drift pertained…" (Peck, 173/*115*). Neville copies this as "divilish drift **nitended**".

Worsley, MSS 47, 55

Shakespeare never used the word 'pertained' but used '**intended**' 18 times.

In the printed text we find "the aspirers' ambition, enflamed and increased" (Peck, 176/*117*) whilst Neville copies this as, "y^e Aspire Ambicon enflamed & **enraged**".

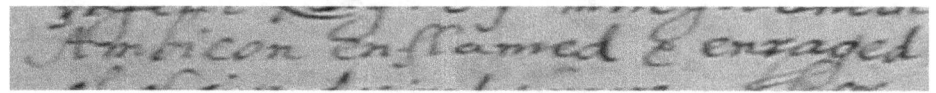

Worsley, MSS 47, 56V

Shakespeare used 'increased' just once, but '**enraged**' 16 times.
In place of the printed "plots, packs and preparations to most **manifest** usurpation" (Peck, 179/*118*) Neville writes, "Plotts, pranks & p^rparacõns".

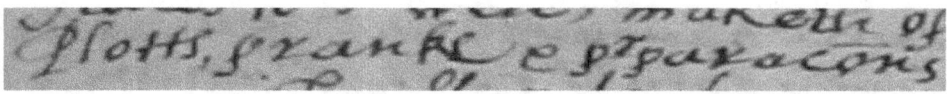

Worsley MSS 47, 58

Shakespeare used 'packs' once and 'pranks' 9 times. In *Henry VI* part I Gloucester says 'pranks' just six lines before the word '**manifest**' (3.1.15).

Neville changes the word 'diffidence' (Peck 180/*119*) to 'defyance'.

Worsley MSS 47, 58

Whilst Shakespeare used 'diffidence' twice he used 'defiance' 11 times: again in changing the text as he copies, Neville alters it in the direction of Shakespeare's word preferences. Likewise Neville substitutes 'behouldnige' for the text's 'bounden' (Peck 181/*119*):

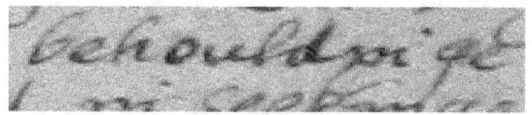

Worsley MSS 47, 58V

Shakespeare used 'bounden' twice and 'beholding' 32 times. Furthermore Neville changes 'assail' to 'assaulte' (Peck, 181 /*119*):

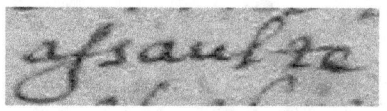

Worsley MSS 47, 58V

Shakespeare used 'assail' 6 times and 'assault' 17 times. Neville alters the printed text from "been nigh" (Peck, 182/*120*) to "byn by":

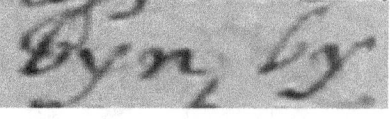

Worsley MSS 47, 59

Shakespeare never used "been nigh" but used "been by" three times. Neville changes the printed word 'pretext' (Peck, 186/*122*) to 'pretence':

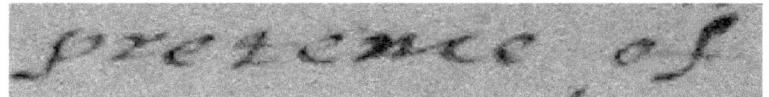

Worsley MSS 47, 61

Shakespeare used 'pretext' just once whereas he used 'pretence' ten times (twice as "pretence of"). Furthermore Brenda James has shown this word is used by Neville in his letters (James, 2008, 246).

In the printed text the word 'mislike' (Peck, 187/*123*) is used: Neville changes this to 'dislike':

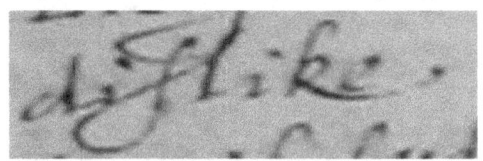

Worsley MSS 47, 61V

Shakespeare used 'mislike' 4 times and 'dislike' 18 times. James (2008, 250) has noticed Neville's preference for words beginning with 'dis-'.

In *Leicester's Commonwealth* we read of the dangers of favourites and how in Henry VI's reign:

"Queen Margaret's too much favor and credit … towards the Marquess of Suffolk that after was made Duke, by whose instinct and wicked counsel she made away first the noble Duke of Gloucester and afterward committed other things in great prejudice of the realm…" (Peck, 188/*124*).

This is enacted in Shakespeare's *Henry VI* part 2. Neville varies the above text, changing "committed other things in great prejudice" to "she committed vnto him great matters **preiuditiall to** the Realme" (Peck, 188/*124*).

Worsley MSS 47, 62

Shakespeare used 'prejudicial' in *Henry VI* part 3: Richard Neville, the Earl of Warwick says:

Suppose, my lords, he did it unconstrain'd,
Think you 'twere **prejudicial to** his crown? (1.1.143)

In less than 100 lines Queen Margaret comes on stage and speaks of "stern Falconbridge" (1.1.241), who was a Neville.[22] Furthermore we can see that Neville writes the words "most sinfull & wicked" at the end of the above quotation. The printed original reads, "most impious and sinful" (Peck, 188/*124*). Shakespeare used 'impious' 8 times but 'wicked' 60 times (five of which are "most wicked").

In the text the word 'compassion' occurs (Peck, 190/*125*). Neville substitutes 'affection':

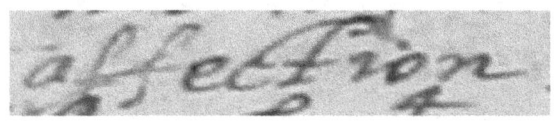

Worsley MSS 47, 63

Shakespeare used 'compassion' 10 times and 'affection' 78 times. Furthermore on the same page (Peck, 190/*125*) Neville changes 'enormous' to 'niurious':

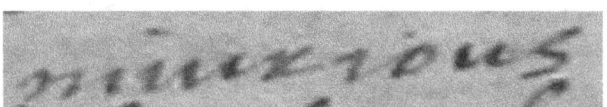

Worsley MSS47, 63

Shakespeare used 'enormous' just once, but **'injurious'** 17 times. Just three lines later Neville adds the phrase, "with oppression and extorte means" to this passage from the printed text: "not only by spoiling and oppressing almost infinite private men, but also whole towns, villages, corporations,

22    According to Hattaway (1993, 83) this was either William Neville, admiral of the Channel fleet in 1462 or Thomas Neville, "vice admiral of the sea" later, or his father Lord Thomas Falconbridge who was sent to sea by Richard Neville, Earl of Warwick. There is indeed some confusion about identity and parentage here: Thomas, Bastard of Fauconberg, was an illegitimate son of William Neville, Lord Fauconberg and Earl of Kent. (An alternative spelling of Fauconberg was Falconbridge.)

and countries, by robbing the realm with inordinate licenses, by deceiving the crown…" (Peck, 190/*125*).

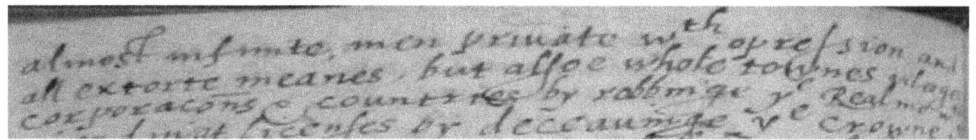

Worsley MSS 47, 63V

Shakespeare used the word 'extort' 4 times including when Cymbeline says, "the **injurious** Romans did **extort**…" (3.1.46) Thus in his additions to the text Neville has used 'injurious' and 'extort' within four lines.

Neville substitutes 'matter' for the word 'affair' (Peck, 192/*126*):

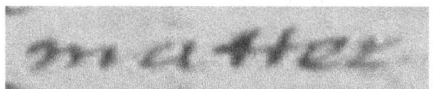

MSS 47, 64

Shakespeare used 'affair' 12 times but the word 'matter' 341 times. Again Neville substitutes 'beleeued' for 'trusted' (Peck, 193/*126*):

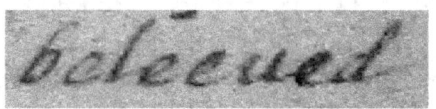

Worsley MSS 47, 64V

Shakespeare used 'trusted' 11 times and 'believed' 19 times. Furthermore Neville changes 'odible' to 'odious' twice in two pages (Peck, 194/*127*):

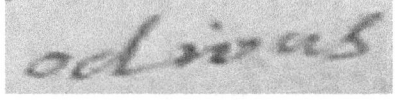 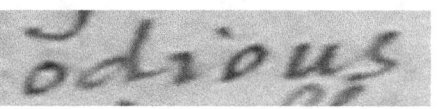

Worsley MSS 47, 65     Worsley MSS 47, 65V

Shakespeare never used 'odible' but wrote 'odious' 9 times.

Occasionally Neville substitutes a word that Shakespeare used less often than the word in the text, for example 'affections' (38 times, 61V) for 'favour' (123 times: Peck, 187/*123*). He sometimes omits words or whole lines, makes mistakes, some of which he corrects by deleting words, others of which are passed over as if he is in a hurry. On one occasion he substitutes a word which Shakespeare never uses: instead of 'inculcating' (Peck, 186/*122*) he writes 'nisultacõn':

Worsley MSS 47, 61

Shakespeare never used 'inculcating'. The OED states that the earliest use of 'insultation' was 1513 and the word was very common in the 17[th] Century.

**Conclusion**
The bias in the words substituted by the person making the Worsley MSS 47 copy of *Leicester's Commonwealth* is in the direction of Shakespeare's vocabulary. Coupled with the evidence of Neville's use of 'ni', 'hmi' and the abbreviation of words beginning with 'pre/pro/par' in both *Sir Thomas More* and Worsley MSS 47 (see chapter 3 and above), this offers further evidence supporting James' discovery that Henry Neville was the writer Shakespeare. It also offers us a window into his subconscious choice of vocabulary.

## Chapter 6

### Annotator A: Worsley MSS 36

"…read the subtle secrecies
Writ in the glassy margent of such books."

*Rape of Lucrece* (99)

Worsley MSS 36 is an elegant, neat, careful copy of *Leicester's Commonwealth*. The writing is delicate, accurate and, I suggest, feminine. It is my view that this copy was made by Anne Killigrew. However for this chapter, and to preserve an openness rather than presume I am right, I will call the Annotator 'A' (which could stand for Anne!). Because I think A is a woman I will used the feminine pronoun.

A does not copy all the printed annotations nor does she reproduce all those that B creates. She is an accurate copier and when B departs from the printed text she stays closer to the original. Her spelling is more modern. Her innovations and changes therefore have a particular significance. The first is when she uniquely identifies Queen Bertha, the wife of King Ethelbert, as converting her husband. Whilst annotator B fails to copy the printed annotations referring to several women (Mary Tudor (twice), Lady Dudley and Blaunch) A does note these. On one occasion she does not note Arbella which B does, but later she copies annotations referring to her. Twice she adds or corrects a historical detail, adding Henry VI to one note and changing Richard 2 in the printed text to R 3 (37V)[23].

**Unique Annotations**
A is the only annotator to note the Isles of Wight, Jersey & Guernsey (21V). Sir George Carew was Captain of the Isle of Wight until 1603 (Peck, 1985, 205). He had travelled round Europe with Neville (James & Rubinstein, 2005, 74) and became Lord Hunsdon in 1596. Hunsdon was Lord Chamberlain and took over the Blackfriars theatre, including the rooms covered by Sir Henry Neville's 1560 lease. The Isle of Wight was where the Worsley family lived, into which Neville's daughter married, and so took ownership of these annotated manuscript volumes after Neville's death. The Earl of Southampton, Henry Wriothesley, later became the Governor

---

23   The numbers in brackets refer to the pages of the manuscript: see appendix 1.

of the Isle of Wight and his deputy was a Worsley, the brother of Neville's son-in-law. We know that Neville visited the Isle of Wight.

Sir Amias Paulet, the Captain of Jersey, was known to Neville and his father: he had been ambassador to France when Neville first visited on his continental tour and became custodian of Mary Queen of Scots after Sir Henry Neville and Ralph Sadler, (who had briefly looked after her in 1584-5), until her death. Sir Thomas Leighton was Captain of Guernsey and in *Leicester's Commonwealth* he is identified as Leicester's brother-in-law, talking with Sir Henry Neville, "on the terrace at Windsor" (Peck, 128/*86*). Annotators A & B both note and name "S$^r$ Henry Neuill" (who is not identified in the printed annotation, 32). In 1578 Leighton married Bess Knollys, daughter of Sir Francis, who lived near the Nevilles in Berkshire (Peck, 1985, 203-4). Malvolio may be modelled on Sir William Knollys (James & Rubinstein, 2005, 133). Thus we can see there are connections between the incumbents of all three islands and the Neville family.

**A's annotations altering the printed text**
A copies a number of annotations in the printed version which B, in Worsley MSS 47, does not. For example the printed annotation is, "Bastardies lauful stops." A writes, "Bastardies Law=full Estoppell" (46). B does not have this note.

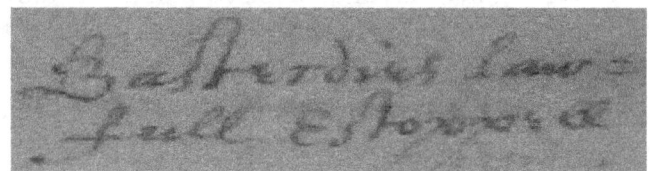

Worsley MSS36, 46

A notes six 'poysonings' whereas the printed text mentions three and B four. She alone uses the more modern spelling of Kenelworth (as opposed to Killingworth by B and in the printed text).

**Annotations shared with B (Worsley MSS 47)**
There is a series of four consecutive annotations in Worsley MSS 36 and 47 that show the annotators were working together. An example of this is when A accurately transcribes the printed annotation as, "Leyc: called the harte & life of the court" (18) whereas B writes, "Leic: the lief & harte of the courte" (19), reversing the words "heart and life" which could quite naturally happen when listening to a reader.

We can see this in reverse when perhaps B is reading. One printed annotation reads:

"The vvordes of the Lord Northe, to M. Poolie. Poolie tolde this to Syr Robert Iermine."

B copies this, changing it, "The words of the Lo: North to Poolie **reported** by Poolie to S$^r$ Ro: Jermyne" (32).

In reading aloud B would have said, "Robert" (which he abbreviates) and so A writes this full name as 'Robert'. She changes the spelling of Poley, but keeps the word '**reported**': "The wordes of the Lo: North, to Poley **reported** by Poley to S$^r$ Robert Jermin" (32).

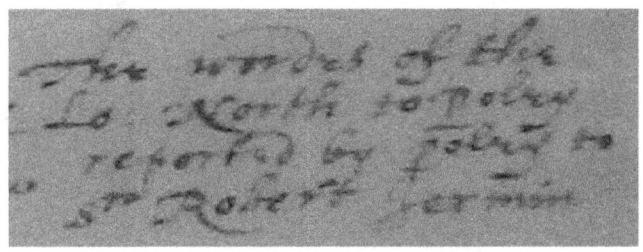

Worsley MSS36, 32

We can see a process of Chinese whispers here, as B reads out the annotation, writes his own version and A copies him with her own changes.

B accurately copies the printed annotation, "The intolerable licentiousnes of Leic carnalitie" (14). A however writes, "The Licentiousnes of Leyc: Carnallity, intolerable" (12V).

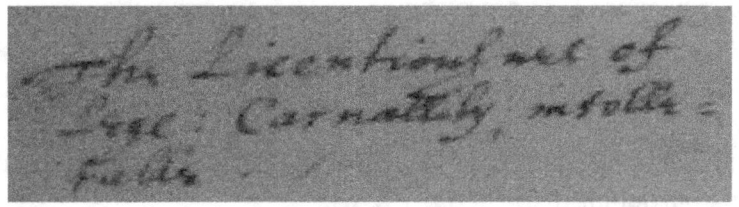

Worsley MSS36, 12V

B accurately copies the printed annotation, "The undutiful devise of naturall yssue, in the state of succession" (33V). He only makes one change when he substitutes the abbreviation 'state' for 'statute'. A's version however casts her as the inaccurate listener, "The undutifull devise of my Lo: of Leic:" (33). The very next annotation confirms that B is reading. He accurately copies, "the 3 argum$^{te}$ nature of the cause it selfe." (34) whereas A makes an alteration to, "3 argum$^t$, the nature & state of y$^e$ matter it self" (33V). Normally so accurate a copier such a change can only be explained by A hearing, rather than seeing, the annotation to be copied. Looking at these annotations I am sure the book was passed backwards and forwards between A and B; there may even have been a third person reading sometimes.

One annotation in the printed version reads:

"The vvords of Mistres Anne VVest Sister vnto this holie Countesse."

A copies this as, "The speeches of M$^{trs}$ Anne West of her sister Lettice." (32V)

B writes, "The speach of Ann West to her sister Lettice". (32)

Both A and B use the word 'speech/es' and name 'Lettice'. A however is closer to the printed text in using the plural 'speeches' instead of 'words'. B therefore copies A, further changing the preposition from 'of' to 'to'.
The next annotation is one that is not found in the printed version but shared by A and B who write, "An audatious & most undutiful speach." Given that the word here is again 'speach' perhaps this represents an exclamation by A as she was reading. Speeches are also made by actors: we do not refer to their words.
Just one page later it seems they have swapped over the task of reading out the text because B is more accurate. The two printed annotations read, "The first argumēt The Nature of ambttion." and "The second argument, Leycester particular disposition."

B accurately copies these as, "1 argum$^{te}$ the nature of Ambicõn" and "2 argum$^{te}$ his particular disposicon" (32V).

A however misses out the word 'argument', copying simply, "1, y$^e$ nature of ambition" and "2, his pticuler dysposicon" (33).

111

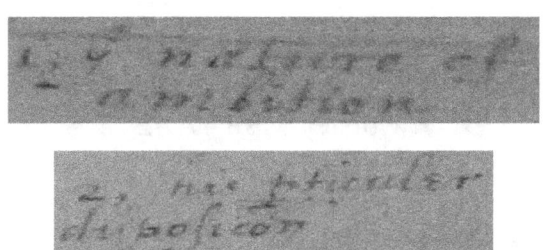

Worsley MSS 36, 33

Both of them then miss a printed annotation. Next B copies part of one that A does not and then again B is the more accurate copier in reproducing the next three annotations. This confirms that A and B passed the task of reading out the text back and forth between them.

They share another annotation not in the printed text. A's version, "Inordinate affection by the prince to a peculiar and wicked person." (62V) is identical to B's except that B capitalises Prince. Another shared annotation is "His oath prophaned." (66V). B spells this differently: "his oathes profaned" (65V). Neville here chooses the plural 'oathes'.

A shares with B the use of X for Christ: in one annotation they both call Sir Christopher Hatton, 'xpõfer' (55).

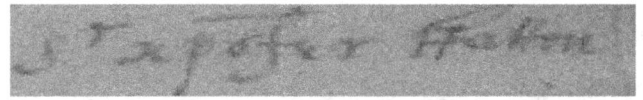

Worsley MSS36, 55

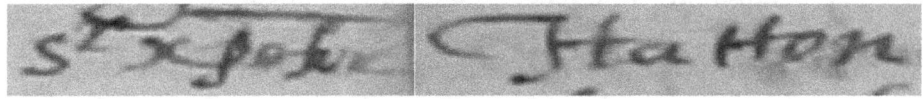

Worsley MSS47, 55

On another occasion A uses the X whilst B calls him 'Christo:'. B uses X in the text for Xmas and Xpians (Christian).

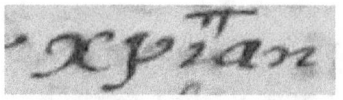

Worsley MSS 47, 42

The annotator of Halle's *Chronicle* also uses X for Xmas (Henry V, f.xliii. Keen and Lubbock change this to 'Christmas' so missing the significance of the use of a Greek letter). 'Xp' are the Greek letters for 'Ch' and 'r' (hence 'Xpofer' for 'Christoper' above) and the use of the X alone stands in for 'Christ'. Neville knew Greek: there is an encrypted Greek inscription on his portrait at Audley End House, Essex.

On two occasions A and B swap over the order of annotations: for example two consecutive printed annotations are:

"The example of Iulius Cesars destruction.

To much cõfidence very perilous in a Prince."

A and B have these in reverse order. Similarly in the printed text we find two adjacent annotations are:

"The diuers operations of Poyson." and "Doctor Baylye the yonger."

A and B both reverse the order with B writing:

"Young Do<sup>r</sup> Bayley" and "Diverse opacõns in poisons". (11V)

A chooses a different word to indicate the doctor's youth:

"Do: Baylye Junior." and "Diuers operacõns of poyson." (10)

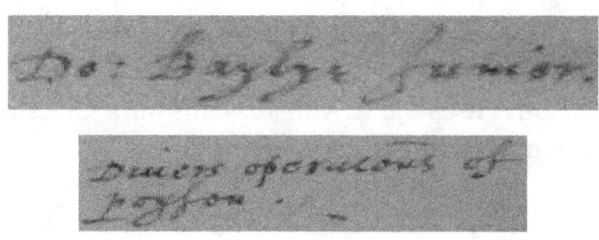

Worsley MSS 36, 10

I suggest this is further evidence of a relationship between them as they copy.

**Conversations between A and B**
One printed annotation reads, "Ley puissance in the priuie Coũcell." B's version is, "His puissance in the privy chamber" (19). A seems to be between these. She uses the word 'chamber', crosses this out and reverts to 'cõnsell': "Leyc: puissance in the privy [chamber] cõnsell." (18V). Is this correction evidence of Neville reading out the wrong word and Anne correcting it?

One printed annotation reads, "The most abiect behavior of Duke Dudley in aduerse fortune."

A's version is: "The base & abiect behauior of Dudley ni his owne aduersity". (56)

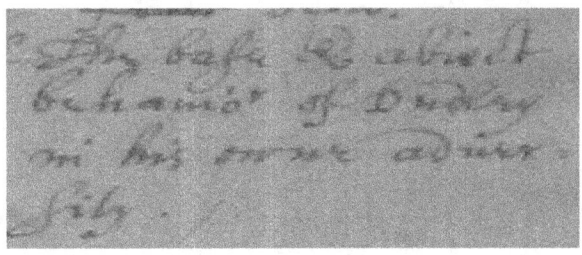

Worsley MSS36, 56

B writes: "The base & abiect behavio[r] of D: Du: ni his downefall and adversitie". (56)

Clearly there is a relationship between the latter two but it is arguable which came first.

**A's annotations and the Northumberland Manuscript (NHMS)**
One startling discovery of this research was that the Northumberland Manuscript version of *Leicester's Commonwealth* seems to be substantially based on Worsley MSS 36. The evidence for this is in comparing some of the surviving annotations on the Northumberland Manuscript with those on Worsley MSS 36. We can see that they are closer than those of the printed version or Worsley MSS 47.

NHMS Folio 81:       1 ye nature of ambition
Worsley MSS 36:      1, y$^e$ nature of ambition
Printed:             The first argumẽt The Nature of ambttion.
Worsley MSS 47:      1 argum$^{te}$ the nature of Ambicõn

A in Worsley MSS 36 and the Northumberland Manuscript (NHMS) scribe are the only annotators to use the words "1 ye" and they use the same spelling of 'ambition'.

NHMS Folio 81:       his pticuler positiõ
Worsley MSS 36:      his pticuler disposicon
Printed:             Leycester particular disposition.
Worsley MSS 47:      his particular disposicon

A and NHMS are the only annotators to use the abbreviated spelling 'pticuler'

NHMS Folio 83:       y$^e$ practice of K.R.3. for dispatching of his wief
Worsley MSS 36:      The practice of K.R.3. for dispatching of his wief
Printed:             The practice of K. Richard for dispatching his vvyfe.
Worsley MSS 47:      The practise of Ri: 3 for dispatching his wief

A and NHMS are the only annotators to use the abbreviations "K.R.3." and write "**of** his wief".

NHMS Folio 83:       a new triuni = betwene Leyc Talb & y$^e$ old Coun of Shrew
Worsley MSS 36:      A new triumvirat, betweene Leyc: Talbot, & the old Coũtesse of Shrousbury.
Printed:             A nevv Triumuirate betvvẽ Ley. Talbot, & the Coũtesse of Shreusbury.

Worsley MSS 47:   the triumvirate betwene Leic: talbott, and the countess of Shrewsburie

A and NHMS are the only annotators to use the word 'old' of the Countess.

NHMS Folio 83: his sleight to bring ye crowne to himself
Worsley MSS 36: His sleight to bring the crowne to himselfe.
Printed: The sleightes of Lei. for bringing al to himself.
Worsley MSS 47: His strength to bring all to himselfe.

A and NHMS are the only annotators to use the singular 'sleight' and the word 'crowne'.

There is only one annotation used in the NHMS and the printed version that is not in Worsley MSS 36 or 47: "Papistical blessing" (folio 85). This means NHMS cannot be based solely on Worsley MSS 36. The scribe must have had access to the printed version at some time whilst basing his copy mostly on Worsley MSS 36.

A comparison of the handwriting (and spelling) makes it clear that the annotators of Worsley MSS 36 and Northumberland MS are two different people. It is however notable that neither of these annotations are copied by B in Worsley MSS 47.

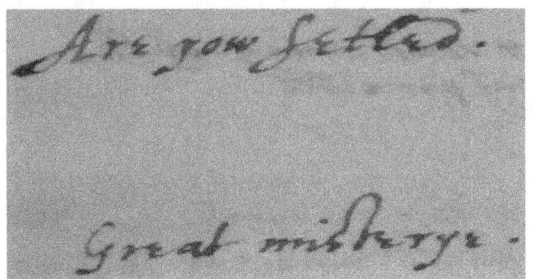    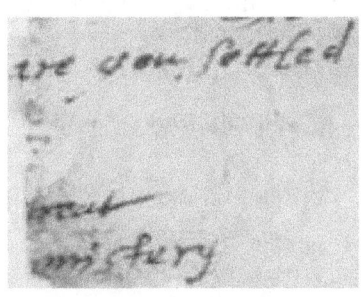

Worsley MSS 36, 39V                Northumberland MS

The printed annotations are: "ARE YOV SETLED?" (in capitals) and "A great misterye." It is clear that A is closer to the printed version, in having just one 't' in 'setled' and a final 'e' on 'misterye'. Therefore I am able to assert that Worsley MSS 36 was the prior copy and the Northumberland Manuscript based on it.

Whilst there may have been different scribes employed to make the Northumberland Manuscript there is a demonstrable relationship between Annotators A, B and C. Thus it can be seen that these three manuscript copies of *Leicester's Commonwealth* are linked. The Northumberland Manuscript has Neville's name at the top and has been regarded since at least 1904 as originally belonging to Henry Neville. The evidence I have presented here confirms Brenda James' view that the Worsley MSS 36 and 47 were originally owned by Neville. On the front cover of the Northumberland Manuscript we can see that someone is practising William Shakespeare's signature.

**Conclusion**
Henry Neville married Anne Killigrew in December 1584. If Annotator A is Anne Killigrew then perhaps these copies of *Leicester's Commonwealth* were made soon after they were married, unless this was one premarital activity that, however dangerous, was acceptable, namely reading and writing together. Such a shared activity does raise the intriguing possibility that Anne helped Neville write the works of Shakespeare. Her focus then in her annotations of *Leicester's Commonwealth* on the named women might be the first hint that the powerful portraits of women in the plays were not the sole creation of a male writer but collaboratively created by Anne and Henry. Given that A clearly took great care in her copying of *Leicester's Commonwealth*, did she also act as Neville's writing partner?

A alone notes the surname of the duke of Suffolk. One annotation in the printed version reads:

"The punishemẽt of VVilliã Duke of Suffolke."

B copies this exactly: "The punishm$^{te}$ of W$^m$ Duke of Suff:" (62V)

A however adds his name: "The punishmt of W$^m$ **de La Poole** Duke of Suff:" (63V)

Worsley MSS36, 63V

Shakespeare names "William de la Pole" five times in *Henry VI* parts 1 & 2. I have previously traced the connections between the Nevilles and the De La Poles (Casson, 2009, 178).

# Chapter 7

## Look About You

"**look about you**: security gives way to conspiracy."
*Julius Caesar* (2.3.7)

*Look About You* was published anonymously in 1600. It is a historical comedy set in the reign of Henry II. It has been described as "superior to most other minor Elizabethan dramas... in structure, characterisation, and style" (Logan & Smith, 1975, 170) and "very cleverly constructed and plotted" (Nelson, 1962, 142). The authorship has been attributed to Antony Munday and Henry Chettle (Logan & Smith, 1975, 171). I will dispute this attribution. I will examine the text for evidence of Henry Neville as the author and *Leicester's Commonwealth* as a source. I will also explore the links between this play and other early works which I have previously identified as by Shakespeare-Neville (Casson, 2009).

**History**
Henry II (1133–1189), the great-grandson of William the Conqueror, was the first Plantagenet King[24]. He married Eleanor of Aquitaine and they had eight children including Henry, Geoffrey, Richard (the Lion Heart) and John. Attempting to ensure a stable transition in the succession, Henry had his eldest son, Henry, crowned as joint King. He was known as "Henry the Young King". In 1173, young Henry and Richard rebelled against their father. Amongst the Young King's supporters was Robert, the Earl of Leicester. Henry II crushed the rebellion and then forgave his sons for their disloyalty. However, he placed Eleanor under house-arrest for fifteen years for encouraging her sons to rebel. In 1182, the Plantagenet princes began fighting each other for their father's possessions on the continent. The danger of civil war was only averted when Henry the Young King died in 1183. The final battle between the Princes was in 1184. Geoffrey and John invaded, but Richard, an accomplished military commander, expelled his brothers. Geoffrey died two years later, leaving only Richard and John. Henry II died in 1189. Richard succeeded but when he died in 1199, John became King, taking the throne from his nephew, Arthur, Geoffrey's son, whom many regarded as the true heir.

---

24 From: http://en.wikipedia.org/wiki/Henry_II_of_England accessed 20/1/2009

**The plot of *Look About You***
The play opens with Robin Hood, also identified as Robert, Earl of Huntington, visiting a Hermit with a letter from Prince Richard requesting that Skink attend Parliament. It is not clear whether Robin knows that the Hermit is in fact Skink himself in disguise. He has been in hiding since poisoning King Henry II's mistress, Rosamond, on the orders of the Young King Henry and his mother, Queen Elinor. In Parliament we see the two Kings, the princes Richard and John, and assembled peers, including the Duke of Gloster[25], the Earl of Leicester and Sir Richard Faukenbridge. Bills are presented including one for the release of the Queen from prison. Skink is given a royal pardon and the Young King grants him a manor that belongs to Gloster in compensation. Gloster objects and assaults Skink. Gloster is arrested and sent to the Tower. He asks that his sister, Lady Faukenbridge, be told of his arrest so she can plead for his release. Redcap, a stuttering runner, is sent with a message. Prince Richard, who is in love with Lady Faukenbridge, promises to use his influence to get Gloster released. Skink, now a fugitive again, changes clothes with Redcap and thus is admitted to Lady Faukenbridge who sends him to visit Gloster. She meanwhile is attended by Robin and the amorous Prince Richard. The latter is unsuccessful in his attempt to seduce her and departs to effect her brother's release, leaving Robin to press his suit.
Gloster, in prison, changes clothes with Skink and so escapes. Prince John visits Skink, thinking he is Gloster. He leaves his cloak and hat whilst he goes to visit another prisoner. Skink is therefore able to escape disguised as Prince John.
We then see the Young King, Queen Elinor and the Earl of Leicester plotting Gloster's death. King Henry II enters and they argue. Prince John appears in Gloster's discarded gown and is mistaken for him. John reveals his identity and furiously demands Gloster's death. A search is ordered.
We return to Lady Faukenbridge who conspires with Robin, asking him to take her place, so she can visit "the holy hermit" to discover from his clairvoyant wisdom what will happen next. Her brother Gloster arrives. She disguises him with a beard to look like her husband and so helps him escape detection during a search of the house.
Skink appears disguised as Prince John. Sir Richard Faukenbridge enters wearing a gold chain, which Skink 'borrows' (in his persona as John). Faukenbridge leaves and Gloster enters in his Faukenbridge disguise. He also mistakes Skink for Prince John. When Skink mentions the chain again

---

25     I have retained the spellings in the 1600 quarto.

Gloster asks for it back and Skink, breaking it in half, exits. The real Prince John enters. Gloster, as Faukenbridge, makes friends with the Prince and, offering to reveal Gloster's supposed hiding place in a tavern, goes off to effect an arrest. The real Faukenbridge enters and the plot thickens with more confusion about the gold chain before Prince John realises there has been a deception and they all go in search of the fugitive. Gloster and Skink escape again, tricking their pursuers.

Meanwhile Robin, disguised as Lady Faukenbridge, copes with Prince Richard's arrival by feigning sickness. Skink, back in his hermit disguise, receives visits from Lady Faukenbridge, disguised as a merchant's wife, and from Prince John and Sir Richard Faukenbridge, both of whom take a fancy to the disguised Lady Faukenbridge and separately arrange to meet her later. Skink then disguises himself as a falconer and entraps John and Sir Richard, making them fall into concealed pits on the heath, and then robbing them.

Prince Richard's courtship of Lady Faukenbridge (the disguised Robin) is interrupted by the real Lady Faukenbridge (disguised as a merchant's wife). Her husband arrives in hot pursuit and the multiple confusions of identity result in farce. Gloster, disguised as a hermit, meets Prince Richard who is disguised as a servant. Gloster attempts to rob the Prince and they fight. Robin, not recognising the Prince, comes to Gloster's aid. When Richard reveals his identity all three are reconciled. When the Prince and Robin leave, Gloster returns to his disguise as a hermit. Skink enters, also disguised again as a hermit, and there follows confusion as to who is the 'real' hermit. The rival Earls of Leicester and Lancaster enter. The two hermits are unmasked and both are arrested.

Meanwhile, back at the Faukenbridge household, Lady Faukenbridge persuades Prince Richard to abandon his seduction and they all set off to the tavern to enjoy teasing Prince John.

The final scene is one of great splendour and drama at court. The Kings, Queens, Princes and Earls meet in celebration of the Young King's birthday. The old conflicts are replayed and the twists of the plot explained. The Young King, Queen Elinor and the Earl of Leicester call for the execution of Gloster and preparations are made to cut his hand off. King Henry II, Lady Faukenbridge and Prince Richard plead for mercy. The situation is transformed when the Young King, suddenly giving up his pride and power, acknowledges his royal father's sovereignty. The play ends in happy celebration, penance for past wrongs, forgiveness, peace and unity, although the villainous Prince John and his vicious Queen mother nurse their fury at defeat.

This summary does not include all the comic complications and tricks of the plot. Framed by the serious historical drama of the two kings it is a farce about disguise and confusion of identity but there is clearly a political subtext.

## Historical figures in *Look About You*: fact and fiction

### 1) Robert Huntington/Robin Hood

*Look About You* begins with Robert, the Earl of Huntington. During Henry II's reign David of Huntington (c. 1144 –1219) was the brother of King William I of Scotland (Barber, 2003, 139). The writer of *Look About You* is clearly not referring to this man. His Huntington is fictional and identified as Robin Hood. As stated in chapter 2, the contemporary Earl of Huntington, Henry Hastings, is a major figure in *Leicester's Commonwealth*. He was Leicester's brother-in-law and a claimant to the throne through his ancestor Edward IV (Peck, 104/72). There is documentary evidence that Neville's father knew the Earl of Huntington: in a letter to Sir Ralph Sadler dated 16/1/1580, Elizabeth I instructed that, "Henry Nevill shall from hence resorte to a house of o$^r$ cousin the **Erle of Huntingdon** in Leicestershire named **Ashby**" (British Library: Additional MS 33594, folio 14). One of the annotations in Worsley MSS 47 reads, "**Ea: Huntnigt:** preparacõn at **Ashbye**."

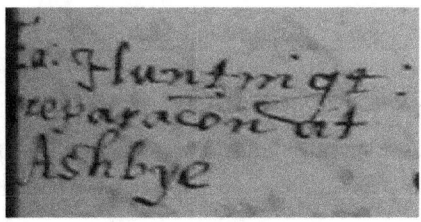

Worsley MSS 47, 22

In the printed version he is identified as "My L. of Hũtington", rather than as an 'Earl' (as he is named in the play) and this annotation.

In *The Two Gentlemen of Verona* (c1592-3) Shakespeare refers to Robin Hood. The banished Valentine meets a group of outlaws in the forest who invite him to be their leader, saying, "By the bare scalp of Robin Hood's fat friar, This fellow were a king for our wild faction!" (4.1.36). In *As You Like It*, the exiled duke and his men "live like the old Robin Hood of England"

(1.1.111). *As You Like It* was written the very same year as *Look About You* was published. In 1599 the unhappy Neville, (like Jaques), had the idea of escaping to the forest, as evidenced in his letter to Cecil that he would rather "be a hermit in Ashridge or the forest…" than continue as Ambassador (James & Rubinstein, 2005, 131). Given the hermit disguises in *Mucedorus* and *Look About You* and the hermit in the forest in *As You Like It*, this reference is particularly striking.

Nelson (1962, 141) stated that the Robin Hood legend "provided either the main plot or an important subplot of at least seven plays written between 1590-1601". He lists *George a Greene* (c1590, which has been attributed to Robert Greene); George Peele's *Edward I* (c 1592-3) which "contains one scene where the Welsh rebels play a Robin Hood disguising game"[26]; a lost play *The Pleasant Pastoral Comedy of Robin Hood and Little John* (1594). Antony Munday and Henry Chettle wrote two plays about Robin Hood: *The Downfall of Robert the Earl of Huntington* (written, or revised, according to an entry in Henslowe's diary in 1598) and *The Death of Robert Earl of Huntington*. Both were published in 1601. I shall examine these last two later. The question is, where does *Look About You* fit into this series? I believe it was the very first, which possibly explains why it has virtually none of the Robin Hood legend in it, showing him simply as a young man.

Nelson (1962, 142) pointed out that Richard Grafton was the source of the suggestion that Robin Hood was an Earl. Grafton's *Chronicle* (1569) was a source for *Henry VI* part 2, which Shakespeare is believed to have written by 1590.[27] This evidence, that Shakespeare used Grafton as a source, as early as the late 1580s, would then support the possibility of an early date for the play (see below).

## 2) Robin Goodfellow

In Anthony Munday's play *Fedele and Fortunio* (1585) there is a reference to "Robin goodfellowe Hobgoblin" (LION). Munday influenced Neville's play *Locrine* (see below) and they co-operated on *Sir Thomas More* (see chapters 3, 5 and 8). "Robin Good-fellow" is also mentioned in *Look About*

---

26    From: http://www.lib.rochester.edu/camelot/teams/dowdeint.htm accessed January 2009

27    From: http://www.shakespeare-w.com/english/shakespeare/source.html accessed 22/2/2009

*You* (2089). This is the very name given to Puck in *A Midsummer Night's Dream* (1594-6):

> Either I mistake your shape and making quite,
> Or else you are that shrewd and knavish **sprite**
> Call'd **Robin Goodfellow**... (six lines cut)
> Those that **Hobgoblin** call you and sweet Puck. (2.1.34)

In *Look About You* Redcap "runs like **hob-goblin** up and down the heath" (2603)[28]. The word '**spright**' is used twice in *Look About You*. The OED tells us 'Redcap' is the name of a sprite or goblin. This may be related to the red fly agaric mushroom (used as a hallucinogenic by Lapp shamans[29]). James (2008, 40) suggested that Marston's appeal to a poet he called 'Rufus' was a reference to Neville's red hair so we may wonder whether the name 'Redcap' appealed to a red-head!

A comic poem, *Pimlyco or Runne Red-cap*[30], published in 1609, testifies to the enduring popularity of *Look About You*. At the very end of the poem there is a verse:

> Run, (Red-cap) Run, amongst the Rest
> Thou art nam'd last, that once were best,
> But (Red-cap) now thy woll is worne
> By Pimlyco is Red-cap thorne.

Furthermore the poem contains a reference to the comic waiter at the Salutation pub in *Look About You*:

> Drawer need not baule Anon, Anon,
> Each Guest for his owne Drink does run.

The poem also mentions Lothbury (where Neville lived for a time) and Shakespeare's popular play *Pericles*. Perhaps it is simply a coincidence that one extant copy of this poem is at the Henry Huntington Library in California!

In *Look About You* Prince John says, "Wink at my mirth; 't may make

---

28   All line references are from Greg (1913).
29   Shakespeare mentions Lapland sorcerers in *The Comedy of Errors* (4.3.11).
30   Copy accessed through EEBO at John Rylands Library, Manchester, 14/4/09. See Bullen, 1891.

**amends**, so thou and I, and our friends, may **be friends**" (2145). This recalls Puck's epilogue:

> Give me your hands, if we **be friends**,
> And **Robin** shall restore **amends**.     (5.1.423)

Clearly there is a relationship between these two texts but it is not clear which came first. In fact the first Quarto of *A Midsummer Night's Dream* was published in 1600, the very same year as *Look About You*. According to the LION database no other writer used 'friends' near 'amends' between 1584-1600. However in a letter dated 7/8/1599 Neville used the word 'Friends' 25 lines before 'Amends' (Winwood, 1725, Vol 1, 85).

### 3) Robert, Earl of Gloster

Robert, the first Earl of Gloucester, Henry II's uncle, was the illegitimate son of Henry I (Barber, 2003). During Henry I's reign he was a successful military commander and regarded as "a man of proved talent and admirable wisdom" in the contemporary source, the *Gesta Stephani*. Present at Henry I's deathbed, he was a supporter of his half sister, the Empress Matilda's claim to the throne but he was defeated by Stephen. Matilda gave up all hope and fled to Normandy after Robert's death. Matilda was Henry II's mother. Matilda's husband, Geoffrey of Anjou, was known as Plantagenet and so Henry II was the first Plantagenet king. He was born in France and Robert had taken him back to England when he was nine.

Robert was alienated by Stephen's favouritism towards the twins, Waleran and Robert de Beaumont, the latter being the 2$^{nd}$ Earl of Leicester. There followed a civil war during which Robert, Earl of Gloucester, took Leicester's lands in Dorset for his own[31]. However he was not able to defeat Stephen and died in 1147, when Henry II was just 14 years old. His appearance in *Look About You* is therefore an unhistorical fiction and he is made brother of the fictional Lady Faukenbridge. She is given the title of Countess of West-Hereford. Roger Fitz Miles de Gloucester (son of Robert) was given the Earldom of Hereford by the Empress Matilda, for his support for her claim to the throne, so the playwright may be confusing Robert and Roger, father and son.

Geoffrey of Monmouth described the real Robert Earl of Gloucester as one

---

31     From: http://en.wikipedia.org/wiki/Robert,_1st_Earl_of_Gloucester accessed January 2009

of the 'pillars' of the English King. In *Look About You* Gloster himself says, with heavy irony:

> Here's like to be a well stayed **common wealth**,
> Wherein proud **Leicester** and licentious John
> Are **pillers** for the king to lean upon.   (433)

Geoffrey of Monmouth is a known source for Shakespeare and in *Henry VI* part 2, Humphrey, Duke of Gloucester, speaks to the, "Brave peers of England, **pillars** of the **state**…" (1.1.74). Neville, as author of *Locrine* (see below), also drew on Geoffrey of Monmouth (Casson, 2009, 103). In *Locrine* the word '**pillar**' is used twice with the meaning of supporting the state, for example, Assarachus says:

> Now who is left to helpless Albion?
> That as a **pillar** might uphold our **state**…   (5.2.3)

In *Look About You* Gloster is repeatedly identified as a bastard, as when Prince John complains, "The bastard is escaped in my clothes" (914) and when Henry the Young King says twice, "I do desire the death of bastard Gloster" (1019, 1021). The bastard Earl then is related to a fictional Neville (Lady Faukenbridge) and to an actual Plantagenet king, and is an enemy of the Earl of Leicester, a disguiser and a powerful truth teller: this all begins to make sense when we put Neville (who used disguise, was himself illegitimate and descended from the Plantagenets) into the frame as author and politician. Shakespeare created a series of figures who fearlessly speak Truth to Power, starting with the Bastard Fauconbridge in *The Troublesome Raigne* and *King John* and continuing with plain Thomas of Woodstock, and John of Gaunt in *Richard II*. *All these figures were related to Neville.* Furthermore Neville spoke Truth to Power in the person of James I: indeed the King invited Neville to do so, preferring his plain speaking to Francis Bacon's 'extravagant stile' (Casson 2009, 172). "Sir Henry Neville did directly answer" (Winwood, 1725, Vol 3, 235).

The contemporary Duke of Gloucester was Henry Percy, 8th Earl of Northumberland (1532-1585), who married Catherine Neville, daughter of John, the 4th Baron Latimer. He was involved with Charles Paget and Mary Queen of Scots and died in the Tower on June 21st 1585. Thus, at the very time I have suggested *Look About You* was written, a real Duke of Gloucester had been arrested, dispatched to the Tower and died (whether murdered or by suicide is not clear)[32].

---

32   From: http://www.luminarium.org/encyclopedia/northumberland8.htm accessed 6/6/09

**4) Sir Richard and Lady Marian Faukenbridge**
The Faukenbridges are unhistorical fictions. Lady Faukenbridge is named as Marian. (This might further confuse her identity with Maid Marian in the Robin Hood legend.) She is identified as Countess of West-Hereford. Sir Richard Faukenbridge is identified as a knight of the Cross and Lord of the Cinque Ports.

What then is the meaning of these fictional interpolations? When we put Henry Neville into the picture all these make sense. Fauconberg was a Neville family name since William Neville married Joan de Fauconberg in 1429 during the reign of Henry VI. Identifying Lady Faukenbridge as the Countess of West-Hereford links her to Robert Devereux who was Viscount of Hereford at the time of the play. Devereux was of course the Earl of Essex. (John Neville held the barony of Essex during the reign of Edward III.) Neville had known Devereux from at least 1583 when they travelled to Scotland together. By giving this title to Lady Faukenbridge he is allying a hidden Neville to a hidden Devereux. By 1600 when the play was published, Neville was himself a knight, a supporter of the earl of Essex and one of Lords of the Cinque Ports. In one of the annotations in the Tower Notebook (Worsley MSS 40, 1602) Neville wrote, "Barons 5 ports the canapie". Brenda James noticed the references in the Tower Notebook to the Lords of the Cinque Ports carrying the canopy over the monarch at the coronation: a role pondered by Shakespeare in Sonnet 125 and mentioned in *Henry VIII* (James and Rubinstein, 2005, 46).

The bastard Fawconbridge/Faulconbridge appears in *The Troublesome Raigne* and *King John*. He is the son of Richard the Lionheart and Margaret Faulconbridge. Her husband is Sir Robert, so the names have been changed: Lady Faulconbridge's first name changes from Marion to Margaret, Sir Richard to Robert and the spelling of Faulconbridge is different. The title page of *The Troublesome Raigne* spells this as Fawconbridge. The First Folio *King John* spells it Faulconbridge.

The Faulconbridge name appears in the following plays between 1591-1600:

| **Order of printing** | **Suggested order of writing** |
|---|---|
| *The Troublesome Raigne*, 1591 | *Look About You*, 1585-6 |
| *Henry VI* part 3, 1595 | *The Troublesome Raigne*, 1587-8 |
| *Love's Labours Lost*, 1598 | *Henry VI* part 3, 1589-91 |

*Edward IV*, 1599/1600 (Heywood/Chettle)
*Henry V*, 1600
*The Merchant of Venice*, 1600
*Look About You*, 1600

*Henry VI* part 1, 1623
*King John*, 1623

*Henry VI* part 1, 1589-92
*King John*, 1593-6
*Love's Labours Lost*, 1594-5
*The Merchant of Venice*, 1596-7
*Edward IV*, 1598-9
*Henry V* 1598-9

In other words Shakespeare ceases using the Faulconbridge name after 1599. Four plays containing it were printed for the first time in 1600: *Look About You, The Merchant of Venice, Henry V* and *Edward IV*. The writer using the name Faulconbridge repeatedly in the late 1580s and 90s was Shakespeare and the name contained a hidden connection with the Neville family. *Edward IV* has been attributed to Thomas Heywood and others: it was registered in 1599 and printed the next year (Ribner, 1965, 272). The bastard Faulconbridge in this play is the real historical figure, not a fictional character. He was Thomas Neville who led an army in support of Henry VI and failed in his siege of London. He was then captured and beheaded by the forces of Edward IV (Trace, 1968, 62). Perhaps after this play, which again pointed to a Neville, the bard decided not to use the name again (see appendix 9).

In 1607 George Wilkins' play *The Miseries of Enforced Marriage* (based on *The Yorkshire Tragedy*, see Casson, 2009, 195) was published. Wilkins' use of the Faulconbridge name is not in the text of the play but in the margin: one character is called 'Lord' in the play but identified as Faulconbridge to readers. No one in the theatre would know this hidden identity. A fantastical novel, by an anonymous writer, embroidering the Faulconbridge legend, *The Famous History of George Lord Fauconbridge* appeared in 1616 (see appendix 6). Is it purely a coincidence that this is the year following Neville's death, indeed the very year William Shakespeare from Stratford died?

One of the manuscript copies of Shakespeare's popular second sonnet, dating from the 1630s (Add. MS 10309, British Library: Taylor, 1986), was owned by Margaret Bellasys, who was probably the daughter of Thomas Bellasys, first Lord Fauconberg. The fourth Earl of Yarborough, the owner of the Worsley Manuscripts examined in this book, married Marcia Pelham in 1886. In 1903 she was granted the barony of Fauconberg which had been in abeyance for four hundred years.[33] Thus the Neville manuscripts were held by a family who managed to reclaim the Fauconberg name!

---

33      http://en.wikipedia.org/wiki/Earl_of_Yarborough accessed 31/3/09

## 5) Robert, Earl of Leyster

Robert de Beaumont, the 3rd Earl of Leicester, was one of the principal followers of Henry the Young King. He was defeated in 1173 and imprisoned for five years. He had little influence in the remaining years of Henry II's reign, but was restored to favor by Richard I (the Lion Heart). In 1190 Robert went on pilgrimage to the Holy Land, but he died on his return journey.[34] Thus his role in the play is also not historically accurate as he is fictionalised as an enemy of Gloster, perhaps conflating him with his father, the 2nd Earl. We can therefore see that the writer brought him into the play in order to dramatise a court rivalry between a dangerous Earl of Leicester and a bastard related to a hidden Neville.

### *Leicester's Commonwealth* and *Look About You*

Just before the section on King John in *Leicester's Commonwealth*, the writers mention Henry II: "since the Conquest, it appeareth plainly in King Stephen and King Henry II, both of them born out of English dominions and of parents that at their birth were not of the English allegiance, and yet were they both admitted to the crown" (Peck, 160/*106*). Richard I is also mentioned in a discussion about the laws of succession.

In *Look About You* there are a number of specific references to material in *Leicester's Commonwealth*. The word 'commonwealth' is used twice. The Earl of Leicester is associated with murder and specifically with poison. Referring to the poisoning of Rosamund, Leicester himself complains:

> What vollumes will be writ, what lybels spred
> And in each lyne our state dishonoured!     (127)

This sounds very like *Leicester's Commonwealth*. Gloster warns Henry II:

> Ther's more infectious breaths about your throne.
> Leyster is there; your enuious Sonnes is there;
> If them you can endure, no poyson fear.     (324)

---

[34]    http://en.wikipedia.org/wiki/Robert_de_Beaumont,_3rd_Earl_of_Leicester accessed 20/1/09

Skink, the poisoner, play acting to save his skin, covers himself in pig's blood as if he had been attacked, and pretending to shout at his attacker, cries, "Ide breake the neck of yee downe the stayres…" (1571). This is an extraordinarily daring reference to the accusation in *Leicester's Commonwealth* that Leicester had his first wife murdered by a servant pushing her down some stairs so that she broke her neck.

Perhaps the playwright got away with this by putting it into a scene of high farce. Gloster refuses to drink wine offered by Leicester. He says, "I'll count it poison" (501) and flings it to the ground. In *Leicester's Commonwealth* poisoned wine is suggested as the cause of the Earl of Essex's death. Gloster accuses Leicester of being a liar and threatens him:

> First, through a crimson sluice,
> Ile send thy hated soul to those black fiendes
> That long have houered gaping for their parte,
> When **tyrant** life should leaue thy **traitor** heart!   (2670)

In *Leicester's Commonwealth* Leicester is accused of being a tyrant. His father and grandfather are accused of being traitors, "the one being a cozener and the other a tyrant" (Peck, 193/*127*).

The word 'faction' is repeatedly used in *Leicester's Commonwealth* to describe the different groupings supporting rival claimants to the throne. In one passage there is an alliterative run of words beginning with 'f': "a fast obliged friend, the other a fellow or follower in faction" (Peck, 99/*69*). In *Look About You* the word is used four times in four lines about the different factions at court including the alliterative, "thy false father's faction" (990). This is in a scene where Gloster's death is plotted: clearly the playwright wishes the audience to understand the dangers inherent in factionalism. In *Leicester's Commonwealth* Leicester's faction is said to have a watchword which is "Are you **settled**?" or "Whether you be **settled** or no" (Peck, 142/*96*).

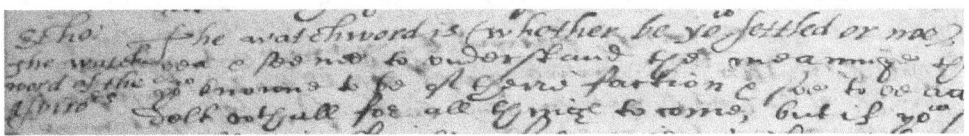

Worsley MSS 47: 39V

In the final speech of *Look About You* King Henry II say:

> I am new crowned, **new settled** in my seate.
> Lets' all to the Chappell, there giue thankes and praise,
> Beseeching grace from Heauen's eternal Throne,
> That England neuer know more Prince then one.   (3209)

Here the history-as-metaphor dissolves into current political concerns: for the unity and peace of the realm and not to have two Princes: i.e. not to have the kingdom divided or shared between Elizabeth I and the Earl of Leicester. Another possibility is that the last line refers to an incident when Elizabeth boxed the ears of Lettice and banished her from court, commenting that as "but one sun lighted the sky," so she would "have but one Queen of England"[35]. Lettice had married Leicester in 1578 and the Queen's jealousy was further inflamed by her sumptuous wardrobe and her habit of riding in carriages through London so that people mistook her for the Queen.

In *Leicester's Commonwealth* it is stated that Ambrose Dudley (the Earl of Warwick and Leicester's brother) was given land belonging to Lord Berkeley (Peck, 123/*83*). In *Look About You* the disreputable Skink is given land that belongs to Gloster. As we saw in chapter 1, Neville had reasons to dislike Ambrose.

**Neville Connections**
Sir Ralph Sadler and Sir Henry Neville (Neville's father) were given custody of Mary Queen of Scots 1584-5. There is a letter dated December 1583 from Elizabeth I asking Sadler and Neville for their assistance in this matter in the State Papers at the Public Records Office in Kew, London (Lemon, 1865, 142). Elizabeth's letter authorising the transfer of Mary's custody is dated 1/4/1584 (Hicks, 1964, 149). From September 1584 to January 1585 Mary was in their care (Lovell, 2005, 338). Thus at the very time *Leicester's Commonwealth* was published and the Worsley manuscript copies made, Neville's father was partly responsible for an imprisoned Queen.
From January 1585 Sir Amias Paulet was appointed Keeper of Mary Queen of Scots. He refused Elizabeth's suggestion that he kill Mary. Perhaps the line in *Look About You* where the unscrupulous Skink speaks of killing Rosamond is a reference to this, "At a queen's bidding I did kill a quean"

---

35       From: http://www.berkshirehistory.com/bios/lknollys.html

(391). Such a monarch's request to a servant, to assassinate a rival claimant to the throne, troubles the consciences of Hubert in *The Troublesome Raigne/King John*, the play which is a sequel to *Look About You*. Paulet had sufficient conscience to refuse to gratify his sovereign. Perhaps only someone in Neville's position could have known about such a secret request from the Queen to eliminate her rival.

In 1584 Neville became member of Parliament for New Windsor. Thus we can see that the scenes in Parliament early in the play could be based on his own experience of procedures in the House of Commons. Lord Faukenbridge puts forward a bill "for the releasement of the queen" (75). We hear M.P.s grumbling as they debate and of "the tricks that pages pass the time in Parliament" (561). Such details might well be observed by a new M.P..

Henry II's poisoned mistress, Rosamund, was buried at Godstow Priory, "only a short distance up-river from Gloucester Hall", Oxford (Foster, 1981, 118). Dr. Thomas Allen left a note of the design on her headstone. Neville knew Allen (see chapter 3). Thus Neville, an Oxford graduate, could well have been aware of the resting place of this figure whose death is recalled repeatedly in *Look About You*. Furthermore Neville could trace his family history back to Henry II's reign when his ancestor, Alan de Neville, had been the King's Chief Forester (James, 2005, 59).

Robert Huntington (Robin Hood) is described in the play as a ward of Prince Richard. In 1581 Henry Wriothesley, the young Earl of Southampton, became a ward of Lord Burghley and in 1585 entered St John's College Cambridge. Neville met Wriothesley at Burghley's house when he was a boy: since Neville was away in Europe from 1578 until 1583 this meeting must have been between 1583-5. Wriothesley was a strikingly beautiful youth. In the play Richard likens Robin to Cupid (Love):

> Be gone sweete boy to Marian Faukenbridge,
> Thou lookest like loue perswade her to be louing.   (410)

Wriothesley was close to the Earl of Essex: perhaps the relationship between Robin and Richard in the play mirrors that relationship. Shakespeare-Neville certainly loved Wriothesley as is evident in his sonnets and the dedications of *Venus and Adonis* and *The Rape of Lucrece*. In the play Robin dresses up as a woman, impersonating Lady Faukonbridge. There is a portrait of the young Henry Wriothesley, looking so feminine that for many years it was misidentified as a woman. Attributed to John de Critz, it is owned by the Cobbe family (see Fields, 2006, 117).

The Young King Henry grants the Lordship of Rowden to Skink thus depriving Gloster of his land and causing him to assault Skink. At the time of the play the Rowden Lordship was in the possession of the Vaux family who were barons of Har**rowden**. Sir Nicholas Vaux appears in Shakespeare and Fletcher's *Henry VIII*. His son, Thomas Vaux, was a poet and is misquoted by the gravedigger in *Hamlet*. Another Vaux appears in *Henry VI* part 2 (3.2.371). This was probably William Vaux, a Lancastrian, who was killed at the battle of Tewkesbury in 1471. According to Warren (2003, 220) Shakespeare's chronicle sources do not mention him so this suggests some special knowledge of the Vaux family which Neville may well have had. Catherine, daughter of William Vaux, the third baron, married another Sir Henry Neville, who later became the 7th Lord Abergavenny, in about 1615. This suggests at least some familiarity between the families before that date.

Begor pointed out that the role of the Earl of Lancaster in the play is an unhistorical fiction as the Earldom was only created in 1267, long after the reign of Henry II. "No doubt the depiction of an old Lancaster supporting the ruling monarch owes something to the fame in Elizabethan times of John of Gaunt" (Begor, 1965, 20). Neville was a descendent of John of Gaunt. He notes his name in the margins of his copy of *Leicester's Commonwealth* (Worsley MSS 47). Shakespeare was to give a great patriotic speech to Gaunt in *Richard II*.

In *Look About You* there are brief but characteristic references to falconry, a sport Neville knew and Shakespeare used as a source of imagery.

**The date of *Look About You***
As the play was published in 1600 Begor thought it had been written in 1598-9. Lancashire suggested the play referred to the monarchical aspirations of the Earl of Essex (Logan & Smith, 1975, 173). Begor (1965, 54) thought the play reflected a quarrel between Elizabeth I and Essex in 1598; she equated the rebellious Young King Henry with Essex and saw the scene of Henry's submission to his father as advice to Essex (Begor, 1965, 10-11). Jones suggested the play dated from 1595, noting that Robin is an immature character whom we see grown up in the Munday and Chettle

plays (Nelson, 1962, 141). Furthermore the play "is an excellent example of the comedy of disguise, and as this form had lost its early popularity by 1600, the play must have been written before this date. The play is so full of quick changes of costume that it may be indentified with the lost play *The Disguises*, known to have been performed in 1595" (Nelson, 1962, 141). However, when we realise *Leicester's Commonwealth* is a source, we can see that although analogous with Essex's ambitions (and so making the printing in 1600 topical), the play refers explicitly to the Earl of Leicester, the factions and divisions in the realm and an imprisoned Queen: all themes of 1584-7.

As I have discovered a relationship between this play and *Leicester's Commonwealth* the earliest possible date for its composition would be 1584. I suggest the play was written in 1585-6. This would be shortly after Neville had met Henry Wriothesley. Taking history as metaphor I note that the play depicts a Queen being held in prison for fomenting rebellion. This Queen survives, indeed is released from prison. I suggest this is a reference to Mary Queen of Scots' imprisonment. As she was executed in 1587 the play must predate that event. King Henry threatens to execute Elinor:

> If thus she moue me,
> Ile haue her head, though all the world reproue me.    (1127)

The imprisoned Queen is under threat of execution in the play but does not face a capital charge, so the play would predate Mary's trial in 1586. The appearance of an Earl of Leicester suggests a date before his death and, as there is also no hint of any Armada, the play was probably written before 1588. When I had dated *Mucedorus* to 1584-5 and *Locrine* to 1587-88, I was aware of a gap between these two early plays. I therefore wondered if there was a play that would fit into that gap. I have previously noted the links between *Mucedorus* and *Leicester's Commonwealth* (Casson, 2009, see appendix 7). Furthermore in *Locrine* there is Queen Estrild who is kept hidden underground for years and who later commits suicide when unsuccessful in battle with the Queen Guendoline (who is specifically associated with Elizabeth I). I therefore suggested Estrild was Mary Queen of Scots and this dated that play after her execution. *Locrine* and *The Troublesome Raigne of John* (which I date to 1587-8) both contain references to foreign invasion and possibly to the Armada (1588). These facts would then suggest a probably date for the creation of *Look About You* as 1585-6.

Another probable source for *Look About You* is Holinshed's *Chronicles* which was published in 1587. Holinshed describes an incident when Henry II served the Young King at table and the young man's arrogance shocked observers (Holinshed, 1976, 130). We see this in the play. Holinshed of course was an important source for Shakespeare's history plays. Bate (1997, 201) and others have pointed out that Shakespeare "was the only dramatist of the age who returned frequently to that foundation-text of Tudor ideology, Holinshed's *Chronicles*" (Egan, 2006, 61). Since Neville's father-in-law, Killigrew, was involved in editing this edition, Neville would have had access to the book whilst it was in preparation so this source would not rule out the early date.

*Look About You* is the first part of a trilogy: *The Troublesome Raigne of John King of England*, parts one and two, complete a story of the fictional Faulconbridge family and follow on from the history depicted in *Look About You*. We see the young irascible Prince John of *Look About You* become the insecure tyrant King John in *The Troublesome Raigne*. The latter begins many years after *Look About You*. Lady Faulconbridge confesses that she did in the end give in to Prince Richard's amorous attentions and so conceived a bastard son, Philip. By the time the play opens Richard is the late lamented Lionheart, whose crown has been inherited by King John.
When we consider history as metaphor we can see Leicester as King John, a usurper, and young Prince Arthur as James I (both born outside England and linked as such in *Leicester's Commonwealth*). There is a foreign invasion, religious conflict, and enemies within the state: all is saved by the loyal bastard. Thus we can date *The Troublesome Raigne* to 1587-8 and this suggests an earlier date for *Look About You*, namely 1585-6. *Leicester's Commonwealth* was not so named until 1586 and as the word 'commonwealth' is used twice in the play this might point to the later date but as the word is used in the tract itself this is not conclusive. One name might confirm this: the character Skink is an invention of the playwright. Begor suggested that this name comes from 'skinker', a tapster. She noted that a colonel Skink served in the British army in the Low Countries in 1586. A skink is also the name of a lizard which would suit the character's nature. Skink is like the Vice, a rogue hero. Begor (1965, 592) stated that rogue hero literature was popular in the late 16th Century. Shakespeare's Richard III is an example of such a character. In *Henry IV* part 1, Prince Hal speaks of "an under-skinker" (2.4.24).

In the First Folio, the spelling of Gloucester evolves from Gloster in Henry VI parts 1, 2 and 3 (written c 1589-91), to Glouster in Richard III (c 1592) and finally to Gloucester in Henry V (1599). The annotator of Halle's *Chronicle* wrote a note about "the murther of brother Thomas Woodstocke duk glocester" (Keen & Lubbock, 1954, 128). As I have dated the Halle annotations to c 1594-8 this spelling fits into this sequence. In *Look About You* the name is spelt Gloster: my suggestion of an early date for *Look About You* therefore fits with plays written towards the end of the 1580s. There remains the possibility that Neville revised *Look About You* in about 1599 prior to its publication when he was using *Leicester's Commonwealth* vocabulary in *Julius Caesar* and *Henry V*. However he did not change the spelling of Gloster!

*Look About You* was printed in 1600 "as it was lately played by the right honourable the Lord High Admiral his servants". After his arrest following the Essex Rebellion in 1601, Neville was placed under house arrest "at the Lord Admiral's house in Chelsea" (James & Rubinstein, 2005, 146).

Because Begor (1965) has a very different view of the date of *Look About You* I examine the question further in Appendix 5.

**The title**

"Look About You" could mean "Watch Out!" or "Beware!" The poet warns. It could also mean "Look! It's about **you**!" In the latter case it could be a warning to Elizabeth I or a message to the Earls of Leicester and Huntington, or to the audience. This however would be a very high risk strategy. It may be that the use of hilarious comedy is designed to disarm the threat of political censorship.

"Look About You" could also mean "Search!" as when Gloster says, "Come looke about, search euery little corner" (1227). The play has several searches in it as when Redcap searches for Gloster; Robin goes in search of Skink; and Gloster, disguised as Faukenbridge, pretends to search for Gloster.

The title is used repeatedly throughout the play as a catch phrase. It is also used by Shakespeare in *Julius Caesar* which was written the year before *Look About You* was printed (2.3.7, quoted at the start of this chapter); in *The Taming of The Shrew* Grumio says, "Master, master, **look about you**: who goes there, ha?" (1.2.139) and in *All's Well That Ends Well* a soldier says, "So, **look about you**: know you any here?" (4.3.316). According to LION no other writer of 1584-1600 used the phrase "look about you" except Shakespeare. In *The Troublesome Raigne* Lewes says to Arthur, "'tis time to looke about" (Sider, 1979, 69, line 186).

## Themes in *Look About You* and Shakespeare

**Disguise and confusion of gender and identity**

*Look About You* has been described as "the best complex disguise play of its period" (Logan & Smith, 173, 1975). The play does not just use disguise for fun: it is also about the confusion which happens when identity and gender are disguised. Disguise is of course a major theme of Shakespeare's plays, with women dressing as men; Falstaff disguising as a woman; Henry V and Henry VIII both going in disguise; tragic and comic effects result from mistaken identity (Hero in *Much Ado About Nothing*, Cloten in *Cymbeline* and two sets of twins in *The Comedy of Errors*). In *Look About You* Gloster says he, "wil be a **proteus** euery houre" (1513). Prince John describes Gloster as "He that **changes** himself to sundry **shapes**" (2121). Richard, the villainous Duke of Gloucester in *Henry VI* part 3 says he will, "**Change shapes** with **Proteus**" (3.2.192). In *The Two Gentlemen of Verona* the disguised Julia, revealing her true identity, confronts Proteus:

> Behold her that gave aim to all thy oaths,
> And entertain'd 'em deeply in her heart.
> O **Proteus**, let this habit make thee **blush**!
> Be thou ashamed that I have took upon me
> Such an immodest raiment, if **shame** live
> In a **disguise** of love:
> It is the lesser **blot**, modesty finds,
> Women to **change** their **shapes** than men their minds. (5.4.)

Elements of the Shakespearean blot image cluster are immediately apparent and the speech brings together characteristic themes of young Shakespeare: oaths, disguise and shame which we see in *Look About You* (see below).

Neville's grandfather, Edward went in disguise to a masque at Cardinal Wolsey's house: this scene is shown, disguised itself (so that Neville is removed from the story) in *Henry VIII* (see Casson, 2009, 175). In a diplomatic letter dated 24/9/1599, Neville writes of a Mr. Honniman using a disguise in secret service work. In another of 22/10/1599 he informs his reader that Monsieur de Betunes "came to London in disguised Manner as a Scottish-man". On 20/11/1599 Neville tells us, "I thinck of a disguising" (Winwood, 1725, Vol 1, 107, 124, 133). If Neville, who successfully disguised his identity as a poet/playwright, is accepted as the writer, then it is no surprise that this early play should be concerned with disguise and confusion of identity.

**Oaths and Chastity**

The swearing oaths is connected with chastity as Lady Faukenbridge resists Prince Richard's blandishments:

Richard:        Lady Faukenbridge,
           Did you not ioyne your faire white hand?
           **Swore** that ye would **foresweare** your husbands bed,
           If I could but finde out Gloster?
Lady F:    I **swear** so?
Richard:              By heauen
Robin:     Take heed, its a high **oath** my Lord.           (2704)

Robin confesses it was he in disguise as Lady Faukenbridge that made this promise. The good Lady then regrets she is not free and resists Richard's "desire unchast" and "unlawful sute", offering, should her husband die, to become his wife rather than his 'harlot': "that shame shall neuer dwell vpon my brow" (2728). This recalls Lady Elizabeth Grey resisting Edward IV in *Henry VI* part 3. Lady Elizabeth refuses to be Edward's 'concubine' (3.2.98), a word that is used four times in *Look About You.* Just 30 lines later in *Henry VI* part 3, Gloucester uses the hyphenated word 'unlooked-for' (3.2.131) which occurs in *Look About You* (see below). Lady Grey accepts marriage, just as Lady Faukenbridge suggests she would. Is it only a coincidence that a Duke of Gloucester appears in both plays? We see just such a confrontation between an importunate man and a resistant woman in *Richard III, The Rape of Lucrece, Edward III* and *Measure for Measure*. In *Edward III* (which was written 1592-3) when the Countess of Salisbury resists the King's advances, links are made with the Rape of Lucrece, as they are by Lady Fauconbridge in *The Troublesome Raigne*. This preoccupation with chastity in marriage matches Neville's experience of being illegitimate: his father was still married to his first wife, Winifred, when Henry was conceived by Elizabeth Gresham. Thus it is not difficult to see the connections with Neville's own life when we consider that his own father made love to his mother before they were married and Neville had to bear the secret life-long shame of bastardy, as is evinced in Shakespeare canon.

Furthermore the recurrent theme of oath-swearing can be seen in the political context of the time. In October 1584, after the Throckmorton plot of 1583 and the assassination of William of Orange, Walsingham and Cecil proposed an oath in Parliament, the Bond of Association, whereby MPs swore revenge against anyone who made an attempt to kill the Queen or usurp the throne (Hadfield, 2005, 18). Neville was a new MP at this time.

**Bastards**

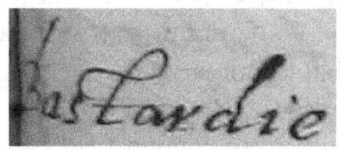

Worsley MSS 47, 46[36]

In *Look About You*, *The Troublesome Raigne*, *King John*, *Much Ado About Nothing* and *King Lear* there are bastards. Whilst this alone need not suggest the plays are connected, when we examine the texts we can see very clear connections. With Neville as the common author these are immediately apparent and explained. Gloster is the bastard in *Look About You*. His sister marries Lord Faukenbridge (a Neville family name). She later gives birth to the Bastard Fauconbridge (between the plays). In *King Lear* Gloucester's bastard son Edmund cries "Gods, stand up for bastards!" We do not know if Neville cast a revising eye over the old text of *Look About You* before it was published in 1600 but it definitely predates *King Lear*. It is startling then to read in *Look About You* that Gloster is threatened with having his eyes put out (836). Arthur is likewise threatened in *The Troublesome Raigne* and *King John*, demonstrating further connections between these plays and *Look About You*.

In *Look About You* a bastard (Gloster) is both a commentator on, and involved in, the action, just as in *The Troublesome Raigne* and *King John*. Furthermore in *The Troublesome Raigne* the Bastard Fauconbridge and his brother Robert are brought onto the stage by the Earl of Salisbury. This man was William Longsword, the bastard son of Henry II and therefore King John's half brother. He married Ela, the Salisbury heiress. Richard Neville, the Earl of Salisbury (1400-60), appears in the plays *Henry VI* parts 1 & 2. Perhaps only Neville, the bastard writer with a family connection to the

---

36    'Baſtardie' is exactly the spelling used in the first quarto of *Titus Andronicus* (Malone Society reprint, 2003, line 2160).

Earldom of Salisbury, could enjoy the secret irony of a bastard introducing a bastard to the King.

**The Royal Succession and Division of the Realm**
Discussion of the succession was forbidden by Elizabeth I. It was of course the core concern of *Leicester's Commonwealth* and a major theme for Shakespeare's plays. In crowning his son, Henry II had attempted to ensure a smooth succession but in fact promoted division. In the play Henry the Young King asks for half the realm (203). Gloster snorts, "Nay, giue him all, and he will scant be pleas'd" (206). Holinshed (1976, Vol 2, 148) stated that the young king "openlie demanded to have the whole rule committed to him". Another incident taken from Holinshed is when "King Henry the father served his sonne at table". The Young King's disdainful behaviour is commented upon by Holinshed (1976, 130-1). In the play it is again Gloster who laments Henry II's self abasement when the King kneels to serve the Young King, exclaiming, "O hell! O tortor!" (3051). James (2008, 246) noted that both Shakespeare (46 times) and Neville (in a letter dated 6/6/1599) used the word 'torture'. If my early date for *Look About You* is accurate this would be his first use of the word.
There is a political connection between *Look About You* and *King Lear*. In the former the king gives up power to his son, in the latter the king gives his power to his daughters. In both the theme of the dangerous transmission of royal authority is illustrated by the consequences, of threats to stability and the peace of the realm. There are other connections between the plays, which I will note later.

The interweaving of these themes, of disguise, oaths, chastity, bastards and inheritance, make sense when we put Neville into the frame: these were key issues in his life and so may be taken as indicators of his authorship.

**Plot devices in *Look About You* and Shakespeare**
**The gold chain**
In *Look About You*, Skink (in disguise) tricks Sir Richard Faukenbridge into giving him a gold chain, Gloster (in disguise) gets half of it from Skink. There is further recrimination about this gold chain due to the confusion of identity resulting from the disguising. This is almost exactly what happens in *The Comedy of Errors*, in which the confusion of identity arises from the two sets of identical twins being mistaken for each other as the gold chain passes between them. Hazlitt (1874) referred to *The Comedy of Errors* in his edition of *Look About You*. In *Look About You* the word 'goldsmith' is used

twice. Shakespeare uses it 8 times, all of which are in *The Comedy of Errors*. In *Arden of Faversham* there is also a 'goldsmith' (2.1.21). Bradshaw, the goldsmith in *Arden*, sells stolen plate that belonged to Sir Anthony Cooke, who was Neville's mother-in-law's father (Casson, 2009, 162). I suggest that *Arden* was written just after *Look About You* (see chapter 10).

**The pits**
Skink tricks both Prince John and Faukenbridge so they fall into pits on Blackheath. He then robs them. Likewise, in *Titus Andronicus*, Martius and Quintus fall into a pit in which Bassianus already lies dead. This darkly comic scene has tragic results but both scenes are about innocent men falling victim to Machiavellian villains.

**Cutting off hands**
In *Titus Andronicus* three hands are cut off. In *Look About You* Gloster's hand is nearly cut off and we recognise another recurring theme in early plays. In *Edward III*, Warwick links the themes of oaths and dismemberment when he says, "What if I swear by this right hand of mine, to cut this right hand off?" (2.1.352).
In 1579 John Stubbe wrote a pamphlet objecting to Elizabeth's proposed marriage with the Duke of Anjou. Elizabeth was incensed. She wanted to have Stubbs executed. In *Look About You* the cruel Queen Elinor demands, "Off with his hand, then with his head" (3041). I note that both Queen's names begin with the letters 'Eli'. Stubbe was arrested and sentenced to have his right hand cut off. The sentence was carried out with surgeons present to prevent him bleeding to death. In *Look About You* a surgeon is called upon to "make a mark" (3110).
Stubbe's pamphlet was called *The Discoverie of a **Gaping Gulf***, and it is perhaps recalled in the lines:

>men hate adulterous sin,
>Count it a **gulfe**, and yet they needs will in. (143)

The word '**gaping**' also occurs in the play (2671). Stubbe remained in the Tower until 1581. In 1589 he became MP for Great Yarmouth (Mears, 2004). Neville had become an M.P. in 1584, so they probably met in Parliament, if not before.

**The emerging blot image cluster**

This Shakespearean image cluster places the word '**blot**' in relation to 'heaven/sky', 'night', 'moon', 'constancy/inconstant', 'disguise' (mask), 'winter/coldness', frost, 'sovereign/king', 'eye', 'sun' and 'cheeks' (face/complexion), (Muir, 1960, 22: in Egan, 2006, Vol 3, 284). The words '**stain**' and '**spot**' are also used with these images. The imagery contrasts the wish to hide the shame of a blot/stain/disgrace (by disguising, darkness, night, cloud) and the revealing of a blushing shamed face to the eye of day (= sun = sovereign) (Casson, 2009, 198).

Is this image cluster to be found in *Look About You*? There are indeed elements of this cluster, like fragments that are beginning to coalesce, in the play. For example:

Henry:     Why does not Gloster weare a Coronet?
Gloster:   Because his **Souereign** doth not weare a crown.
Henry:     By **heauen** put on thy Coronet, or that **heauen**,
           Which now with clear [arch]³⁷ lends vs this light,
           Shall not be **courtain'd with the vaile of night**,
           Eare on thy **head** I clap a burning Crowne.   (2851)

The circumstances are shameful: the bastard Gloster is embarrassing the Young King because he has shamed his royal father by his rebellion. According to LION no other writer of the period 1584-1599 used the word 'curtain'd' except Shakespeare, who used it twice, the earliest of which is in *Titus Andronicus*, referring to hidden sexual behaviour. Skink also uses this curtain image with two other blot cluster words, "Til **nights blacke**

---

37    'Arch' is an editor's guess for a missing word. Were the word 'eye', it would fit the blot cluster. "Clear eye" is in *The Comedy of Errors* (3.2.62). Two lines later the word 'heaven' is repeated twice. Shakespeare uses the "eye of heaven" in *The Rape of Lucrece*, *Richard II*, *King John* and Sonnet 18. Eyes were thought at the time to send out beams of light so this image of the sun as an eye lending light would be appropriate at the time. Indeed just before "clear eye" in *The Comedy of Errors* there is "your **eye**… your beams, fair **sun**… **clear** your sight…**wink**, sweet love, as look on **night**" (3.2.55-58). As Skink uses the words "**clear sky**" this would be an alternative to 'clear eye' and still fit the blot cluster. Falstaff says "clear sky" in *Henry IV* part 2 (4.3.50).

hand **curtaine** this to **cleare sky**." (1305)[38] In T*he Rape of Lucrece* there is an instance of the blot cluster where this word occurs:

> Look, as the fair and fiery-pointed **sun**,
> Rushing from forth a **cloud**, bereaves our sight;
> Even so, the **curtain** drawn, his **eyes** begun
> To **wink**, being **blinded** with a greater light:
> Whether it is that she reflects so bright,
> That dazzleth them, or else some **shame** supposed;
> But **blind** they are, and keep themselves enclosed.   (372)

In *Look About You* Robin says, " he did **winke**, the **blinde** man had an **eye**" (2428). Both passages refer to a man's lustful gaze. Twice in *Henry V* Shakespeare uses the word 'wink' near 'blind' (5.2.296, 302-6) in a scene when Henry is wooing Kate.

The word 'shame' is used 13 times in the play, along with 'ashamed' and 'shameless'. For example Robin argues with Richard, dissuading him from his seduction of Lady Faukenbridge, using the words 'unchastity', 'shameless', 'sinne', 'staine', 'blemmish', 'untaynted' (696-708). Other blot cluster words that are used in the play include: 'heaven', 'sky', 'night', 'inconstant/constant', 'disguise', 'winter', 'cold', 'frosty', 'sovereign', 'king', 'eye', 'sun', 'cheek', 'blush', 'disgrace' and 'cloudy'. Only the moon is missing.

'Cloudy' is used twice of the face. Richard says, "let one cloudy frowne Shaddow the bright sunne of thy beauties light" (2222, thus combining the blot cluster ideas of 'cloud', 'face', 'sun', and 'shadow'). Shakespeare uses 'cloudy' 16 times, half of which refer to facial expressions of emotion varying from shame to melancholy and anger.

In such an early play I would not expect to find the full cluster but clearly the elements are there and these can be seen to evolve in the next plays to become the full blot cluster. Sams (1986, 250) found this cluster in *Edmund Ironside*, and pointed out that the words "twenty thousand" also occur, connected to the blot cluster. In *Look About You* "twenty thousand" is used twice. I have found elements of the blot cluster and the words "twenty thousand" in *Locrine* (Casson, 2009). The annotator of the Halle's

---

38    In *The Troublesome Raigne* we read, "**Night** had shadowed all the earth with sable **curtains** of the **black**est hue" (Sider, 1979, 160, 42).

Chronicle noted "20,000 men of scottes" in the margin.

Halle's *Chronicle*, Henry IV, fxviii[a]

"Twenty thousand" also occurs in *The Troublesome Raigne*. Furthermore the elements of the blot cluster are to be found in that play, as when the bastard confronts his mother about the hidden shame of his bastardy and the following words appear: 'blotteth', 'heaven's', 'blush', 'shroud', 'stain'd', 'king'. The passage occurs between a Phaeton image and a reference to the rape of Lucrece.

Professor Kenneth Muir, in *Shakespeare as Collaborator* (1960) remarked: "the presence of image clusters is one of the strongest arguments for Shakespeare's authorship" (Armstrong, 1979, 203). Furthermore, "As no two poets employ the same image clusters, therefore work of doubtful provenance can be assigned to a poet with certainty if it contains clusters, or exhibits principles of cluster formation, characteristic of writings known to be authentic" (Armstrong, 1979, 198).

**Comparable vocabulary in *Look About You* and Shakespeare**
One of the most poetic of speeches in the play is when Richard is courting Robin who is dressed as Lady Faukenbridge, (so the scene is comic). He says:
>Under the upper **heaven**, nine goodly **spheres**,
>Turne with a **motion** ever **musicall**,
>In Pallaces of Kings, meliodious **sounds**,
>Offer pleasures to ther soveraignes **eares**.
>In Temples, milke white clothed **queristors**,
>**Sing** sacred Anthemes bowing to the shrine,
>And in the feelds whole **quires** of **winged** clarkes,
>Salutes the morning **bright** and Christaline... (2185)

This may be compared with a passage from *The Merchant of Venice*:

>Here will we sit and let the **sounds** of **music**
>Creep in our **ears**: soft stillness and the night
>Become the touches of sweet harmony.
>Sit, Jessica. Look how the floor of **heaven**

> Is thick inlaid with patines of **bright** gold:
> There's not the smallest **orb** which thou behold'st
> But in his **motion** like an angel **sings**,
> Still **quiring** to the young-eyed cherubins… (5.1.54)

I have highlighted words that occur in both. Instead of '**spheres**' in the first we have '**orbs**' in the second. The situation is comparable: the wished for harmony of lovers is expressed in metaphors of the music of the spheres, singing and celestial figures/birds. If *Look About You* was written a decade before *The Merchant of Venice* (1596) the similarity of these passages shows the germination of poetic diction in the young bard and we can see how his skill developed over time. I have suggested that *Look About You* was written before *The Troublesome Raigne*. It is therefore relevant here to compare a passage in that play with the above. The bastard Faulconbridge falls into a trance in which his real identity as the illegitimate son of Richard (the very person who speaks the first speech above) is revealed:

> Me thinkes I heare a hollow Eccho **sound**,
> That *Philip* is the Sonne unto a King:
> The whistling leaves upon the trembling trees,
> Whistle in consort I am Richard's Sonne:
> The bubling murmur of the waters fall
> Records *Philippus Regius filius*:
> **Birds** in their flight make **music** with their **wings**,
> Filling the ayre with glorie of my birth:
> **Birds**, bubles, leaves and mountains, Eccho, all
> Ring in my **eares**, that I am Richards Sonne.
> Fond man, ah whether art thou carried?
> How are thy thoughts ywrapt in Honors **heaven**?

Instead of a 'quires'/'queristors' we have a 'consort'; instead of 'motion', 'flight'; instead of 'bright', 'glorie'. There is also the shared vocabulary of 'sound', 'music', 'wings', 'ears', 'heaven'. The heavenly choir is here a flock of birds which is what Richard, in the speech from *Look About You*, calls "whole quires of winged clarkes" (a pun on larks). In all three speeches Nature's music (of the spheres, birds, leaves, waters) is heard. In the last the poetic soul of the bastard Faulconbridge is speaking in an inspired trance: the disguised, illegitimate Neville is emerging as a poet. This link between *The Merchant of Venice* and the three Fauconbridge plays (*Look About You*,

*The Troublesome Raigne* and *King John*) might be explained by the fact that *The Merchant of Venice* is believed to date from the period just after *King John*: 1596-7. Neville would have been re-reading *The Troublesome Raigne* as he revised it to create *King John*. Indeed *The Merchant of Venice* was printed the very same year as *Look About You*, 1600. Furthermore in *The Merchant of Venice* the young English baron who is a hapless suitor for Portia's hand, is called Falconbridge (1. 2. 66)!

The above passages are especially important in considering the suggestion that Munday and Chettle wrote *Look About You* (see below) because there is a comparable passage in *The Downfall of Robert the Earl of Huntington* (written 1598, published 1601).

> Marion, thou seest, though courtly pleasures want,
> Yet country sport in Sherwood is not scant;
> For the soul-ravishing delicious **sound**
> Of instrumental **music**, we have found
> The **winged quiristers** with divers notes
> Sent from their quaint recording pretty throats,
> On every branch that compasseth our bow'r,
> Without command contenting us each hour.   (Thorndike,1902, 63)

This passage was definitely written after *The Troublesome Raigne* and *The Merchant of Venice*. Begor however suggested that *Look About You* was written after *The Downfall of Robert the Earl of Huntington*, despite it being published a year before. These passages however make very clear that *Look About You* is much closer to *The Merchant of Venice* and *The Troublesome Raigne*. All three use the words '**ears**' and '**heaven**', which Munday and Chettle do not. *The Downfall of Robert the Earl of Huntington* seems rather to depend on *Look About You* which uses the words '**queristors**' and "**quires** of **winged** clarkes". The poetry of *Look About You* is clearly superior.

**Words and phases**

I will now focus on rare words and pairs of words to show there is a relationship between *Look About You* and canonical Shakespeare.

The stuttering Redcap says "Ile ca ca caperclaw to to tone of yee," (2610) meaning he will hit one of the two hermits. The OED states that 'caperclaw' is a variant of 'clapperclaw', meaning to claw or scratch with open hand and nails. In fact 'caperclaw' is first noted as occurring in a Martin Marprelate pamphlet *Hay any Work for Cooper* in 1589. Nashe used the word 'clapper-claw' in 1590. Shakespeare uses it in *The Merry Wives of Windsor* (2.3.59, believed to date from 1598) and it occurs in the introductory epistle to *Troilus and Cressida* (1609) as 'clapper-clawd'. If the date I have proposed for *Look About You*, 1585-6, is accurate then it would be the very first usage.

Gloster says, "**Worse** is a brewing, and yet not the **worst**." (268). Shakespeare uses 'worse' near 'worst' six times, in four of which the word 'worse' occurs before 'worst'. For example in *King Lear* Edgar says:

> And **worse** I may be yet: the **worst** is not
> So long as we can say, 'This is the **worst**.'     (4.1.27)

Henry the Young King says, "Where **strength** wrongs **weakness**, it is mere **oppression**" (2985). In *Richard II* the Bishop of Carlisle tells of how:

> fear **oppresseth strength**,
> Gives in your **weakness strength** unto your foe…    (3.2.180)

Henry the Young King speaks of, "**extreme extremitie**s" (3063). The Chorus in *Romeo and Juliet* says, "Tempering **extremities** with **extreme** sweet" (2 Prologue). In *Love's Labours Lost* the King says, "The **extreme** parts of time **extremely** forms all causes…" (5.2.734).

The Young King Henry insists, "add not **oil to fire**. **Wrath's kindled** with a word" (970). Richard II speaks of "**Wrath-kindled** gentlemen" (1.1.152). In *King Lear* Kent says, "Bring **oil to fire**" (2.2.74). Marlowe had used "wrath-kindled" twice: in *Ovid's Elegies* and *Tamburlaine* II (LION).

Skink, talking to the stuttering Redcap, wishes his "Pyanet **chattering**" (535) would safely deliver him from danger. According to the OED, 'pyanet' is a variant of magpie. There is a related image in *Henry VI* part 3, where: "**chattering** pies in dismal discords sung" (5.6.48). Published in 1595 as *The True Tragedy of Richard Duke of York* this clearly predates Thomas Nashe's *Summer's Last Will and Testament*, which appeared in 1600, where he writes, "vain chattering pies" (1173).

Skink uses another rare word 'helter skelter' which later appears in *Henry IV* part 2, with a hyphen:

> Sir John, I am thy Pistol and thy friend,
> And helter-skelter have I rode to thee… (5.3.90)

Gloster, meeting Skink, complains he is "half strangled with the **Garlicke breath**" (1293). In *A Midsummer Night's Dream* Bottom tells the actors, "eat no onions nor **garlic**, for we are to utter sweet **breath**" (4.2.40). In *Coriolanus* Menenius complains of "The **breath** of **garlic**-eaters!" (4.6.102).

Rosamund (34) is described as "red cheekt". In *Venus and Adonis* Adonis is also described as "Rose-**cheek'd**" (3). In *Look About You* Lancaster, defending the King's mistress, says:

> Had never King a Concubine but he?
> Did *Rosamond* begin the fires in **Fraunce**?
> Made she the Northerne borders reeke with flames?
> **Unpeopled** she the townes of Picardy?
> Left she the wives of **England husbandles**?

I have shown in my previous book that Shakespeare used sequences of five rhetorical questions (Casson, 2009, 127-8). The bard uses **'unpeople'** four times including in *Henry VI* part 3, just one line away from France, and two from England, when the king says:

> No: first shall war **unpeople** this my realm;
> Ay, and their colours, often borne in **France,**
> And now in **England** to our heart's great sorrow,
> Shall be my winding-sheet. (1.1.126)

Shakespeare also used 'unpeopled' 4 times, three of which include images of war. He used 'husbandless' (157) just once in *King John* (3.1.14), a play which, like *Look About You*, includes members of the Faulconbridge family.

King Henry says, "It's **iniust Justice**" (3105). In *The Rape of Lucrece* Tarquin "**justly** thus controls his thoughts **unjust**" (189). In two plays Shakespeare juxtaposes 'rest' and 'unrest' (*Richard III* and *Titus Andronicus*). The word 'unrestful' occurs in *Look About You* (1.1.8). In three early works he puts 'gentle' and 'ungentle' in the same line (*Henry VI* parts 2 and 3 and *Titus Andronicus*). This recalls a similar juxtaposition of words in *The*

*Troublesome Raigne* when John says he is, "contented uncontent".

In *Look About You*, Gloster says, "presently sir off with your coate. Nay quicke, **uncase**" (818). In *The Taming of The Shrew*: Lucentio says, "Tranio, at once **uncase** thee; take my colour'd hat and cloak" (1.1.207). Both are urgent, both mention a garment. In *Edmund Ironside* Edricus says, "My will is that you will **uncase**, for I mean to change apparel." (3.5.179) Again there is a sense of urgency and all three lead to disguising. When the word 'uncase' is used in Munday's *The Downfall of Robert, Earle of Huntington* (867) it simply refers to undressing, with no sense of urgency nor of disguise. A full list of **'un'** words in *Look About You* is in appendix 4.

**Vocabulary used in *Look About You*, Worsley MSS 47, Shakespeare and Neville**

The word '**maintenaunce**' is used three times in *Look About You* (218, 339, 2341). This word occurs three times in *Leicester's Commonwealth*. It is also used by the annotator of Worsley MSS 47 who spells it with Neville's characteristic 'au' as in the *Look About You* quarto: '**mayntenaunce**'. It is also used three times in early Shakespeare plays: *The Two Gentlemen of Verona* (1.3.68); *The Taming of The Shrew* (5.2.149) and *Henry IV* part 1 (5.4.20). The word '**deluded**' is used twice in *Look About You* (2717-8). Shakespeare used **deluded**' in *Henry VI* part 1 (5.4.76) and in *Edward III* (5.1.6). Neville used '**delude**' in a letter of 1/11/1599 (Winwood, 1725, Vol 1, 126). The word '**deludeinge**' is used in one Worsley MSS 47 annotation (see chapter 3).

**The Language of *Look About You* and Neville's letters**
Brenda James (2008, 246-252) drew up a list of words and phrases habitually used by Neville in his letters that are to be found in Shakespeare. Several of these occur in *Look About You*. These include '**exceeding**', '**clean**' (meaning completely, as in "I clean forgot") and "**let slip**".

Gloster speaks of his "**exceeding** zeale" (3190).

Skink, fleeing the prison, is "**cleane** out of winde and raine" (2052).

'Slip' is used six times: "I would **slip** the collar" (480); "**give** us **the slip**" (845); "if now you **slip** the time, Gloster will **slip** away" (1330); "I'll see him **slip** a string though I **give** my service **the slip**" (1457). In the section of *Sir*

*Thomas More* written by Hand D (seen by many scholars as Shakespeare) are the words, "to **slipp** him lyke a hound" (Crystal, 2008, 37). Neville, in a letter dated 13/11/1599 writes that someone had "**given** me **the slipp**" (Winwood, 1725, Vol 1, 128) and in another letter, "having **let slip** the best opportunity" (James, 2008, 250).

At the end of the play Henry II speaks of, "**Unlookt for** peace, **unlookt for** happy dayes" (3207). In the 1609 edition of the Sonnets, we find, "**Unlookt for** ioy" in sonnet 25. In *Henry IV* part 1, Falstaff says "honour comes **unlooked for**" (5.3.60). In *The Rape of Lucrece* there is "**unlooked-for** evil" (846). The phrase is used ten times by Shakespeare, all of these are in early works. In *King John* it is used twice (2.1.79, 560). Richard Neville, the Earl of Warwick, uses the words "**unlook'd for** friends" in *Henry VI* Part 3 (5.1.14). Neville used "**Unloked for**" in a letter dated 1/11/1599 (Winwood, 1725, Vol 1, 126). In the 1609 edition, Sonnet 7 includes the spelling '**Vnlok'd**' (Vendler, 1999, 74).

In a letter of 18/6/1613 Neville wrote, " if our business **be dispatcht**" (Winwood, 1725, Vol 3, 463). In *Look About You* Skink says of his day's activities, "In halfe an houre al wil **be dispatcht**" (1997). The spelling is the same in letter and play. I will now examine links between *Look About You* and other plays I have identified as Neville's early work.

### *Look About You* and *Mucedorus*

In 1598 the first quarto (Q1) of *Mucedorus* was published anonymously. Just two years later *Look About You* appeared, also anonymous. These plays both date back to the period before Neville chose the name 'William Shakespeare'. If, as I suggest, *Look About You* was written immediately after *Mucedorus* there should be detectable links in themes and vocabulary between them and indeed they are there. First there is clear evidence that both plays were influenced by *Leicester's Commonwealth* (see Casson, 2009 and appendix 7). Both use disguise and state that the sources of such costumes are masques. In *Look About You* Lady Faukenbridge gives her brother Gloster a disguise of a false beard and wig. Gloster asks, "But prethee where hadst thou this beard and haire?" She replies, "Prince Richard wore them hether in a **maske**" (1194-5). In *Mucedorus* Anselmo offers to disguise the hero in a costume that, "twas a Shepherds, Which I presented in Lord Julio's **Mask**" (Q3: 1.1.49). There are men disguised as hermits in both plays.

More specific echoes include cannibalism. In *Look About You* Prince John says, "Blood, I could eat these rogues" (932). He then threatens that he will, "**dash** your **branes out**" (950). In *Mucedorus*, Bremo, the cannibal, threatens Amadine that he will "beat **out** thy **brains**" (3.3.32). In *Locrine* Humber threatens Strumbo, "I'll **dash** thy cursed **brains**" (4.3.81); Strumbo protests, "**Dash out** my **brains**?"(4.3.86). Juliet fears she will "**dash out** my desperate **brains**" in *Romeo and Juliet* (4.3.) and Leontes threatens to "**dash out**… the bastard **brains**" of his daughter in *The Winter's Tale* (2.3). "I dasht the braines out of a brat," says Doncaster in Munday's *The Death of Robert, Earle of Huntington* (line 636). Not only was this written years later but it is not a threat but a report of past action.

Shakespeare and Neville (in his letters) use many words beginning with 'dis'. In *Mucedorus* there are 23 'dis' words used 35 times. In *Look About You* there are 23 used 38 times. Nine, nearly half, of these words are found in both plays. I have put the usage in canonical Shakespeare in [square brackets].

| *Mucedorus* | *Look About You* |
|---|---|
| disdainer [0], disdained [3] | disdaine x 3 [41] |
| disgrace [52] | disgrace x 6 |
| disguise [19], disguised x 3 [17] | disguise x 4 |
| dislike x 4 [18] | dislike x 2 |
| distress x 2 [16], distressed x 6 [10] | distrest |
| dismayed [1] | dismaying [0] |
| disposed [27] disposition [46] | dispos'd [0] |
| displeasure [42] | displeasure x 3 |
| disturb'd [7], disturbance [0] | disturb [13] |

The language of *Look About You* is simpler than most Shakespeare: this is understandable when it is dated immediately after *Mucedorus* and before *Locrine* right at the start of his writing career. Jupin (1987, 37-54) has been able to show quite what a sophisticated play *Mucedorus* is and how in exploring the relationship between Comedy and Tragedy (Envy) it has an underlying structure that belies its simplicity (Casson, 2009, 88). Likewise *Look About You* has a complex structure and interplay of ideas that at first sight are not apparent.

### *Look About You* and *Locrine*
*Locrine* was published as by W. S. in 1595. I have previously shown it is an

early work by Neville (Casson, 2009). Both *Look About You* and *Locrine* have Queens who are cruel, and who are imprisoned and both plays show the dangers of dividing the kingdom. Both have Holinshed as a source. In *Locrine*, which is a tragedy, there is a conscious, Senecan development of poetic rhetoric. The plays share specific vocabulary.
In *Look About You* Gloster says of Redcap, "He's ever running but he makes small haste." (788). In *Locrine* Strumbo says, "the more haste the worst speed" (1.3.34).
In *Look About You* Block says, "my **muse** shall me **invoke**" (1461). The word '**rhymer**' is used within the previous 100 lines (1379). In Shakespeare's Sonnet 38 I have found:

> Be thou the tenth **Muse**, ten times more in worth
> Than those old nine which **rhymers invocate**…

In *Locrine* the word **invocate** (4.2.147) is used and I have previously shown how this usage matches Shakespeare's (Casson, 2009).

In *Look About You* King Henry speaks of "twenty thousand valiant men" (237) and Robin says, "We have twenty thousand at our call" (2803), referring to troops. I have shown this figure occurs in *Locrine*, *Edmund Ironside*, *Richard II* and *Hamlet* about troops (Casson, 2009).

Speaking of his enemy, Humber evokes Briareus in *Locrine*. He says Albanact,

> Heaps hills on hills, to scale the **starry** sky,
> As when **Briareus**, armed with an hundreth **hands**,
> Flung forth an hundreth mountains at great Jove…   (2.6.7)

In *Look About You* Prince John, in one of his rants, wishes he could attack his enemy Gloster:

> Or get seditious hundreth thousand **hands**,
> And like **Briareus**, battle with the **Starres**,
> To pull him downe from heaven if he were there…   (1091)

Shakespeare mentions Briareus (and his "many **hands**") once in *Troilus and Cressida* (1.2.29). In *The Troublesome Raigne*, cursing because of her enemies' triumph over her son, Constance evokes Briareus, who,

"Beleaguers all the Skie" (Sider, 1979, 57, 462).

In *Look About You* John wishes:

> O would I were a **Basiliske,** to **kill**
> These gleare ey'd villaines. (1722)

The **basilisk** appears in *Locrine, Edmund Ironside, Arden of Faversham* and in *Henry VI* part 2, where Henry says, "come, **basilisk**, And **kill** the innocent gazer with thy sight" (33.2.). The phrases have the same structure and focus finally on the sight of the basilisk's victim.
In *Look About You* Skink says:

> Far enough and well, flye **one foote** more,
> Would I were halfe so far without the doore. (881)

In *Locrine* Humber asserts that, "Yet would we **not** start back **one foot** from them" (2.2.76). Sams (1986, 261) pointed out the similarities between the following passages in *Edmund Ironside* when Edricus says, "Yet fled I **not** a **foot**" (5.1.93) and in *Henry VI* part1 when the Dauphin says he will not "go back **one foot**" (1.2.21) and in *Henry VI* part 3 when Richard cried, "Charge! And give no **foot** of ground" (1.4.15). In a letter dated 15/5/1599 Neville wrote that the King of France "had **not** styrred **one foote**" to greet the Spanish Ambassador (Winwood, 1725, Vol 1, 20).

### *Look About You* and *Arden of Faversham*
My dating suggests these plays were almost contemporary, *Arden of Faversham* being written between 1586-90. Both have Holinshed as a source. Perhaps the most startling link between these two works is the covert reference to the seeming murder of Leicester's first wife as told in *Leicester's Commonwealth*. In *Arden of Faversham* Shakebag, the villain, brags that he has killed the widow Cambly, "I spurned her **down the stairs**, And **broke her neck**," (5.2.9). In *Look About You* Skink shouts, "I'd **break the neck** of ye **down the stairs**…" (1571). In *Leicester's Commonwealth* the words are: "she had the chance to fall from a pair of **stairs** and so to **break her neck**" (Peck, 81/58). This shows how close the two plays are; whilst the word order of *Arden of Faversham* is closer to *Leicester's Commonwealth*, the phrase in *Look About You* preserves the same present tense of '**break**'.

In *Look About You* the word 'copesmates' is used twice and 'copesmate' once. In *Arden of Faversham* Mosby contemptuously dismisses Alice with, "Go, get thee gone, a **copesmate** for thy **hind**s" (3.5.104). When Lady Faukenbridge uses this word in *Look About You* we find it is close to the word 'Hind' (the name of a tavern):

> Nay Madam he is hard by, there must be Reuelles at the **Hind**e to night;
> Your **copesmate** there, Prince John. (2385)

In both plays the word is also used in the same context, of infidelity. Shakespeare calls Time "**copesmate** of ugly Night" in *The Rape of Lucrece* (925). The word '**hind**' also occurs in *The Rape of Lucrece* (543).
In both plays we find pig's blood used as a disguise/decoy by people wishing to escape. In *Look About You* scenes are set in a tavern, the Salutation; indeed it is named four times. In *Arden of Faversham* Shakebag suggests the murderers meet at the Salutation to eat and plan. (The Salutation is also mentioned in Ben Jonson's *Bartholomew Fair* but this dates from 1614.)
In *Look About You* Rosamund is named as Clifford's daughter (Walter de Clifford, also known as Walter Fitz Richard). The *Arden* playwright invents a 'Lord Clifford' to replace the real Lord North. In 1587 George Clifford, Baron of Westmoreland, sat on the commission which tried Mary, Queen of Scots, and attended her execution.
I have also found the following words are used in both plays: copesmate, counterfeit, greedy, gaping, slip, harebrained, unkind, undeserved, unlucky, dislike, discharge, dishonoured, (see Appendix 4 for lists of 'un'' and 'dis' words).
Of these words the following are also to be found in *Leicester's Commonwealth*: copesman, counterfeit, greedy, slip, dislike, discharged.

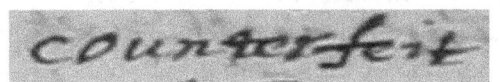

Worsley MSS 47, 50

In *Look About You* John says, "This changing counterfeit" (1599). The word 'counterfeit' occurs 8 times in the play. Shakespeare uses it 45 times.

### *Look About You* and *Edmund Ironside*
Both plays include disguise and the cutting off of hands. Both have ruthless, but darkly comic, villains (Skink and Edricus). In *Look About You* the comic servant Block's name is the subject of jokes. The word 'block' is

immediately associated with 'head' as in, "**Blocke** by the commission of his **head**" (560) and "let **blocks head** be made a chopping **blocke**" (582). There are also '**block-heads**' (1721) and "that **blockehead Blocke**" (1779). In *Edmund Ironside* I find '**block-heads**'[39] (2.2.71) and Edricus, struggling for inspiration as a writer, seeks:

    A thing that would put spirit in a **block**
    And be a whetstone to a blunter **head**. (3.5.125)

In *Coriolanus* there is 'block-head' (2.3.26). In the final scene of *Look About You* Henry the Young King orders:

    **Bring** forth a **blocke**, wine, water and towell,
    **Knives**, and a Surgion to binde up the vaines,
    Of Glosters arme: when his right **hand** is off… (1968)

In *Edmund Ironside* Canutus orders, "**bring** an axe, a **block** and **knife**" in order to cut off two hostages' hands (2.3.20). The association of 'block' and 'head' is a grimly comic reminder that Neville's grandfather was beheaded: a fact that I have linked with the many severed heads in the early History plays (Casson, 2009, 161). In *Richard III* Hastings accepts his imminent execution with, "Come, lead me to the **block**; bear him my **head**" (3.4.107). In *Henry VI* part 2 Suffolk says, "Let my **head** stoop to the **block**" (4.1.125). The Halle's *Chronicle* annotator also notes executions. When we bring this interest in execution together with disguise we have two crucial Neville themes in both plays.

In *Look About You* Skink visits Gloster in prison, disguised as Redcap. Gloster asks him to swap clothes so he can escape. He says, "off with your coate. Nay quicke, **uncase**, I am bold to borrow it" (617). In *Edmund Ironside* Edricus orders Stitch, "My will is that you will **uncase**, for I mean to change apparel" (3.5.179). As he changes clothes Stitch says, "since there is **shift** but I must change **shifts**" (33.5.184). In *Look About You* Henry the Young King speaks of "**shifts** in other mens disguise" (2942).

In *Look About You* there are 22 'un' words used 27 times (see Appendix 4). Six of these are to be found in *Edmund Ironside* (in which there are 36 'un'

---

39    According to LION no other writer between 1584-1600 uses 'block-head' with a hyphen. Without a hyphen it appears Robert Greene's *Friar Bacon and Friar Bungay* (written about 1589, published 1594).

words used 39 times). I have listed the number of times the words are used in the Shakespeare canon [in square brackets].

Unheard: [4]
Uncase: [1]
Unkind: [29] also found in *Arden of Faversham, Locrine*
Untutor'd: [5]
Undeserved: [5] also found in *Arden of Faversham*
Uncivil: [8] also found in *Locrine, Troublesome Raigne, Edward III*
According to LION no other writer apart from Shakespeare uses the words 'uncase', 'uncivil' and 'untutor'd' during the period 1584-1600. What are the chances of two different authors using six identical words, three of which are exceedingly rare?

### *Look About You*, *The Troublesome Raigne* and *King John*

*Look About You* is historical farce. *The Troublesome Raigne* is a history play with elements of farce. *King John* is a history play with some underlying dark humour provided by the bastard Faulconbridge. In all three plays the Faulconbridge family are centre stage. All three have a tyrannical Queen whose name begins with the letters 'Eli'. Taking the history as metaphor I note that in *The Troublesome Raigne* and *King John* there are two rival queens, one of whom is imprisoned and later dies, an invasion that is repulsed, an army that is drowned, and a tyrant that dies: all these images fit the period of 1586-8. Campbell (1968, 136, 142, 149) showed how the author of *The Troublesome Raigne* compressed history to more accurately mirror the events of 1587-8. *Tamburlaine* was on stage in 1587. The writer of *The Troublesome Raigne* refers to Marlowe's play in the opening prologue. *Tamburlaine* was printed in 1590, three years after it first appeared. If we allow a similar time lapse for *The Troublesome Raigne*, which was published in 1591, we would reach back to 1588.

There is no hint of Lady Fawkenbridge giving in to the amorous Richard in *Look About You*, indeed the opposite. She stoutly resists. There are then good reasons for thinking that *Look About You* predates *The Troublesome Raigne* (TR). Begor (1965, 39) stated that the romantic subplot of *Look About You* "conforms in all major background details to the Bastard material in TR and KJ[40], especially TR". I therefore suggest the dates of composition are as follows:

*Look About You* 1585-6;

---

[40] KJ = *King John*

*The Troublesome Raigne* 1587-8.
*King John* 1593-6.

There is a continuity between these three plays: all three look at similar themes and share characters: Queen Elinor, Prince/King John and Lady Faulconbridge appear in all three. A bastard is an important figure in each: first Gloster, then Faulconbridge. Together these plays provide us with special insight into the development of Shakespeare's technique.

There are nine 'dis' words that are found in both *Look About You* and *The Troublesome Raigne*, the same number as shared by *Look About You* and *Mucedorus*, indeed four are shared by all three plays, again I have listed the number of times these words occur in canonical works in [square brackets]:

| **Look About You** | **The Troublesome Raigne** | **Mucedorus** |
|---|---|---|
| dishonoured [3] | dishonour [44] | |
| disdaine [41] disdained | disdain, disdain'd [9], disdained [3] | disdainer [0], |
| disgrace [52] | disgrace | disgrace |
| discharge [30] | discharge, discharging [1] | |
| dispatch [70] | dispatch | |
| discovered [9] | discovered | |
| distrest [0] | distress'd [7], distressed [10], distress [16]; | distressed distress |
| disturb [13] disturbance [0] | disturb, disturber [0] | disturb'd [7], |
| dispute [5] | dispute | |

*The Troublesome Raigne* has higher numbers of both 'dis' and 'un' words, suggesting it was written later (see Appendix 4). If we then compare this with the vocabulary of the Munday and Chettle plays we find that *The Downfall of Robert the Earl of Huntington* has five of these words, while *Death of Robert Earl of Huntington* has only two. In other words just in terms of 'dis' words *Look About You* and *The Troublesome Raigne* are closer (see appendix 4). Furthermore there are just five of these 'dis' words in *King John* confirming that on this measure again *Look About You* is closer to *The Troublesome Raigne*.

I have found the following vocabulary is shared between the plays and compare these with words used in *King John*, the Shakespeare canon and the two Munday-Chettle plays (Meagher, 1980).

| Look About You | Troublesome Raigne | King John | Shakespeare canon | Downfall | Death |
|---|---|---|---|---|---|
| murmuring | murmur | murmuring | 4 | | |
| hayre-brain'd, hot-braind | brainsick | pure brain | hare-brain'd hair-brain'd brain-sick 5 hot brain | | |
| beare a braine | catch the brain | catch | bear a brain | | braine |
| my braine flowes | | | my brain more busy | | |
| seare thy braines | hatch'd in thy brain | hatch | sear me to the brain | | the braines |
| Briareus | Briareus | | 1 | | |
| strangled | strangle | strangle | strangle 7 strangled 7 | | strangling |
| bloud-sucker | bloodsucker | | 1 | | |
| curtaine | curtain | | 15 | | |
| hasty | hasty | hasty | hasty 20 | hastily | hasted |
| deluded | delude, deludes | deluded | 1 | | delude |
| brawles | brawls | | 6 | | |
| captive Queene | Queene... captive[1] | | 1 | | Queene... prisoner;[2] captives |
| orisons | orisons | | 5 | | |
| bacon fletches | rib of bacon | | bacon 3 | | |
| daintiest | daintie | | daintiest 2 dainty 21 | | |
| horror | horror | horror | 13 | | horrid |
| tortor | tortures | torture | torture 30 tortures 4 | | |
| stocke | stock | | 31 | | |
| cloudy frowne | cloud to frown | frown 4 clouds | cloudy brow | gloomy clouds | cloude clowdy |
| clipping | clip | | clip 10 clipping 1 | | |
| pollicy/ pollicie* | pollicie* | policy | 45 | | policy |
| prosper | prosper ous | | prosper 24 prosperous 25 | | |
| mute | mute | | 19 | | |
| rumour | rumor | rumour | 10 | | |

| swallow | swallowed | swallowing | swallow 16 swallowed 9 | | |
|---|---|---|---|---|---|
| munition | munition | munition | 2 | | |
| shamelesse | shamelesse | | shameless 7 | | |
| Total 29 | 27 | 14 | | 2 | 9 |

*Look About You* is undoubtedly closest to *The Troublesome Raigne*. There thus arises the probability that they were written by the same person who created the Faulconbridge family story. Furthermore even though the revised *King John* has fewer of the words shared by *Look About You* and *The Troublesome Raigne* it nevertheless has more than either of the Munday-Chettle plays (or indeed both taken together). We can also see that the vocabulary of *Look About You* is canonical.
*Copying *Leicester's Commonwealth* Neville uses the same spelling of 'pollicie':

Worsley MSS47, 42

This is the spelling used in the first quarto edition of *Titus Andronicus* (1594, line 669, Malone Society Reprint, 2002) and in the 1609 edition of sonnet 118. The annotator of Halle's *Chronicle* uses the spellings 'policie' and 'pollicye' (Henry V, f.xb and f.la, Keen and Lubbock, 1954, 138, 149).

**Anthony Munday and Henry Chettle**
*Fidele and Fortunio* or *The Two Italian Gentlemen*, a comedy "translated out of the Italian" was published in 1585. The author was identified as A.M., probably Anthony Munday. In it a comic character, Captain Crackstone, uses words later to be found in *Locrine*: 'Cuprit' (instead of Cupid, 2.2.614), 'birdboltes' (4.5.1353) and 'constulted' (5.4.1752). In *Locrine* Strumbo, another loquacious comic character, speaks of 'Cuprit' and 'birdbolts' in the same line (1.3.14) and 'constultations' in the same speech, just 9 lines earlier (1.3.5). We can have little doubt therefore that the author of *Locrine* (which I have dated 1586 onwards) knew Munday's


(Footnotes to table above)
1        "Queene Elianor, Though she be captive"
2        "Queene Elianor, are you a prisoner?" line 1769; "Queene their prisoner" 1802. The word 'captives' is not linked to the word 'Queene'.

play. *Fidele and Fortunio* is about rivals in love and there is no sign that the author was aware of or referring to political events: the play would have been written at least a year or two before publication and so probably pre-dated *Leicester's Commonwealth* (it was registered on November 12th 1584, which is after the tract was published). It is relevant here because it shows Munday writing during this period and he has been suggested as the author of *Look About You*. He is the acknowledged author of the plays *The Downfall of Robert the Earl of Huntington* (written, or revised, according to an entry in Henslowe's diary in 1598) and *The Death of Robert Earl of Huntington*, both of which are about Robin Hood and published in 1601. Munday may have been helped by Henry Chettle[41]. Despite the fact that *Look About You* was published before these two Robin Hood plays, Begor believed it was written after them and depended upon them. However, she stated that, "All evidence points to a single author" (Begor, 1965, 78). Nevertheless, unable to identify that author, she suggested that the play was plotted by Munday and written by Chettle.

The possibility of political awareness in relation to *Leicester's Commonwealth* in these plays might be demonstrated by a reference to Cynthia and Endimion in *The Downfall of Robert the Earl of Huntington* when the usurping Prince John compares himself to Endimion and names his mother, Queen Eleanor, as Cynthia (line 1202). Whilst this seems to echo Lyly's reference to Endimion and Cynthia in his play (see chapter 1) it is hardly a political comment, rather a tired conventional image. Indeed as John is Eleanor's son it is hardly comparable to the relationship between Elizabeth I and the Earl of Leicester. A 'watchword' is also used (line 1575) by Friar Tuck but this does not equate with the 'watchword' in *Leicester's Commonwealth*. Munday's plays are mythic English stories of the noble outlaw and the promised return of the saviour King Richard. They are conventional, using these references as established clichés and the plays are inherently politically conservative: wicked figures are forgiven and re-incorporated into the state of harmony. The Earl of Chester says, "Subjects must not choose what king they list" (line 1074). Several scholars have suggested that Munday was appealing to a Protestant non-Conformist audience (Bevington, 1968). Dutton & Howard (2006, 31) point out that

---

41  From: http://en.wikipedia.org/wiki/The_Downfall_and_The_Death_of_Robert_Earl_of_Huntington#cite_note-13 **accessed January 2009**

the sixteenth Century Earls of Huntingdon were associated with the Puritan cause. Gabrieli & Melchiori (1990, 16) suggest Munday was appealing to a puritanically inclined City middle class audience and that the plays denounce "the prevarications of Church and State against the rights of the individual". The politics of *Look About You* are very different from this: Huntington is a cross dresser (hardly the act of a Puritan!). The play is concerned with a usurping king, a wicked, imprisoned queen and problems of loyalty and the succession.

The use of disguise in *The Downfall* and *The Death* is brief and perfunctory and does not lead to major complications. Despite some similarities *Look About You* is actually a very different type of play. There are no bastards and no Faulconbridges in Munday's plays.

I therefore propose that the idea that Munday and Chettle might have written *Look About You* is based on no evidence other than the name 'Robin Hood' appearing in all three plays: by that token one might as well say *As You Like It* or *The Two Gentlemen of Verona* were written by Munday and Chettle. In any case whilst Robin Hood does appear in *Look About You* none of the other stock characters such as Friar Tuck, Will Scarlet and Little John (who do appear in the Munday plays) are present. I therefore suggest the attribution of *Look About You* to Munday and Chettle is a mistake.

**Anticipating Shakespeare**
Previous scholars who have suggested Munday and Chettle authored *Look About You* have missed the significance of the much stronger links with *The Troublesome Raigne*, and therefore *King John*, through the story of the Faulconbridges. Having found clear evidence of the influence of *Leicester's Commonwealth* that also has been overlooked, I have been able to propose an earlier date and provide evidence that this play is a very early work by the bard. Thus links to later Shakespeare plays are explained by the emerging ideas of a young poet anticipating rather than copying later works. Several scholars have noted links with *Henry IV* part 1, including Prince John's resemblance to Hotspur (Logan & Smith, 1975, 170-4); the behaviour of the drawer, who like Francis cries, "Anon, anon, sir," in response to orders; the drawer swearing on the Bible; the use of sugar; Faukenbridge's bluffing claim that he recognised his disguised wife, "**I knew thee**, Moll… I wink'd at all," (Nelson, 1962, 142) recalls Falstaff response when the fact that he was duped is exposed, "**I knew ye** as well as he that made ye,"

(*Henry IV*, part 1, 2.4.263) and there is a reference to the Prodigal son in both. *Henry IV* was written in the autumn of 1597, by my reckoning, ten years after *Look About You*, which would explain why it is more sophisticated. I have already found clear evidence that Strumbo in *Locrine* (c 1586-9) repeatedly anticipates Falstaff (Casson, 2009). *Locrine* definitely predates *Henry IV*, by up to ten years.

In *Look About You* Gloster says:

> **Blow winde**, the youngest of King Henries stocke,
> Would possibly fitly serve to make a weather-cocke.      (297)

This recalls Lear's great cry, "**Blow winds** and crack your cheeks! Rage! Blow!" (3.2.1). Macbeth cries, "**Blow, wind**! come, wrack! At least we'll die with harness on our back" (5.5.51). In *Julius Caesar* Cassius says, "**Blow wind**, swell billow and swim bark!" (5.1.66).

John replies to Gloster:

> **Gape earth**, challenge thine owne as Gloster lyes,
> Pitty such mucke is cover'd with the skies.      (299)

Anne Neville, responding to Richard III (another Duke of Gloucester), begs, "**earth, gape** open wide and eat him quick" (1.2.63). Marlowe uses "Gape, earth" in *Tamburlaine* I (2660) and "Earth, gape" in *Dr. Faustus* (2030). Peele used "gape earth" in *Edward I* (LION).

The playwright of *Look About You* strangely anticipates later works by the bard. We see ideas which he later develops, just as Handel progressively recycled melodies from early operas to later works. I therefore propose that *Look About You* was written at the very start of Shakespeare-Neville's career. It was probably his second play (after *Mucedorus*), indeed his first history which combined farce with politics as a method of getting its message across without incurring the wrath of the authorities. As the audience laughed the political ideas were smuggled in. In our own times Dario Fo has used farce in this way. *Look About You* is in effect a subversive satire in which the truth telling bastard Gloster escapes to tell the tale.

**Conclusion**

Shakespeare was a playwright who combined Holinshed with Grafton and Geoffrey of Monmouth as sources, used the Faulconbridge name repeatedly, wrote parts for bastards, made Robin Goodfellow, as Puck, a major figure in *A Midsummer Night's Dream*, was concerned with oaths, chastity and the royal succession, used cutting off hands, disguise, gender/identity confusion, a gold chain and pits in the earth as plot devices, developed the blot cluster and used falconry as a source of imagery. We can see all these in *Look About You* and, furthermore, evidence of Henry Neville as the hidden author and *Leicester's Commonwealth* as a secret source. It is a complex, very funny play that deserves to be better known, performed and further studied.

**Chapter 8**

Hand D in *Sir Thomas More* and Worsley MSS 47

"Here's a paper written in his hand…"
*Much Ado About Nothing* (5.4.86)

The only surviving manuscript believed to be by Shakespeare is the three pages written by "Hand D" in *Sir Thomas More*, a play by Anthony Munday (with help from Henry Chettle, Thomas Dekker, Thomas Heywood and Shakespeare). It is preserved in MS Harley 7368, at the British Library. It was written in about 1592-3. The manuscript was first mentioned in 1728[42], in the diary of the Oxford antiquarian, Thomas Hearn (Gabrieli & Melchiori, 1990, 1). It was acquired by the British Museum in 1753. Of the three pages by Shakespeare just one, folio 9, is clear (the other two are faint and smudged). I have already introduced the links between Worsley MSS 47, the Halle *Chronicle*, the Northumberland Manuscript and the Hand D section of *Sir Thomas More* in chapters 3 and 4. These manuscripts have never been compared before so my discoveries are groundbreaking. I have been able to identify Hand D as Henry Neville, based on his habits of writing 'in' as 'ni' and abbreviating words beginning with 'pro/par/per'. It is possible that Neville wrote more than just the Hand D section as parts of the manuscript are by Hand C, who has been identified as an anonymous copyist (Gabrieli & Melchiori, 1990, 23). More's soliloquy at the start of Act 3 has been seen as possibly by Shakespeare. Nosworthy concluded that not only was "Addition II (Hand D) by Shakespeare, but that Addition III (Hand C) was probably written by him as well and then copied into the manuscript by a playhouse scribe" (Ribner, 1965, 210). I will provide new evidence for this below.

There are two plot devices in the play that are characteristic of early Shakespeare-Neville: a premonitory dream and a meeting between two men, one of whom is a disguised substitute for the real person. Foreboding dreams are to be found in *Arden of Faversham, Henry VI* part 2, *Richard III, Julius Caesar, Henry VIII* and *Thomas of Woodstock* (Casson, 2009). Disguises are used in many plays and mistaken identity is common (for example in *The Taming of The Shrew, The Two Gentlemen of Verona, Henry IV* part 1,

---

42   This is the very year that *Double Falshood*, the lost *Cardenio*, was published by Lewis Theobald (Casson, 2009).

*Henry V* and *The Comedy of Errors*). Henry Neville's grandfather, Edward, used disguise and was mistaken for Henry VIII (whom he resembled) on more than one occasion and one of these, at a banquet given by Cardinal Wolsey, is behind an incident in Shakespeare's *Henry VIII* and *Thomas of Woodstock* (Casson, 2009). In *Henry VIII* Cromwell announces that "Sir Thomas More is chosen Lord Chancellor" after Wolsey's fall (3.2.393).

### *Sir Thomas More* and *Thomas of Woodstock*

*Thomas of Woodstock* is an anonymous play that has recently been identified as by Shakespeare in a major four volume study by Michael Egan (2006). Bevington examined the political themes that recur in these two plays. "*Woodstock* upholds an ideal of old-fashioned nobility as England's best hope for justice." "Another public figure who grows to heroic stature as intermediary between an angry people and their monarch is the title figure of *Sir Thomas More*" (Bevington, 1968, 251, 253). Sir Thomas More is a man who stands up to a king and is a whimsical wit, joking even as he ascends the scaffold. He is a figure related to other loyal citizens (several of whom do indeed have a sense of humour) who confront a monarch (such as the Countess of Salisbury in *Edward III*, John of Gaunt in *Richard II*, Falconbridge in *King John*, Kent and the Fool in *King Lear*). Plain Thomas of Woodstock is also a jocular truth teller who confronts a monarch. Like Thomas More he tries to calm the rebellious commons; they are both noble men who act as an intermediary between the people and the King. In both plays the signing of documents is crucial: Thomas More refuses to subscribe to an unspecified royal article and in *Thomas of Woodstock* the people are forced to sign blank charters. Both welcome players into their houses, have a sense of humour, the common touch and worried wives who have fearful dreams. Both are killed by tyrannical monarchs. *Sir Thomas More* was written within a year of *Thomas of Woodstock*, both have been dated to 1592-3. Both were so politically sensitive that they were not published and survived in manuscript only. Both plays were censored by Sir Edmund Tilney, the Master of the Revels, whose remarks and cuts are visible on the manuscripts. Bevington (1968, 256) showed that *Sir Thomas More* is more conservative and orthodox than *Thomas of Woodstock*, which does seem to sanction rebellion, but both plays examine how the failure of a monarch to redress grievances can lead to civil unrest.

Neither play was identified as by Shakespeare for centuries. In my previous book I showed that there is evidence pointing to Neville's authorship of

*Thomas of Woodstock* (Casson, 2009). Now I can show that the Hand D section of the *Sir Thomas More* manuscript is comparable with Henry Neville's own hand writing, as seen in the Worsley MSS 47 (see below).

## The *Henry VI* trilogy and Worsley MSS 47

I have already shown the connections between Worsley MSS 47 and the *Henry VI* trilogy in chapters 2, 3 and 4. Helgerson (2006, 35) saw Duke Humphrey in *Henry VI* part 2 as the first of the series of noble figures who "mediate between king and commons… To serve the public good is, as these men understand it, the true purpose of government". He made links between *Henry VI* part 2, *Sir Thomas More*, *Thomas of Woodstock* and *Look About You*. Indeed Humphrey is a Duke of Gloucester, just as those other blunt truth tellers, Thomas of Woodstock and Robert of Gloster in *Look About You*. *Henry VI* part 2 was published anonymously in 1594 as *The First Part of the Contention betwixt the two Famous Houses of York and Lancaster*. Therefore, since *Sir Thomas More* and *Thomas of Woodstock* were written in 1592-3, any similarities between them either were drawn from manuscripts, performances or shared authorship. Duke Humphrey's wife has a dream which she interprets as prophetic. He also has a premonitory dream and is killed. Duke Humphrey's death is referred to in *Leicester's Commonwealth* (Peck, 188/*124*). Just after his body is discovered in Shakespeare's play, by none other than Richard Neville, the Earl of Warwick, "Nevil's noble race" is mentioned (*Henry VI* part 2, 3.2.214). Later in the play Jack Cade leads a rebellion. Like Lincoln, who leads the riots in *Sir Thomas More*, he ultimately is defeated and both are killed. The *Henry VI* trilogy is a powerful warning against civil strife. There is a continuity between these plays which is suggestive of shared authorship. This can be demonstrated in the use of metaphors.

Oak trees are mentioned five times in *Thomas of Woodstock*. The King uses the oak as a metaphor:

> as a fearful thunderclap doth strike
> the soundest body of the tallest **oak**,
> yet harmless leaves the outward bark untouched… (4.3.180)

Speaking of his fall from royal favour, Sir Thomas More says:

> thinke when an **oake** fals vnderwood shrinkes downe

> and yet may liue though brusd, I pray ye striue
> to shun my ruin for the **ax** is set
> euen at my **root** to fell me to the ground. (Gabrieli & Melchiori, 1990, 224)

In *Henry VI* part 3 a messenger says:

> many strokes, though with a little **axe**,
> Hew down and fell the hardest-timber'd **oak**. (2.1.54)

In the next scene George says, "We set the **axe** to thy usurping **root**..." (2.2.165). According to the LION database Shakespeare is the **only** playwright to use the words '**oak**', '**axe**' and '**root**' together between 1585-1625. The words '**axe**' and '**root**' are both in *Look About You*. The authors of *Leicester's Commonwealth* used tree metaphors and the idea of 'extirpation' ("to root up, root out", OED) that were later used by Shakespeare (see chapter 2). Neville was a forester, responsible for the royal forest at Windsor. Thus we can see a continuity between *Leicester's Commonwealth*, Worsley 47, *Look About You*, the *Henry VI* trilogy, *Sir Thomas of Woodstock* and *Sir Thomas More*.

**The Mores and the Nevilles**
I noted in chapter 5 that Neville added the following to the text of his copy of *Leicester's Commonwealth*: "Look in ~ Rastalles abridgm^te".

Worsley MSS 47, 47

John Rastell, Sir Thomas More's brother-in-law, was a lawyer, playwright and publisher. Neville had clearly read Rastell's three volume legal encyclopaedia, the *Graunde Abridgement*, and refers to it here (Guy, 2009, 104). Neville's grandfather, Edward, probably knew Rastell as they both went to the Field of the Cloth of Gold in 1520. Indeed Thomas More was also present. Shakespeare tells of this diplomatic extravaganza in *Henry VIII*. The Duke of Norfolk describes the "earthly glory" of the event to Lord Abergavenny, who was none other than George Neville, brother of Edward. George Neville, Baron Bergavenny was Lord Warden of the

Cinque Ports and son-in-law to the Duke of Buckingham, who is also present in this scene. Later we witness Buckingham's fall. Thomas More's father, John, who had been Buckingham's solicitor, was one of the judges at his treason trial (Guy, 2009, 71). Henry VIII gave Thomas More the manor of Southborough, Kent, out of the lands forfeited by Buckingham (Guy, 2009, 132).

One of More's undersheriff colleagues in the court for "poor men's causes", Thomas Neville, was elected Speaker of the House of Commons, knighted and became a royal counsellor (Guy, 2009, 56, 165). Sir Thomas Neville was Speaker from 1515 and was followed, in 1523, by Sir Thomas More. More was invited to join the King's Council in 1516, and finally agreed to do so in 1518 (Guy, 2008, 57). More and Neville were clearly friends as Neville's servants were mentioned in a comic Christmas entertainment at More's house in 1525 (Guy, 2009, 165). Thomas Neville had a successful career, unaffected by the disgrace of one brother (George) and the execution of another (Edward). He became wealthy and Charles Brandon, the Duke of Suffolk, pawned jewels worth £ 700 with him (ODNB, Davies, C. Vol 40, 543). Brandon is mentioned in *Leicester's Commonwealth*:

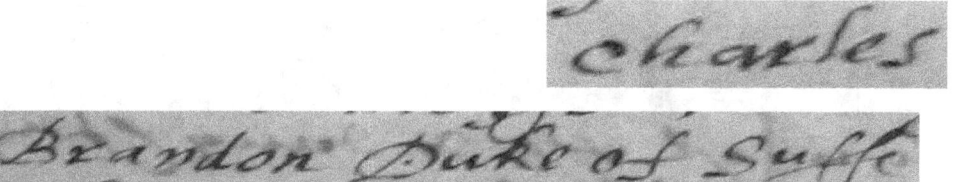

Worsley MSS 47, 44

Brandon appears on stage in *Henry VIII*. His father William, appears as Henry VII's standard bearer at Bosworth in *Richard III* (5.4.4.) and is killed in battle (5.7.14). Thomas More's *History of King Richard III* was a source for Shakespeare's *Richard III* (Guy, 2009, 123). Thus we can see links between the More and Neville families and Shakespeare's plays.

Let us now look at the handwriting of folio 9 of the manuscript of *Sir Thomas More*.

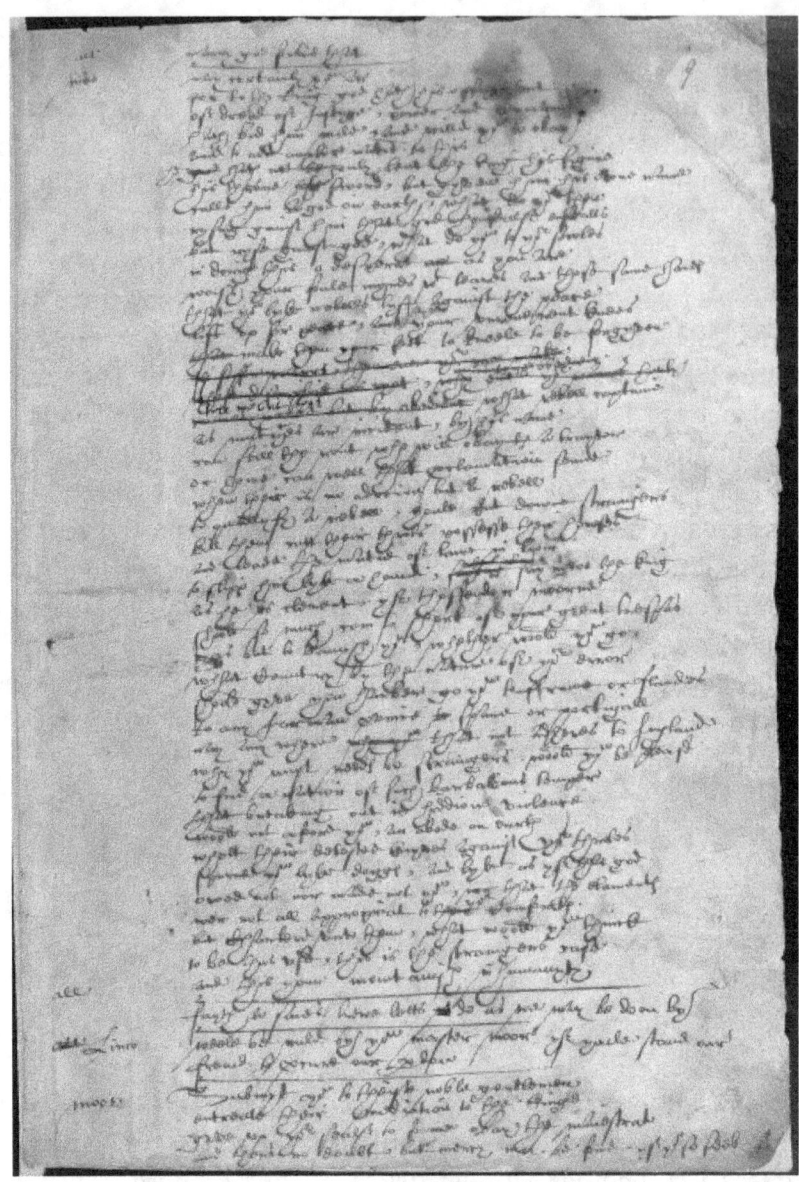

Folio 9 of the Hand D section in *Sir Thomas More* in Harley MS 7368
© The British Library Board.

The following transcription of this text is mainly from Crystal (2008, 37-8) checked against Greg (1923) and my own reading, which has taken into account Neville's characteristic spellings of 'in' words as 'ni', 'hmi' for 'him' and shortened words beginning with 'pro/par': for clarity I have emphasised these words by **emboldening** them. Previous editors have corrected these spellings without realising their significance.

All:    marry, god forbid that.

Moo(r): nay certainly yoᵘ ar,
    For to the **knig** god hath his offyc lent
    of dread of Iustyce, power and Comaund
    hath bid him rule,  and willd yoᵘ to obay          5
    and to add ampler matie to this
    he [god] hath not [le] only lent the **knig** his figure
    his throne [z] [&] swoord, but gyven **hmi** his owne name
    calls **hmi** a god on earth, what do yoᵘ then
    rysing gainst **hmi** that god **hmisealf** enstalls     10
    but ryse gainst god, what do yoᵘ to yoʳ sowles
    **ni donig** this o desperrat [ar] as you are.
    wash your foule mynds wᵗ teares and those same hands
    that yoᵘ lyke rebells lyft **aganist** the peace
    lift vp for peace, and your vnreuerent knees     15
    [that] make them your feet to kneele to be forgyven
    [is safer warrs, then euen yoᵘ can make]
              [in **ni** to yoʳ obedienc.]
    [whose discipline is ryot; why euen yoʳ warrs hurly]
    tell me but this
    [cannot **pceed** but by obedienc] what rebell captaine
    as mutyẽs ar incident, by his name     20
    can still the rout who will obay [th] a traytor
    or howe can well that **pclamation** sounde
    when ther is no adicion but a rebell
    to quallyfy a rebell, youle put downe **stranigers**
    kill them cutt their throts possesse their howses     25
    and leade the matie of lawe **ni** liom
              [alas alas]
    to slipp him lyke a hound, [sayeng] say nowe the **knig**
    as he is clement, yf thoffendor moorne
    should so much com to short of yor great trespass
    as but to banysh yoᵘ, whether woold yoᵘ go.     30
    what Country by the nature of yoʳ error
    shoold gyve you harbour go yoᵘ to ffraunc or flanders
    to any Iarman **pvnice**, [to] spane or portigall
    nay any where [why yoᵘ] that not adheres to Ingland
    why yoᵘ must needs be straingers, would yoᵘ be pleasd     35

```
              to find a nation of such barbarous temper
              that breaking out in hiddious violence
              woold not afoord yoᵘ, an abode on earth
              whett their detested knyves **aganist** yoʳ throtes
              spurne yoᵘ lyke doggs, and lyke as yf that god           40
              owed not nor made not yoᵘ, nor that the elaments
              wer not all appropriat to [their] yoʳ Comforts.
              but Charterd vnto them, what woold yoᵘ thinck
              to be thus vsd, this is the **stranigers** case
              and this your momtanish inhumanity                        45

All:    fayth a saies trewe letts [vs] do as we may be doon by

Linco:  weele be ruld by yoᵘ master moor yf youle stand our
        **frenid** to **pcure** our **pdon**

Moor:   Submyt yoᵘ to theise noble gentlemen
        entreate their mediation to the kinge                          50
        gyve vp yoʳ sealf to forme obay the maiestrate
        and thers no doubt, but mercy may be found yf yoᵘ seek [yt]
```

## Comparisons between the handwriting of *Sir Thomas More* and Worsley MSS 47

These two documents were written up to eight years apart. We would not expect a man's handwriting to remain exactly the same over the period between the ages of 24-31 but similarities would seem to point to the identity of the writer. In both Worsley 47 and *Sir Thomas More* 'Majesty' is abbreviated to 'Matie' (see also Neville's 1601 letter in which this abbreviation is used, appendix 8). Furthermore Neville uses superscript letters to abbreviate 'you' and 'your' in Worsley MSS 47 and similar examples can be seen in *Sir Thomas More*.

  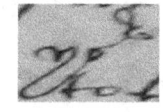

yoᵘ Worsley 47, 19      and 23 yoʳ

"you to yor" *Sir Thomas More*

We can see other similarities. For example, the 'y' that loops back to join the next letter in the words 'you' and 'your' above, and 'traytors/traytor' below, note also the 'v' shape of the upper part of the 'y':

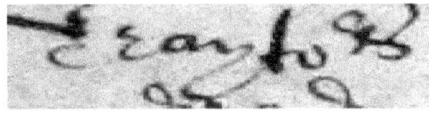  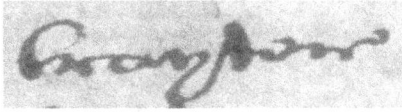

Worsley MSS 47, 3V                              *Sir Thomas More*

The 'p' that joins up with the next letter is visible in 'power', where the 'r' is extended:

  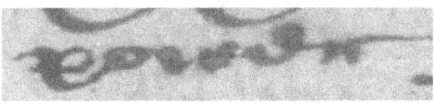

Worsley MSS 47, 19                              *Sir Thomas More*

The 'e' that leans over backwards in 'power' (above) and 'strangers/stranigers', the elongated Elizabethan 's' joining the top of the 't' (see also 'maiestrate' below):

Worsley MSS 47, 8

*Sir Thomas More*

The rising tail of the s at the end of 'strangers/straingers' (above) and 'flaunders' (Flanders) and the form of the 'ers':

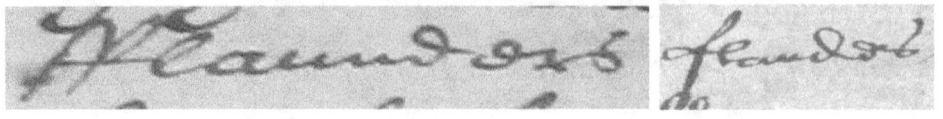

      Worsley MSS 47, 4V                          *Sir Thomas More*

The double 'f' of 'ffaunce' (France):

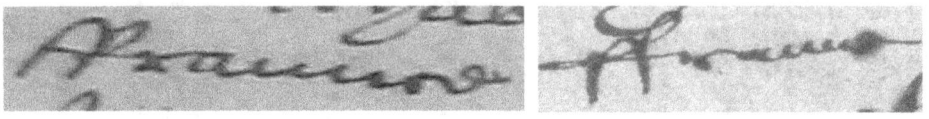

      Worsley MSS 47, 8V                          *Sir Thomas More*

The 'ence' of 'vyolence/violence':

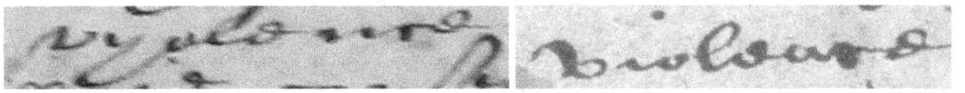

Worsley MSS 47, 14                          *Sir Thomas More*


The 'rate' of 'magistrate/maiestrate':

      Worsley MSS 47, 18V                         *Sir Thomas More*

The 'd' and the extended 't' of 'doubt':

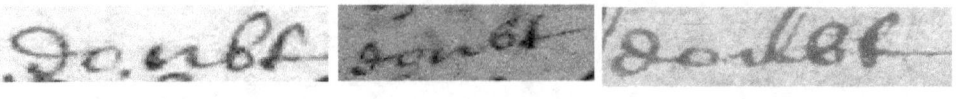

Worsley MSS 47, 5V; 12V                      *Sir Thomas More*

173

The 'erc' of 'mercie/mercy':

Worsley MSS 47, 37V　　　　　　　　Sir Thomas More

And finally, 'noble':

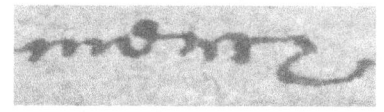

Worsley MSS 47, 12V　　　　　　　　Sir Thomas More

Melchiori (1998, 175) noticed the occurance of a capital C instead of the lower case in the quarto of *Edward III* which was written about the same time as *Sir Thomas More* (1592-3): "This may reflect the author's habit, noted in the three pages of Hand D… of nearly always capitalising initial C not only in nouns and adjectives but also in verbal forms, a feature absent from the rest of that manuscript or in fact from any other manuscript of the time." In Neville's 1601 letter (see appendix 8) the words 'Coullour', 'Commodities', 'Content', 'Complement' are capitalised.

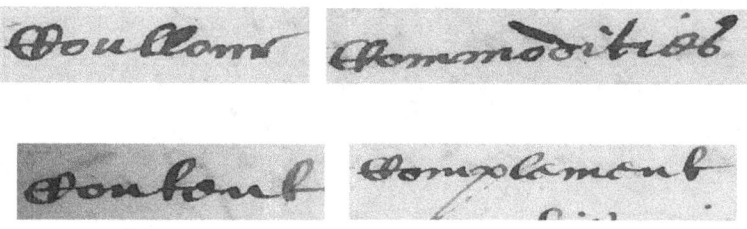

We can compare these with the capital C used by Hand D and in Worsley MSS 47:

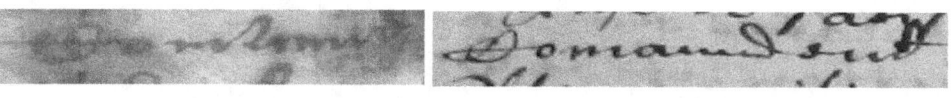

'Comaund' in *Sir Thomas More*　　'Comaundent' in Worsley MSS 47, 18V
Further expert palaeographical research will clarify whether these two

hands belonged to the same person but, by examining these examples, readers can judge for themselves.

**Conclusion**

Previous scholars have agreed that Hand D is Shakespeare but they were only able to compare this writing with the six authenticated signatures by William Shakespeare from Stratford: no other handwriting by him exists. I have now provided the first evidence that this manuscript is by Henry Neville.

**Chapter 9**

Ptolemy and Politike Pamphlets, 1588-9:
Newly Discovered Annotated Books

"I will read politic authors"
*Twelfth Night* (2.5.161)

Whilst researching Thomas Heywood's play *Edward IV* (see appendix 9) I found a reference to a text in the Bodleian Library called *A Politike Discourse most excellent for this time present* (Rowland, 2005). I was intrigued by the mention of this book due to several factors: it was printed in 1589; it was about the relationship between England and France; it was a political document; it was in Oxford and **it was annotated**.

**A source for *Edward III*?**
The first annotation that had made me pause when I read about it in Rowland's edition of *Edward IV*, was the pithy paraphrase, "Great brags... small performance" (p 30). The annotator of Halle's *Chronicle* contrasts 'smalle' and 'gret' in his very first note. In Shakespeare's *Edward III* the King says, "fair **performance** cannot follow promise" (2.1.305). Just four lines earlier the word '**great**' occurs. *Edward III* does have Neville connections: we see the battle of Neville's Cross dramatised and three characters, Salisbury, Montague and Warwick have titles that the Neville family eventually held. One detail is unhistorical: Warwick is made "Warden of the North". The real title holder was Lord Neville who set up the cross to commemorate the victory over the Scots (Melchiori, 1998, 58, 104, 138). Examining *A Politike Discourse* in Oxford I found further connections with *Edward III* that suggested this text might be a source for Shakespeare's play.

In *Edward III* the battle of Crecy is dramatised: the French King John identifies the field of battle (first quarto spelling):

> Now on this plaine of **Cressie** spred your selues,
> And, Edward, when thou darest, begin the fight. (3.3.166)

In the margin of *A Politike Discourse*, on page 31, the annotator underlines the name and writes "Battaile at Cressie" in the margin:

176

*A Politike Discourse*, 31, Bodleian Library, Oxford (4° L. 90. Art)

In the play, after the battle, the Black Prince reports:

> Here is a note, my gracious Lord, of those
> That in this conflict of our foes were slain:
> Eleven Princes of esteem, four score Barons,
> A hundred and twenty knights, and thirty thousand
> Common soldiers; and, of our men, a thousand. (3.4.107)

Just after the above annotation naming the battle in *A Politike Discourse*, the following text is underlined after the words "there were slaine on our side" (that is the French):

"aleuen princes, fourscore barons, a thousãd & two hundred horsemen, & more then thirty thousand footmẽ."

*A Politike Discourse*, 31, Bodleian Library, Oxford (4° L. 90. Art)

In the play the "list of the enemy losses is reproduced verbatim from the sources (Froissart, chapter 132; Holinshed, II, 640) with a single mistake: the knights killed were not a hundred and twenty but twelve hundred (xii.c in Frois., 12 hundred in Hol.)" (Melchiori, 2001, 132). However both these sources only name the 30,000 as 'other' whereas the *Politike Discourse* calls them 'footmen' which is closer to "common soldiers". The word 'footmen' is used earlier in *Edward III* (1.1.140).
Was it just coincidence that this annotator had underlined these numbers? Were there any other signs that this text might be a source for the play? *A Politike Discourse* starts with the French author stating he is motivated by his love of truth and he has overcome his "naturall **loue of his countrie** in composing it." *Edward III* starts with the Frenchman Artois protesting that "**love unto my country** and the right" motivates his support for the English

King. He provides a pedigree, a report on Edward's right by inheritance to claim the French crown. *A Politike Discourse* also outlines the history of the French monarchy and mentions Edward III's magnanimity. In the play the French King John speaks of the ancient Greeks, Charlemagne and prophecies that the Black Prince will drown or be "**hackt a pieces**". In *A Politike Discourse* there are classical Greek references, Charlemagne is mentioned and the French nobility "were there **hewen to peeces**... the King John himself fell into the hands of the Prince of Wales" (= the Black Prince). One passage underlined in *A Politike Discourse* reads, "the Lyon hath plucked vs out of the Eagles clawes" (p 14). A Lyon and an Eagle occur within three lines of each other in *Edward III* (1.1.95/8).

In *The Contre-Guyse* pamphlet in the same volume, the annotator underlines "the wings of their ambition" (p 5). King Edward III speaks of "golden **wings of** fame" (1.1.47). There are a number of words to be found in both the play and the politike pamphlets, for example on page 30 of *A Discourse vpon the present estate of France* one phrase is both underlined and highlighted with a marginal symbol:

÷ woulde obstinate themselves

In the play King Edward says:

> Ah, France, why shouldest thou be thus **obstinate**
> Against the kind embracement of thy friends? (3.3.27)

Another passage underlined in the same pamphlet reads, "The more enemies, the greater glory" (p 29). In *Edward III* the French King John says,

> But, all the mightier that their number is,
> **The greater glory** reaps the victory. (3.1.31)

'Simile' is a marginal annotation drawing attention to a passage on page 40 that is underlined:

a great sympathie or resemblance betweene heaven, mans body, and a monarchy.

In the play, answering King Edward's seductive approach, the Countess of

Salisbury says:

> As easy may my intellectual soul
> Be lent away, and yet my body live,
> As lend my body, palace to my soul,
> Away from her, and yet retain my soul.
> My body is her bower, her Court, her abbey,
> And she an Angel, pure, divine, unspotted:
> If I should leave her house, my Lord, to thee,
> I kill my poor soul and my poor soul me. (2.1.236)

These last three examples occur within ten pages of the same pamphlet. Whilst these shared references may be coincidence or because both play and tract are using the same sources there remains at least a possibility that this text was a source for *Edward III* which, being written in 1592-3, post dates *A Politike Discourse*. Furthermore when we consider history as metaphor we can see that *Edward III*, like *A Politike Discourse*, is concerned with international relations between England, France and Spain. The sea battle of Sluys (1340) is described in the play (3.1.64 - 78) in terms which explicitly recall the English victory over the Armada in 1588. The recognised source for this is the *Discourse Concerning the Spanish Fleet Invading England in the Year 1588,* by Petruccio Ubaldino[43], published in 1590 (Melchiori, 1998, 28; Wentersdorf, 1965, 227 - 31). This is another contemporary political pamphlet which post dates the politike pamphlets and shows the bard consulting contemporary publications as well as the major sources of Froissart, Holinshed and Painter. *Edward III* may also have been written to celebrate the 1591 campaign of Robert Devereux, the Earl of Essex, who had been in command of an expeditionary force sent to France to assist Henri of Navarre. Devereux was a direct descendant of Edward III (as was Neville). Neville was a supporter of Essex and was to become ambassador to France ten years later. His principle task was to ask for repayment of money lent to Navarre, (by then King Henri) in that war, and attempt to negotiate a peace treaty with Spain.

**The politike pamphlets: evidence for the identity of the annotator**
The small volume which contains *A Politike Discourse* (4° L. 90. Art) was printed between 1588-9 and is a collection of 15 political pamphlets, 9

---

43    Reprinted in The Harleian Miscellany, Vol 1, 119-132, London, 1809. There is also a copy in the Bodleian Library.

of which are annotated by the same hand. They focus on the civil wars in France, the relationships between England, France, and Spain, and Henri of Navarre's struggle to unify and stabilise France after the assassination of the Duke of Guise (December 23rd 1588). The Duke was responsible for the St Bartholomew's Day Massacre in Paris, 1572. He also participated in the Throckmorton Plot of 1582 which aimed to assassinate Elizabeth I and place Mary Queen of Scots on the throne. Henry Neville referred to the St Bartholomew's Day Massacre in his diplomatic letters.

There are three types of annotation in these politike pamphlets: underlinings, marginal notes and assorted lines, designs and one pointing hand. In summary the annotations include:

* Political issues concerning war and peace between England, France and Spain.
* Legal issues concerning the succession to the throne. The annotator especially notes the "L(aw) Salick".
* The dangers of factions, usurpation and civil war.
* The annotator notes similes, metaphors, vocabulary, proverbs and turns of phrase.
* He mentions geometry, notes a bastard, a falcon and "disguising his drifts"[44].
* He annotates with the same systematic method, noting points 1,2,3,4 as we saw in the annotations of *Leicester's Commonwealth*, Halle's *Chronicle* and Neville's diplomatic correspondence.
* He has characteristic ways of writing the capital letter N and the number 4 which I recognised from Neville's writings.
* He abbreviated some words beginning with 'pre/par' ('psent'; 'ptend'; 'ptis') and in some instances wrote 'ni' instead of 'in', including the word 'aganist'.
* He twice underlined the word 'cleane' meaning completely/absolutely (in *Discourse vpon the present estate of France*, pages 2 and 20) which is characteristically used by Neville and Shakespeare (James, 2008, 247). On pages 12 and 45 (of *Discourse*) and 15V (of *The Contre-Guyse*) he also wrote and underlined 'pretences', another characteristic word used by both Neville and Shakespeare (James, 2008, 246).

---

44  Shakespeare uses the words 'disguising' and 'drift' within six lines in *The Two Gentlemen of Verona* (2.6.37-43) which was written c 1592 – 3, just after these annotations and contemporary with *Edward III*.

Together these factors seem indeed to point to Neville having been the annotator. I was especially struck by the annotation of "L. Salick." which is on page 13V in *The Contre-Guyse* pamphlet.

*The Contre-Guyse* 13V, Bodleian Library, Oxford (4° L. 90. Art)

The text reads, "the Salike lawe", so the annotator has reversed the word order to note the "L(aw) Salick". This is exactly the word order Neville uses in Worsley MSS 47. The annotator here uses the same spelling and word order as the authors of *Leicester's Commonwealth*: "**the Law Salick**". As we saw in chapter 3, Shakespeare uses this word order. In *Henry V* we find the spelling is "**the law Salike**" (1.2.11) which matches the spelling of *The Contre-Guyse* text.

**The date of the annotations**
The date of the annotations cannot be determined with any certainty: there is no obvious indicator but I suggest they were contemporary, probably made 1589-93 and certainly before Neville went to France as English Ambassador in 1599 (when *Henry V* appeared on stage). The links with *Edward III* suggest a date before 1593.
Neville knew Sir Thomas Bodley, the founder of the Bodleian Library, mentioning him in his letters, and they had both been to Merton College. The Bodleian bought the politike pamphlets in 1841.

**Ptolemy at Merton College**
In Merton College Library there are two books which were given to the library by "Henrici Neuilli". Both are in Greek: one on Roman History (21. DD.6) is unmarked, the other, dated 1588, about the Celestial Geometry of Ptolemy (32.A.4), is annotated by Neville in Latin and Greek. Neville studied astronomy and geometry at Merton under his tutor Henry Savile. The annotations have the familiar systematic quality with items being numbered in the margin. One of the annotations of the *Ptolemiæi Astronomi* includes the abbreviated 'pductu' (instead of 'productu': p 12). Another annotation is of the "insula Meroe" (p 30). Meroe is on the Nile delta. In the play *Locrine*, Albanact says, "I'll pass the Alps to watery **Meroe**…" (2.6.48). In *A Politike Discourse* the words, "*Briareus* (as *Homer* saith) had

an hundred hands" (p 20) are underlined by the annotator. In *Locrine* Humber says, "Briareus, armed with **an hundreth hands**…" (2.6.7). In *The Contre-Guyse*, there is a marginal line against a passage concerning 'Lactance' (p 25V = Lactantius), whom Strumbo mentions by name in *Locrine*. Strumbo refers to a Lactantius text on the Moon, thus connecting him with Neville's astronomical interests. I have dated *Locrine* between 1586-89 with revisions being made until 1595 when it was printed. This dating therefore fits perfectly with these annotations about Meroe, Briareus and 'Lactance' in books printed in 1588-9. I have previously shown that *Locrine* was an early work by Shakespeare with numerous hidden Neville connections (Casson, 2009). Lactantius is also obliquely referred to in *Henry VI* part 1 (dated 1589-92): describing Joan of Arc, the Bastard of Orleans says:

> The **spirit of** deepe **Prophecie** she hath,
> Exceeding the nine **Sibyls** of old Rome…    (1.2.55)

Cairncross (1965, xxxv) pointed out that the source of this was Cooper's *Thesaurus* (1565) where the Glossary gives, under **Sybilla**, "A generall name of all women which had the **spirite of prophecie**: of them (as Varro and **Lactantius** doe write) were tenne... every one of these (as **Lactantius** sayth) prophecied of the incarnation of Christ." Cooper's *Thesaurus* is one of Shakespeare's recognised sources.

## Further discoveries

The very last of the pamphlets, entitled *The Reformed Politike*, was printed in 1589 by Richard Field, at Blackfriars. He went on to print Shakespeare's poems, *Venus and Adonis* (1593) and *The Rape of Lucrece* (1594).

There is more textual evidence for the politike pamphlets being a source for *Edward III* than for Ubaldino's *Discourse Concerning the Spanish Fleet*, which has been accepted as a source. This annotated book in the Bodleian Library is a document which offers further evidence that Henry Neville was Shakespeare. These discoveries suggest there may yet be more books annotated by Neville to be found.

## Chapter 10

A National Treasure

"What sees thou else
In the dark backward and abysm of time?"
*The Tempest* (1.2.49)

The Worsley Manuscript MSS 47 is a major discovery: nothing less than a key source for Shakespeare-Neville's political works. The discovery was made by Brenda James. My detailed examination has led to further confirmation of her findings and established a relationship between the Worsley MSS 47 and 36, and the Northumberland Manuscript copy of *Leicester's Commonwealth*. In claiming *Leicester's Commonwealth* as a stimulus for Shakespeare's work I am not suggesting it was the major source: once inspired to create the bard turned to many sources as he researched his chosen themes, such as Holinshed, Halle, Foxe, and Geoffrey of Monmouth. What I have suggested is that the political ideas and historical references, the language and metaphors of *Leicester's Commonwealth* were triggers to his creativity. It also provides a starting date to that creativity: 1584. The texts I have previously discovered all post date this, starting with *Mucedorus* (see appendix 7). I have also been able to show that the handwriting and spelling in Worsley MSS 47 is similar to that in the annotated Halle's *Chronicle* and the Hand D section of the manuscript of *Sir Thomas More*, thus providing further evidence of Henry Neville's authorship of the works of Shakespeare. Furthermore I have shown echoes of the vocabulary of the Worsley MSS 47 copy of *Leicester's Commonwealth* are to be found in Neville's letters.

The similarity between Neville's handwriting and that of the Hand D section of *Sir Thomas More*, the only manuscript generally accepted as being in Shakespeare's own hand, is clear (see chapter 8). For example:

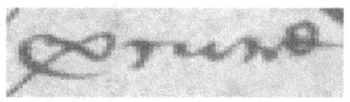

'pcure' (procure), *Sir Thomas More*

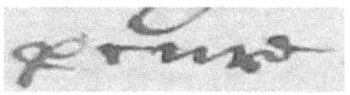

'pcure', (procure), Worsley MSS 47, 8V

Indeed the characteristic use of 'ni' instead of 'in' and the abbreviation of words beginning with 'pre/pra/pri/pro/par/per' point towards the same person being the annotator of Worsley MSS 47, the Hand D section of *Sir Thomas More* and the Halle *Chronicle*. That Neville does not abbreviate words beginning with 'pro/par/por' in his 1601 letter to his boss, Robert Cecil, (e.g.: 'prohibite', 'proceede', 'porcion', 'particular', 'proceednig', see appendix 8) shows that the abbreviations in Worsley MSS47 were a conscious choice whereas the 'ni' habit, which does occur in the 1601 letter, was subconscious. He does abbreviate 'pro/par' in the 1602 Tower Notebook (Worsley MSS 40[45]: e.g. 'pliament' for parliament, 'pbat' for probate, 'pportion' for proportion). Furthermore the fact that there are fewer instances of the 'ni' habit in the Halle annotations, the Northumberland Manuscript, the Tower Notebook and a letter written by Neville in 1613 (Stowe, 174, folio 116, British Library) would suggest a later date for the Halle, as it seems this was a habit Neville gradually grew out of, though in a letter of 1613 there are instances of him writing 'ni' instead of 'in'. So the sequence might well be:

| | |
|---|---|
| Worsley MSS 47: | 1584 - 6 |
| *Ptolemiæi Astronomi* (Merton Library): | 1588 - ? |
| Politike pamphlets (Bodleian): | 1589 - 93 |
| *Sir Thomas More* Hand D: | 1592 - 3 |
| Halle's *Chronicle* (Lancaster): | 1594 - 8 |
| Northumberland Manuscript: | 1596 - ? |
| Worsley MSS 40: Tower Notebook | 1602 - 3 |

The annotations of *Ptolemiæi Astronomi* and the "politike pamphlets" in the Bodleian (4° L. 90 Art), are new discoveries offering evidence for Neville's authorship of *Edward III* and *Locrine*. No one has previously compared the annotated Halle's *Chronicle* with the Hand D section of *Sir Thomas More*. This book offers entirely new evidence of links between these two Shakespeare manuscripts and of how they are connected with the Northumberland Manuscript and Henry Neville's manuscript of *Leicester's Commonwealth* and his letters. All this confirms that Worsley MSS 47 is a national treasure of incalculable value.

If *Leicester's Commonwealth* was indeed a continuing inspiration to

---

45    For more information on the Tower Notebook see James & Rubinstein, 2005, 44-50.

Shakespeare-Neville we should be able to make some predictions, namely:

1) that there would be early works showing evidence of that influence;
2) that there could be some middle works showing evidence of that influence;
3) there might be later works that still showed some signs of that influence.
4) We might also predict the discovery of hitherto unrecognised early works that were substantially influenced by *Leicester's Commonwealth*.

All these predictions come true:

1) There is clear evidence in early works: *Mucedorus*, *Arden of Faversham*, *Edmund Ironside*, *Henry VI*, *Titus Andronicus* and *The Rape of Lucrece*;
2) I have shown there are echoes to be heard in *Henry V* and *Julius Caesar*;
3) Later there are traces in *King Lear*, *Macbeth* and *A Yorkshire Tragedy*.
4) The discovery of *Look About You*, a previously unrecognised early play by the bard, which I have dated back to 1585-6, fulfils the last prediction.

I am now able to further adjust the chronology of Shakespeare-Neville's early works (previously published in Casson, 2009, 228):

*Mucedorus* 1584-5 (published anonymously 1598, revised 1610)
*Look About You* 1585-6 (published anonymously 1600)
*Arden of Faversham* 1586-88, (published anonymously 1592)
*Locrine* 1586-89 (published as by W.S. in 1595)
*Edmund Ironside* 1587-8 (never published, one manuscript in the British Library)
*The Troublesome Raigne of John* 1587-8 (published anonymously 1591 in two parts)
*Hardicanute* 1588-? (the lost second part of *Edmund Ironside*, see Sams, 1986, 19)

*The Taming of A/The Shrew* 1589 (*The Taming of **A** Shrew* published anonymously 1594, *The Taming of **The** Shrew* published in First Folio 1623)

*Henry VI* part 1 1589-1590 (published in the First Folio in 1623)

*Henry VI* part 3, 1589-91, performed from 1590 (published anonymously 1595 as *The True Tragedy of Richard Duke of York* and in the First Folio in 1623)

*Henry VI* part 2 1590-91 (published anonymously 1594 as *The First Part of the Contention betwixt the two Famous Houses of York and Lancaster* and in the First Folio in 1623)

*Titus Andronicus* 1592 (published anonymously 1594)

*Thomas of Woodstock* 1592-3 (never published: one manuscript in the British Library)

*Sir Thomas More* 1592-3 (never published: one manuscript in the British Library)

*Edward III* 1592-3 (registered 1595, first quarto published anonymously 1596)

A scientific theory, if accurate, should lead to new discoveries beyond the immediate scope of the theory. James' discovery, (for the decoding of the 1609 sonnets dedication led to the discovery, rather than a theory), that Henry Neville was the poet who wrote the plays of Shakespeare, has led to many exciting new revelations and, I suspect, more are to come.

# Appendices

To avoid making this book too detailed I have contained extra material in ten appendices. This material could not be left out because it is important evidence for what I have argued and is a resource to future scholars in this field.

Appendix 1: The Annotations of *Leicester's Commonwealth,* Worsley 36 and 47
Appendix 2: The Northumberland Manuscript Annotations
Appendix 3: The Annotations in Halle's *Chronicle* and Worsley 36 and 47
Appendix 4: The Vocabulary of *Look About You*
Appendix 5: The Date of *Look About You*
Appendix 6: *The Famous History of George Lord Fauconbridge*
Appendix 7: *Mucedorus* and *Leicester's Commonwealth*
Appendix 8: Henry Neville's letter, 1601
Appendix 9: *Edward IV*, Thomas Falconbridge, Essex and Neville
Appendix 10: Arbella

## Appendix 1
The Annotations of *Leicester's Commonwealth* in Worsley MSS 36 and 47

I have modernised the Elizabethan long 'ſ' as 's' in all texts. I have endeavoured to follow the spelling of the annotations exactly. In the case of B's habit of spelling words that contain an 'in' as 'ni', such as 'deludenige' (deluding) I have retained these. Some are not certain as this depends on the placing of the dot above the 'i' and in those instances where I am not sure I have erred on the side of caution and chosen to read it as 'in' (see chapter 3).

I have called the annotators of Worsley MSS 36 and 47, A & B respectively. They often follow full stops with a forward sloping dash: . / however I have not included these dashes though they may be significant (for example see appendix 10) .

The pages of Worsley MSS 36 and 47 are numbered only on the first (recto) page. I have numbered the reverse (verso) page with a V to distinguish it from the preceding one. I have used both Peck's (1985) published text and the internet download (http://www.dpeck.info/write/leic-comm.pdf). I have therefore referred to the page numbers as Peck (65/*48*), putting the book page number first, followed by the internet text page number in italics  The 1584 printed copy studied is in York Minster Library Cat No: XXXVII F.21 502305.

| Peck page | 1584 printed annotations & page numbers | Annotator A. Worsley MSS 36 | Annotator B Worsley MSS 47 | Notes |
|---|---|---|---|---|
| 64/*47* | 3<br>The occasion of this conference and meeting.<br>4<br>The persons and place of this conference. | 1V<br>The persons & place of this conference. | 2<br>The occacõn of the conferenc & meeting<br><br>The persons & place of this conferrence | |
| 65/*48* | A Temperat Papist<br>5<br>The boke of iustice<br>6 | 2 | 2V<br><br><br>3 | |
| 66/*49* | The Papistes practizes against the state. | | | |
| 67/*49* | Tvvoe sortes of dealinge against the state. | 2V | 3V<br>2 sortes of dealniges aganist the state | |

| | | | | |
|---|---|---|---|---|
| | Directly.
7
Indirectlye.
 | Directly.
Indirectly. | Directlie
Indirectlie | |
| 68/50 | The state of al subiectes, in a state of different religion. | | | |
| | | | The first kind of treason | B's first independent note shows systematic analysis, see chapter 4. |
| | 8
The seconde kinde of treason | | 4
The 2 knid | |
| | The application of the former example. | | Applicacõn to former exmpls | |
| | 9
Tvvo degrees of treason. | 3V
The degrees of Treason. | Degrees of treason | |
| 69/50 | Feare of forrayne oppressiõ, maketh friĕdship at home. | Feare of forreyn oppression maketh frendship at home | 4V
feare of forraine oppression maketh frnds at home | Neville spells 'forraine' thus in a letter: 26/1/1600 Winwood, Vol 1, 147. The Halle's *Chronicle* annotator spells 'fraunce' with a 'u' as does Hand 'D' in *Sir Thomas More*.

Shakespeare uses 'papist' once in *All's Well That Ends Well*: (1.3.53). |
| | 10
Fraunce | France. | ffraunce | |
| | Flaunders. | Flannders. | fflannders | |
| | Portugall. | Portugale. | Portugall | |
| 69/51 | The old hatred of east Grecians tovvardes the vvest Latins. | The old hatred of Gretians towards yᵉ west Latines. | The oulde hatred of easte gretians towards the west Latins | |
| 70/51 | 11
Not all Papistes properly traytors. | 4
Not all papists proply Traytors. | 5
not all papi: proper trayt: | |
| | The Priestes and Seminaries that vvere executed. | The preests & seminaries that were executed. | the papists & seminaries executed | |

189

| | | | | |
|---|---|---|---|---|
| 71/52 | 12<br>VVise consideratiõs<br>13<br>Misery moueth mercie.<br><br>A good vvishe. | 4V<br>Miserie moueth mercy.<br><br>A good wishe. | 5V<br>Miserie moveth mercie | |
| 72/52 | The nature and practize of the Guineans<br>14<br>The Tyraunt of englishe state.<br><br>Three differences of religion in Englãd.<br><br>The Erle of Leycester. | 5<br>The nature & practice of the Guineans<br><br>The Tyrant of English state.<br><br>3 differences of Religion in Engl:<br><br>The Earle of Leycester. | 6<br>The nature and practices of the Gunians<br><br>The tiranie of the Engli: state<br><br>3 differences of Relligion in England | Shakespeare uses 'tyranny' 37 times: see "the tyranny of the…" in *The Rape of Lucrece* argument. |
| 73/53 | 15<br>The L. Norths pollicie.<br><br><br>A strange speculation.<br>16 | 5V<br>The Lo: Northes Policy.<br><br><br>a strange speculacõn.<br>6 | 6V<br>The Lo: North pollicie<br><br>Beares<br><br>A straunge speculacõn<br>7 | <br><br><br>B. picks out an image. |
| 74/53 | The Q. Ma most excellent good nature. | The Qu: mats most excellent good nature. | Her Ma<sup>ties</sup> most exellent nature | |
| 74/54 | 17<br>Feares that subiects haue of my L. of Leycester<br><br>Sir Francis VValsingham.<br>K. Hen. presage of the house of Dudlei<br>18 | Feares that subiects have of my Lo: of Leyc:<br><br>S<sup>r</sup> Fr: Walsingham.<br>K: Hen: presage of y<sup>e</sup> house of Dudley | feare in subiects<br><br><br>S<sup>r</sup> ffra: Walsing: | |
| 75/54 | Deepe dissimulatiõ | Deep dissimulacõn. | | |

|  |  |  |  |  |
|---|---|---|---|---|
|  | Sir Francis VValsingham. | 6V S^r Fr: walsingham |  |  |
|  | Edmund Dudley | Edmund Dudley | Ed: Dudley 7V Ed: Dudley |  |
|  | (I)hon Dudley. 19 Robert Dudley. | John Dudley. Robt Dudley. | Jo: Dudley Rob: Dudley |  |
|  | The lavv agaynst talking. | The Law against Talking. | Lawe aganist talkers | *Richard III* 'talkers' (1.3.350). |
| 76/55 | Actiõs of Leycester vvherof hee vvould have no speech. | Accõns of Leycester whereof he woulde have no speech. | Actions of Leic whereof he would have noe speech |  |
|  | 20 Leicester Preparatiues to rebellion vpõ Mõsieurs marriage. | 7 Leyc: preparations to rebellion vpon Mons: mariage. | 8 The p^rparacõn of Leic Rebellion upon Mounsiers marriage 8V | "preparation of" in *Antony & Cleopatra* (3.4.26). |
| 77/55 | 21 To Sir Th. Layton. | To S^r Tho: Layton. | Sir Thomas Layton |  |
|  | L. Treasurer. L. Chamberlayne. | Lo: Treasurer. Lo: Chamberleyn | Lo: tresorer. Lo: Chamb: |  |
|  | M. Cõptroler. | M^r Comptroller. 7V | Mr Contro: |  |
|  | Sir Tho. Hibbot. 22 | Sir John Hibbott. | S^r John Hibberd |  |
| 77/56 | Leycester Father a trayterous Papist. | Leyc: father a trayterous papist. | his ffather a trayterous pa. 9 |  |
| 78/56 | The honour and commodities by the mariage vvith Fraunce. 23 | The honour & comõdities by the mariage with France. 8 | The ho: & comoditie by the mariag with ffrance. |  |
|  | Ethelbert Kinge of Kent cõverted An. Do. 603 | Ethelbert K: of Kent converted By Q. Bertha his wief | Ethelbte K: of Kent. | A. picks out Queen Bertha's role. |

| | | Aº. Dmi. 603. | | |
|---|---|---|---|---|
| 79/56 | 24<br>Toleration in Religion, vvyth vnion in defence of our countrie. | Tolleracõn in Religion with union in Defence of our Countrey | tolleracõn of Re: & union ni the defence of y$^e$ countrie | |
| | 25<br>Diuers mariages of her Ma. defeated. | 8V<br>Divers mariages of her Matie defeated. | 9V<br>diverse marr:g her Ma$^{tie}$ defeated of by Leicest | |
| | Leycester deuises to drive avvay all Suters frõ her Ma. | Leyc: device to drive away all suyters fro$^m$ her Matie. | Leic: deviss to driue away all suters from her Ma$^{tie}$. | |
| 80/57 | 26<br>Leycester conuinceth himselfe of impudencie | Leyc: convinceth himselfe 9 of Impudency. | 10<br>his impudent Coniunction w$^{th}$ Dame Letteice | Shakespeare uses 'conjunction' 8 times. |
| | The basenes of Leycester ãcestrors. | The basenes of Leyc: Ancestrors. | his basenes | |
| | Anno 1. R. Marie. | Anõ 1 R. Marie | | A. notes the queen. |
| 81/57 | D. Dale. | D. Dale. | | |
| | D. Julio.<br>27<br>The Archbisshops overthrovv for not allovving tvvoe vvyves to Leycester his Phisition. | D. Julio.<br>The Archbishop Of Cant: his overthrowe for not allowing Leyc: Phisicõ 2 wives. | 10V<br>The overthro$^w$ of Grindal the Archb: of Canter: | B names the Archbishop, who died in 1583. |
| 81/58 | The Lady Sheffield novve Embassdesse in Fraunce. | The La: Sheffeild now Embassadresse in France. | Sheffeild nowe Emba: in ffraunce and Robte Dudley ni Gloucester Hall | B locates the illegitimate Dudley, son of Leicester and Lady Sheffield, in Oxford. |
| | The death of Leycester first | 9V<br>The death of Leyc: his first | The death of his firste Wief | |

| | | | | | |
|---|---|---|---|---|---|
| 82/58 | Ladie and wyfe. 28 Sir Rich. Verney. Balde Butler. The suspicious death of the Lord Sheffield 29 The poysoning of the Earle of Essex. The Shifting of a childe in Dame Lettice belly. The diuers operations of Poyson. Doctor Baylye the yonger. 30 | wief. Sir Rich: Verney. Bald Butler. The suspicious death of the Lo: Sheiffeilde. The poysoning of the Earle of Essex. 10 The shifting of a childe in Dame Lettice Belly. Do: Baylye Junior. Divers operacõns of poyson. | Sir Richard Verneys death 11 Bald: Butler. The suspitious death of my Lo: Sheffeild The poysonnig of my Lo: of Essex The shiftnig of a child in Dame Lettice belley 11V Young Do$^r$ Bayley Diverse opacõns in poysons | |
| 83/59 | Death of Cardinall Chatiliã. Lea. Honnies. 31 Mesteris Draykot poisoned vvith the Earle of Essex. The Erle of Essex speech to his Page Robyn Honnies | Death of Cardinall Chatilion. Lea 10V Hunnis Mtris Draycott poysoned w$^{th}$ the Earle of Essex. The Earle of Essex speeches to his page Rob: Hunĩs. | Lea & Hunnies 12 Mris Dreycott by the Earle of Essex The words of the Earle of Essex vnto yonge Hunnys | Both A & B delay this note: is this evidence of cooperation between them? Robin Hunnis was son of William, Master of the Children's theatre. Shakespeare uses "words of" 14 times; "speech/es to" once. |
| 84/60 | 32 Death of Sir Nicholas Throgmarton. Sir VVill Cycyll novv L. Treasurer. | 11 Death of S$^r$ Nicho: Throckmorton. S$^r$ W$^m$ Cecill late Lo: | 12V S$^r$ Nicho: Throckmort: pisoned by Leic: | |

| | | | | |
|---|---|---|---|---|
| 85/60 | 33<br>The poysoning of Sir Nicholas in a Salate. | Tresõr.<br>Sir Nich: Throckmorton poysoned in a sallet<br>11V | 13 | |
| | The Lord Chamberlayne:<br>34<br>Monsieur Symiers. | The Lo: Chamberleyn.<br>Mounsieur Symiers. | The Lord Chamberlnie<br>Monnsieur Seniors | |
| | The poisoning of Ladie Lenox. | The poysoning of the La: Lenox. | The poysonnig of the Ladie Lineaux | |
| 86/61 | 35<br>Leycester most variable dealing with vvomẽ in cõtracts and mariages. | Leyc: most variable Dealing w$^{th}$ women in contracts & mariages. | 13V<br>His variable dealings w$^{th}$ weo:m contracts and mariages. | |
| 87/61 | cõtractes.<br>Precontractes.<br>Post-contractes. | contracts.<br>pracontracts.<br>12<br>post contract. | contract<br>p$^{re}$contract<br>post contracte | |
| | | | His was brought vp at Gloucester Hall in Oxford | B. provides unique information, referring to illegitimate Robert/Robin Dudley. |
| | Retract.<br>Protract. | Retract.<br>protract. | Retract<br>protract | |
| | Leycester tvvo Testamẽts. | Leyc: two Testaments. | Leic: olde newe Testam$^t$ | |
| | | | Surcontracte | |
| | 36<br>varius Heliogabalus, & his moste infamous death. | Varius Heliogabalus, & his infamous death. | 14<br>The death of Heliogabulus | |
| | An Epitaphe.<br>37<br>A pitteful permissiõ. | An Epitaphe<br>A pittiful pmission<br>12V | A pittifull permition. | |

194

| | | | | |
|---|---|---|---|---|
| | The extirpation of the Tarquinians. | The extirpacõn of the Tarquinians. | The exterpacõn of the Tarqinians | |
| 88/*61* | An. Do. 959. | Anõ. Dmĩ. 959. | Anno 959 | |
| | The intolerable licentiousnes of Lei. carnalitie. 38 | The Licentiousnes of Leyc: Carnallity, intollerable 13 | The intollerable licentiousnes of Leic carnalitie 14V | |
| | Money VVell spent. | Money Well spent. | money well spent | |
| | Anne Vauiser. 39 | Anne Vauasour | Anne vavizor | |
| | The punishmẽt of God vpõ Leycester, to do hym good. | The punishment of god vpon Leyc: to doe him good. | The punishm.<sup>te</sup> of Leic: to doe hmi good. | B. omits God and writes 'hmi' instead of 'him'. |
| | *The children of adulterors shal be consumed, and the seede of a vvicked bedd shal be roted out saith god. - Sap. 3. | | | |
| | | | 15 | |
| | Leycester oyntmẽt. | Leyc: oyntment. | Leic oyntm:<sup>te</sup> | |
| | Leycester bottel. 40 | Leyc: Bottle. 13V | Leic Bottle. | |
| 89/*63* | A pretie deuise. | A pretty device. | | |
| 90/*63* | An acte of Atheisme 41 | An act of Atheisme. 14 | 15V | |
| | The First reason vvhy Ley. slevv his wife by violence, rather thẽ by poysõ. | The first reason why Leyc: slew his first wief by violence, & not by poyson. | The first reason whie Leic: slew his wief rather by vyolence then by violence | B. makes an error in copying. |

| | | | | |
|---|---|---|---|---|
| 91/64 | The second reason.<br><br>Doctor Baylye the elder.<br>42<br>The practise for poysoning the la: Dudlei.<br>43<br>Doctor Babingtõ. | 2 reason.<br><br>Do: Bayley thelder.<br><br>A practice for poysoning the Ladye Dudley.<br>14V<br>Do: Babington. | the 2 reason<br><br>Bayley the elder<br><br><br><br>16<br>Do: Babnigton | A. notes the woman. |
| 92/64 | A Third reason.<br>44<br>The intĕded murder of Mõsieur Simiers by sundrye meanes. | 3 Reason.<br>15<br>The intended murder of Mounsieur Symeers by sundry meanes. | 3 Reason<br>16V<br>The nitended murder of Mounsieur Semiers by sondrie meanes | |
| 92/65 | The intĕded murder of the Earle of Ormond. | The intended murder of the Earle of Ormounde. | the nitended murder of the Earle of Ormonnd<br>17 | |
| 93/65 | VVyllm Killegre<br><br><br><br><br><br>46<br>Preoccupation of her Ma. person. | W$^m$ Killigrew.<br><br><br><br><br><br>15V<br>praeoccupacõn of her Maties person. | Aspirnig by place ing of corrupt servant about her Ma$^{tie}$<br><u>Aspirnig by placnig of occupacõn of her Matie</u> | A. notes Killigrew & corrects spelling.<br>B. deletes this <u>note</u>.<br>Shakespeare uses 'aspiring' 8 times. |
| | An ordinarie vvaye of aspiring by preocupation of the Princes person | An ordinarie way of aspiring by praeoccupation of the princes pson. | An ordinarie waie of Aspiring by occupacõn of the Princes pson | Shakespeare uses 'occupation' 9 times but never pre-occupation. |
| 94/65 | A Comparison.<br>47<br>The vvay of aspirĩg in Duke Dudley.<br>48 | A Comparison.<br>16<br>The way of Aspiring in Duke Dudley.<br>16V | A comparison.<br>17V<br>the waie of aspirenig in D: Dudley | |

| | | | | |
|---|---|---|---|---|
| 95/66 | Leycester povver in the priuy chamber. 49 Leycester married at vvansteade; vvhen her Ma. vvas at M. Stoners hous Doctor Culpeper, Physitian Minister. No sute can passe but by Leycester | Leyc: power in the privy chamber. Leyc: married at Wanstead when her Ma$^{tie}$ was at M$^r$ Ston's house. D. Culpepper, phisition Minister. No suyt can prevayle but by Leyc: 17 | Leic: power in the privie Chamber 18 The mariage at Wansted when her Matie was at Stoners howse. Do: Culpeper phesicon the minister Noe suit can pass ni court but by Leic: | The annotator of Halle's *Chronicle* spells "howses" with a 'w'. Neville uses this spelling in a letter: 8/8/99 (Winwood, Vol 1, 89). |
| 96/67 | Reade Polidore in the 7 yeare of K. Rich 2. and yovv shal finde this proceding of certaine aboute that K to be put as a great cause of his overthrovv. 50 No preferments but by Leycester to Leycestrians. | Read Polyd: in y$^e$ 7th of Ryc: 2 and you shall fynde y$^{is}$ proceeding of some about the King to be putt as a great cause of his overthrowe. No preferments but by Leyc: to Leycestrians. | Noe p$^{r:}$referm$^{te}$ but by Leic: 18V Parties chased from court vpon Leicesters displeasure | Shakespeare uses "chased... from" three times and 'displeasure' 42 times. |
| 97/67 | Leycester anger & insolĕcie. 51 Leycester peremptorie dealing. Breaking of order in her Maiesté hovvsholde. Leycester violating of al ordre in the countrie abrode. | Leyc: anger & Insolency. 17V Leyc: pemptorie dealing. Breaking of order in her Maties houshold. Leyc: violating of all order in the Coũtrey | Le: pemtorie dealings 19 | |

| | | | | |
|---|---|---|---|---|
| 98/68 | 52<br>A Leycestryane common-vvealthe. | abroade.<br>18<br>A Leycestrian comõn wealth. | | |
| | Leicester called the harte and life of the Court.<br>53<br>A demõstratiõ of Leyc Tyrannie in the Court | Leyc: called the harte & lief of the court.<br>A demonstracõn of Leyc: Tyranny in the Court.<br>18V | Leic: the lief & harte of the courte<br>A demonstracõn of Leic: tiranie ni the Courte. | |
| | Leyc. prouideth neuer to come in the Q. daunger againe. | Leyc: provideth never murr to come in the Qu: danger again. | Leic: provideth never to come ni daunger of the Queene againe | |
| 99/68 | Anno Regni. 31.<br><br>54<br>Ley puissance in the priuie Coũcell. | Anõ regni 31 H6.<br><br>Leyc: puissance in the privy *chamber* cõnsell. | His puissance in the privy chamber | A. crosses out *chamber*: is this evidence of A. & B. talking whilst working together? |
| 99/69 | L. Keeper.<br>L. Chamberlaine.<br>55<br>Matters vvherin the Coũcell are inforced to vvink at Leycester | Lo: Keeper.<br>Lo: Chamberleyne.<br>19<br>Matters wherin the counsaill are enforced to winke at Leyc. | Lo: Keeper<br>Lo: Chamblyne<br><br><br>19V | A uses 'en' not 'in'. Neville often uses words beginning with 'in' in his letters. |
| | Leycester intelligẽce vvyth the rebelliõ in Irelande.<br>56 | Leyc: Intelligence w$^{th}$ the rebellion in Irelande.<br>20 | Leic: intellig: with the Re: ni Ireland | |
| 100/69 | Acteons case novv come to England | Acteons case nowe comõn in Englande. | Acteons case in England: | |

198

| | | 19V | | |
|---|---|---|---|---|
| | Saluatore Slaine in his bed | Salvator slayne in his bed. | Salvato$^{rs}$ death | |
| 100/ 70 | Doughty hãged by Drake. | Dowghtie hanged by S$^r$ F$^r$: Drake. | Doughrie hanged by Drake | |
| 101/ 70 | The story of Gates hãged at Tiborne. 57, 58 | The storie of Gates hanged at Tyborne. 20 | The storie of Gates who was hanged at Tiborne. | |
| 102/ 70 | This relation of Gates, may serue hereafter for an addition in the secõd editiõ of this boke. 59 | This relacõn of Gates may serve hereafter for an addicõn in y$^e$ 2$^d$ Edition of this booke. | | |
| 102/ 71 | The deck reserued for Leycester. | The deck reserued for Leyc: 20V | 20V the Deck reserued for Leic: | |
| | Leycester puyssant vyolence vvith the Prince herself. | Leyc: puissant violence with the prince herselfe. | Leicesters puissant vyolence in the Prince herself. 21 | |
| 103/ 71 | The Erle of Sussex his speech of the Er(le) of Leyces(ter). 60 | Earle of Sussex his speach of the Earle of Leyc: | the Earle of Sussex words of Leic: | |
| | The Lord Burghlei. | Lo: Tresor | Lord Tresorer W$^m$ ^ $^{Lo}$ Cecill | B names Cecil. |
| | Leycester povver in the country abrod 61 | Leyc: power in the Countrie abroade. 21 | Leic: power ni the countries abroade. 21V | B. changes the sense of this point. |
| 104/ 72 | Yorke Erle of Huntington. | In yorke Earle of Hunt: | In York the Ea: of Huntnig: | |
| | Barvvick. The L. Hunsdẽ. | Barwicke Lo: Hunsdon. | In Barw: Lo: Hunsdon | |
| | VVales. Sir Hẽry Sidney. The Er. of Pẽbrook. | Wales S$^r$ Hen: Sydney. Earle of Pembrooke. | In Wales S$^r$ Henrie Sidney | |

| | | | | |
|---|---|---|---|---|
| | The vvest. Earle of Bedford. | West Earle of Bedforde Irelande | In the West the Earl of Bedd: In Ireland | |
| | The L. Grey. | Lo: Graye. | Lo Grey | |
| | †Her Ma. (as he saith, for stricking M. Fortescue) called him lame vvretch: that gryeued hym so, (for that he vvas hurt in her seruice at Lyeth) as he said, he vvould liue to be reuenged. 62 | Her Mati as he saith for stryking of Mr Fortescue called him Lame wretch, that greeved him so sore for that he was hurt in her service at Leith as that he said, hee would live to be revenged. 21V | | |
| | *In Scotlãd or elsevvhere, agaynst the next ĩheritors or presẽt possessor. | In Scotland or elsewhere, against the next Inheritor, or pñt possessor. | In Scotla: or elswhere, aganist the right inher: or present possession | |
| 105/ 72 | Sir Ihon Parotte. Sir Edvvard Horsey. Sir Georg Carevv. Sir Amias Paulet. | Sr John parat. Isle of weight Sr Edw: Horsey. Sr George Carey. Gersey & Garnesey | Sr John Parret Sr Edw: Horsey. Sr Ge: Carie Sr Amias Pawlett | A notes the Isle of Wight. A notes Jersey & Guernsey. |
| | Sir Thomas Layton. 63 | Sr Tho: Laighton. | Sr Tho: Laighton | |
| | Her Ma. Stable. Her Armour Munitition, and Artillerye. The Tovver. | Her Maties stables Armour & munition and Artillery. Tower. Sir Owin: Hopton. | 22 Earle of War: Sr Owen Hopton | |
| 105/ | London. Sir Rovvland | London. Sir Rowland | Sr Rowland | |

| | | | | |
|---|---|---|---|---|
| 73 | Heivvard, &c. | Hawarde | Howard | |
| | | 22 | and his | 'Made' as a |
| | Madde Fleetvvood. | Mad | made Recorder. | spelling for |
| | 64 | Fleetwoode. | | 'Mad' occurs |
| | My L. of | My Lord of | Ea: Huntnigt: | in the 1609 |
| 106/ | Hũtingtons | Hunt: - | preparacõn | edition of |
| 73 | preparation | preparacõn | at Ashbye | sonnet 129. |
| | at Ashby | at Ashby. | | 'Recorder' |
| | | | 22V | see: |
| | Killingvvorth | Kenelworth | | *Richard III* |
| | Castle. | castle | | 3.7.26. |
| | Ralphe Lane. | Raphe Lane | | |
| | The offer & | The offer & | The offer & | |
| | acceptation of | accepttacon of | acceptacõn of | |
| | Killingvvorth Castle. | Kenelworth | Killnigworth Casell | |
| | | Castell. | by | |
| | 65 | 22V | Huntnig: | |
| 107/ | The prerogatiue | The prerogative | | |
| 74 | of my L. of | of my Lo: of | | |
| | Leycester. | Leyc: | | |
| | 66 | | | |
| | | | 23 | |
| | Leyc. the | Leyc: the | Leic: the | B. rushing |
| | Starre directorie | starre directorie | starr directorie | so he drops |
| | to Lavvyers in | to Lawiers in | to Lawiers ni | the word |
| | theyr Clients | their clients | their affayres. | 'clients'. |
| | affayres. | affayres. | | Shakespeare |
| | 67 | 23 | | uses |
| 108/ | Ley. furniture in | Leyc: | Leic: furnished | "furnished |
| 74 | money. | furniture w$^{th}$ | w$^{th}$ money ni | with" three |
| | | money. | aboundance | times; |
| | | | | 'abundance' |
| | The sayĩg of a knight of | The saying of | The saynig of | 13 times, |
| | the shyre touching | a knight of the | a knight of the | three of |
| | Leycester | shyre touching | sheere touchnig | which are "in |
| | money. | Leyc: | Leicester. | abundance". |
| | | money. | | |
| | 68 | 23V | 23V | |
| | The infinit vvayes | The infinite | The nifinit waies | Shakespeare |
| | of gayning that | wayes | of gettnig by that | uses 'getting' |
| | Leycester hath. | of gayning y$^t$ | Leic: hath. | 10 times, |
| | | Leyc: hath. | | 'gaining' just |
| | Sutes. | Suyts. | Suites. | twice. |
| 109/ | Landes. | Lands. | | |
| 75 | | | | |
| | Licenses. | Licenses. | Licenses. | |
| | Fallinge out with | Falling out w$^{th}$ | ffallnige out with | |

201

| | | | | |
|---|---|---|---|---|
| | her Ma. | her Matie. | her Ma$^{tie}$ | |
| | Offices. | | offices | Neville uses 'Ecclesiast-icall' in a letter of 5/10/99 & 'Benefices' 27/4/1600. |
| | Cleargie. 69 Benefices | Benefices | Eccliasti: livings Benifices | |
| | Vniuersitie. | Universities. 24 | vniversities | |
| | Oppressions. | Oppressions. | opression | |
| | Rapines. | Rapines | | |
| | Princes fauour. | Princes favour. | Prnice her favor soulde. | |
| 110/ 75 | Presentes. | Presents. | 24 | |
| | Leycester home-gaine by her Ma. fauour. 70 | Leyc: home gaine by her Maties favour. | Leic: home ganie | |
| | A pretye story. | A pretty story. | | |
| | Leycester forraine gayne by her Ma. fauour. 71 | Leyc: forreyn gaine by her Ma$^{ts}$ fauour. 24V | His fforraigne ganie | |
| | Leycester bribe for betrayĩg Callis. | Leyc: bribe for betraying of Callice. | His bribe for the betraynig of Callis 24V | |
| 111/ 76 | Leycester father solde Bullogne. | Leyc: father sould Bulleyn. | his ffath: sould Bullen | |
| | Erles of Arundel and Southamptõ put out of the Councell by D. Dudley. 72 | Earles of Arundell & Southampton put out of the counsaill by Duke Dudley. | E: of Arund: & Southt thrust out of councell | Shakespeare uses "thrust out" four times. |
| | Leycester gayne by fallinge out vvith her Ma. | | Leic: ganie by fallnig out w$^{th}$ her Ma$^{tie}$. | Shakespeare uses "banqueting" twice. |
| 112/ 77 | 73 | 25 | 25 by banquetnig her Ma$^{tie}$ | |

| | | | | |
|---|---|---|---|---|
| | Leycester fraudulẽt chaunge of landes vvith her Maiestie vvhereby hee hath notablye endãmaged the Croune. | Leyc: fraudulent change of lands with her Matie, whereby hee hath notably endamaged the Crown. 25V | Leic chaungnig lands w$^{th}$ her Ma$^{tie}$ whereby he notablye indaungereth the crowne. | Shakespeare uses 'endanger' twice. B uses 'in-daungereth'. Neville often uses words beginning with 'in' in his letters. A uses 'en' not 'in'. |
| | Leycester Licences. 74 Sylkes & Veluetes. | Leyc: Licences. Silkes & velvetts. | Licences Wines oyles and currance. Silkes and velvetts | |
| 113/ 77 | The Tirãnical Lycence of alienatiõ. | The Tyrannicall Lycence of Alienacõn. | Licence of Alienacõn 25V | |
| | Edmund Dudley. 75 Edmund Dudleys boke vvritten in the Tovver. 76 | Edm: Dudley. 26 Edm: Dudleys booke written in y$^e$ Tower. | Edmund Dudley Ed: booke written ni the Tower: Jo: Dudley Ro: Dud: | |
| 114/ 78 | The supplanting of the race of Henrie the 7. The inserting of Hũtingtõ | the supplanting of the race of K. H. 7. the inserting of Huntingdon. | the supyl: of the race of K: H: 7: 26 | A spells Huntingdon with a 'd'. |
| | Edmund Dudleys broode more cũning then hym self. | Edm: Dudleys broode more cunning then himself 26V | Edmunde Dudleys broode more cunninge then hmiselfe. | |
| 115/ 78 | Northũ. & Leicest Vvill rule theyr Prince & not be ruled. 77 Leycester master of arte and a cunning Logitioner. | Northumber-land & Leyc: will rule their Prince and not be ruled. Leyc: a M$^r$ of Arts & a cunning Logitian. | Since A M$^r$ of Arts in Oxford and a cunnnig logitian. | B. notes Oxford. Neville went to Oxford University. |
| | Ley. abusing and spoyling of Oxford. 78 | Leyc: abusing & spoyling of Oxforde. | | B names |

| | | | | |
|---|---|---|---|---|
| | The L. treasurer. | Lo: Tresor. | Lo tresorer Cecill Lo Burleygh 26V | Cecil for the second time. |
| | Cãbrige. 79 The disorders of Oxeforde by the vvickednes of their Chãcellour. | 27 The disorders of Oxforde by the wickedness of theyr chancellor. | Cambridg The discon: ni Oxford by the wickednes of theire cha: the state of the vniuersit 27 | Shakespeare uses 'discontent' and "the state of the" in *King John*. |
| 116/ 79 | Leases. Leycester instruments. | Leases. 27V Leyc: Instruments. Bayley & Culpepper Dee & Allen D. Lopus. D. Julio. | Instrum<sup>ts</sup> for Leases Do: Baylie Do: Culpeper. Dee and Allen ni Gloucester Hall Julio & Lopus | B records Gloucester Hall for the third time and shows an interest in Dr. John Dee. |
| 116/ 80 | 80 *At Digbyes house in vvarvvickshire Dame Lettice laye, and some other such peeces, of pleasure. 81 | At Digbeys house in warw:shyre Dame Lettice lay & some other such peeces of pleasure. | At Digbeys howse ni Warwickshe: Dame Lettis laye | |
| 117/ 80 | The perill of stãding vvith Leicester in any thing. *Poore men resisting VVarwikes inclosure at North hal were hanged for his pleasure by Leycesters authoritie. Great Tyrannie. 82 The Lord Shippe of Dẽbighe and Leyces. oppressiõ used | The perill of standing w<sup>th</sup> Leyc: in anythinge. Pore men resisting war:wicks Inclosure at North Hall were hanged for his pleasure by Leyc: authority. 28 Great Tyranny. The Lordship of Denbigh & Leyc: | 27V poore men resistnige warwicks niclosure at North hall were hanged by Leicest: comaund. The Lo<sup>r</sup> of Denbigh a great gift. his opresion | Shakespeare twice uses 'pleasure' near 'command' in early works. Shakespeare uses "great gift" in |

| | | | | |
|---|---|---|---|---|
| | therĩ 83 | oppression. 28V | there 28 | sonnet 87. |
| 118/ 80 | The Manor of Killĩgvvorth and Ley. oppressiõ ther. | The Manor of Kenelworth & Leyc: oppression there. | The maner of Killingworths oppression | |
| 119/ 81 | The case of Snovvden forest most pittifull. 84 An olde Tyrannical Commission. | The Case of Snowden Forest most pittifull. An old tyrannicall cõmission. 28V | The matter of Snowden a pittifull case | Shakespeare uses "a pitiful case" in *Romeo and Juliet* (4.5.93). |
| | 85 A ridiculous demonstratiõ of excessiue auarice. | 29 A ridiculous demonstracõn of excessive Auarice. | | |
| 120/ 82 | A singular oppression. | A singular oppression | 29 | |
| | 86 Leycester extremly hated in VVales. | Leyc: extreamity hated in Wales. 29V | Leic: extreamlye hated ni wales. | |
| 121/ 82 | The ende of Tyrãts | The end of Tyrants | The end of tirant | |
| | Nero. | Nero. | Neroe. | |
| | Vitellius. 87 | Vitellius | Vtilius | |
| | | | Leander 29V | Shakespeare uses |
| 121/ 83 | A most terrible reuenge takẽ vpũ a Tyrant. | A most terrible revenge taken vpon a Tyrant. | A tiranous reuenge vpon a tirante | 'tyrannous' 14 times, once near 'tyrant'. See *Titus Andronicus*: |
| 122/ 83 | 88 Leyc. oppression of particular mẽ. | Leyc: oppressions of particuler men. | | "revenge upon the ...tyrant" (1.1.140). |
| | M. Robinson. | M<sup>r</sup> Robinson of Drayton in Staff:Shyre | Mr Robnison of Staff: sheere | Sonnet 131 in 1609 edition spells |
| | 89 M. Harcourt. | M<sup>r</sup>. Harecourte | Richard | the word as |

| | | | Paramore Rich: Lea | 'tiranous'. |
|---|---|---|---|---|
| 123/ 83 | Ric. Lee.  Ludouick Greuill. George VVitney.  L. Barkley.  Archbis of Cãtur.  Sir Iohn Throgmarton.  Lane 90 Gifforde. | M<sup>r</sup>. Rych: Lee.  M<sup>r</sup>. Lodiv Greuill Geo: Witney Lo: Berckley.  Grindall Archbyp of Cant:  S<sup>r</sup> Jo: Throckmorton  Giffordes | Lodovick Grenill George Whittney 30 Lo Birkley  Grindall Archb: of Caunterb:  S<sup>r</sup> John Throgmorton. Lanes  Gillfords | |
| 123/ 84 | Sir Drevv Drevvry.  The present state of my L. Leices.  Leycester VVealth  Leycester strength.  Leycester Cũning. 91 | S<sup>r</sup> Drew Drewry. 30V The present state of my Lo: Leyc:  Leyc: wealth.  Leyc: strength.  Leyc: Cunning. | S<sup>r</sup> Drewe Drewrie  His p̃nte state  His wealth  His strength  His connige | |
| 124/ 84 | Leycester disposition.  Causes of iust feare for her Maiesty. 92 A point of necessarie policie for a Prince. | Leyc: Disposicõn.  Causes of feare for her Ma<sup>tie</sup>. 31 A point of necessary pollicey for a prince. | His disposĩcon  30V two poyntes of assurance wch a Prince hath from his subiectes the first 2 | Shakespeare uses 'assurance' 28 times & "from his subjects" in *Pericles* (2.1.100). |
| 125/ 85 | 93 A Philosophicall argumẽt to proue Ley. intẽt of soueraigntie. | A philosophicall Arguem to proove Leyc: intent of soveraignty. | 31 philosophicall argument<sup>ts</sup> to proue his intent to soueraigntie | |

| | | | | | |
|---|---|---|---|---|---|
| 126/ 85 | The preparatiõs of Leyc. declare his intẽded ende. 94 Hovv the Duke of Northũ. dissẽbled his end. | The preparacõns of Leyc: declare his intended end. 31V How y$^e$ Duke of Northumber-land dissembled his ende. | his nitended preperãcon the Duke of Northumber-land dissemblnig his nitents 31V | See *Henry IV* part 1 (4.1.92) 'intended' near 'preparation'. Shakespeare uses 'dissembling' 13 times; "his intents" twice in *Romeo and Juliet*. |
| 126/ 86 | The boldnes of the titlers of Clarence. 95 The abuse of the statute for silẽce in the true succession. | The boldnes of the title of Clarence. The abuse of the stat: for Sylence in the true succession. 32 | ther bouldness The tytle of Clarence The abuse of the statute for silence of the true succession | |
| 127/ 86 | Tvvo excuses alleadged by Leycester friendes. 96 VVhether Leycester meane the Crovvn sincerelie for Huntington or for himselfe. The vvordes of the Lord Northe, to M. Poolie. 97 Poolie tolde this to Syr Robert Iermine. | 2 excuses alledged by Leyc: freinds. Whether Leyc: meaneth the crowne sincerely for himself or for Huntingdon. The wordes of the Lo: North, to Poley reported by Poley to S$^r$ Robert Jermin | two excuses made by his frnds 2 theire resons 1 2 32 The words of the Lo: North to Poolie reported by Poolie to S$^r$ Ro: Jermyne | "excuses mak'st thou" *Venus and Adonis* 188. "He makes excuses" *Rape of Lucrece* 114. Shakespeare never uses 'excuses' near 'alleged'. Shakespeare uses 'reported' 14 times, once as 'reported by'. |
| 128/ 86 | The vvords of Sir Thomas Layton brother in Lawe to my Lord. | The words of S$^r$ Tho: Leighton Leyc: brother in law to S$^r$ Hen: Neuill 32V | the words of S$^r$ Tho: Layton brother ni lawe to my Lord of Leyc: to S$^r$ Henr: Nevill. | A. & B. point out the relationship to Sir Henry Neville. |
| 128/ 87 | The vvords of Mistres Anne VVest Sister vnto this holie Countesse. | The speeches of M$^{trs}$ Anne West of her sister Lettice. | The speach of Ann West to her sister Lettice | A & B name Lettice. |

207

| | | | | |
|---|---|---|---|---|
| 129/ 87 | 98 Three argumētes of Leycesters meaning for himself before Hũtington. | An audacious & most undutiful speach. 3 argumts of his meaning for himselfe before Hunt: | 32V An audatious & most undutifull speach 3 argum$^{ts}$ of his meannig for himself before Huntnigt: | Shakespeare uses 'audacious' 7 times and 'undutiful' once in *Henry VI* part 3 (5.5.33). |
| | The first argumēt 99 The Nature of ambttion. 100 | 33 1, y$^e$ nature of ambition | 1 argum$^{te}$ the nature of Ambicõn 33 | |
| 130/ 88 | The second argument, Leycester particular disposition. | 2, his pticuler dysposicon | 2 argum$^{te}$ his particuler disposicõn 1 2 | |
| | Leycester disposition to tãper for a kingdõ. | | | |
| | I meane the noble olde Erle of Penbrooke. | | Ea: Pembrooke | |
| | The vnduetifull deuise of Naturall issue, in the statute of succession. 101 | The undutifull devise of my Lo: of Leic: | 33V The undutiful devise of naturall yssue, ni the state of succession 4 | |
| 131/ 88 | The marriage of Arbella. | | 5 Arbella | |
| 131/ 89 | The 3 argument. The nature of the cause it self. | 33V 3 argum$^t$, the nature & state of y$^e$ matter it self 34 | 34 the 3 argum$^{te}$ nature of the cause it selfe. | |
| | The nature of olde reconciled enimyty. | The nature of reconciled Enemies | The nature of reconsiled enimi: | |
| 132/ 89 | 103 The reason of Machauel. | Machiavell, my Lo: Leyc: | | |

208

| | | | | |
|---|---|---|---|---|
| | | counsellor | | |
| | The meaninge of The Duke of Northumberland. vvyth Suffolk. 104 Southhovvse. | 34V Hunt: secreat opinion of Leyc: | The meannig of the D: of Northumberland w<sup>th</sup> y<sup>e</sup> Suffc Duk 34V Huntnigtons secret opinion of Leic: | |
| | The meaning of the D. of Northũ. tovvards the D. of Suffolk. | | | |
| 133/ 90 | 105 The practise of K. Richard for dispatching his vvyfe. | The practice of K.R.3. for dispatching of his wife | The practise of Ri: 3 for dispatchnig his wief | |
| 134/ 90 | A nevv Triumuirate betvvẽ Ley. Talbot, & the Coũtesse of Shreusbury. 106 Huntington. | A new triumvirat, betweene Leyc: Talbot, & the old Coũtesse of Shrousbury. 35 | the triumverate betwene Leic: talbott, and the countess of Shrewsburie 35 | The countess was Bess of Hardwick. Shakespeare uses 'sleight/s' once and 'strength' 119 times. |
| | The sleightes of Lei. for bringing al to himself. | His sleight to bring the crown to himselfe. | His strength to bring all to himselfe. | |
| | Scãbling betvven Ley. and Huntington as the vpshot. | | | |
| | Richard of Glocester An. 1 Edvv. 5. | Ryc: Du: of Glou: | Rich: D: of Glouc: | |
| 134/ 91 | 107 2. That the conspirators meane in her Ma. dayes | Ano 1. Ed: 5. 35V That the conspirators meane it in her Maties dayes | Annº 1º Ed: 5 the conspirato<sup>rs</sup> meane it ni her Maties dayes 35V | |
| 135/ 91 | Fovver considerations. 108 | 4 consideracõn | 4 consideracõns | |

| | | | | | |
|---|---|---|---|---|---|
| | A thing vvorthye to be noted in ambitious men. | The story of Duke Hamon a worthy note for an ambitious man | A worthie noate of an ambitious man Hamõn | A&B add the name Hamon correcting the spelling from Aman in the text. |
| | Hest. 5. | Hist: 25. 36 | | |
| | The Percies. | The Perrceys | The Peirceyes ni K: Ric 2 and K.Hen: 4 36 | |
| | The Neuiles. | The Neuills | The Nevills w$^{th}$ Hen: 6$^{th}$ And Edw: 4$^{th}$ | |
| 136/ 91 | Leycester hatred to her Ma. | Leyc: hatred To her Matie. | | |
| | The euill nature of ingratitude. | The evill nature of Ingratitude. | the nature of nigratitude. | Shakespeare uses 'ingratitude' 21 times but never with 'evil'. |
| 136/ 92 | Leycester speeches of hir Ma. in the tyme of his disgrace. 110 | Leyc: speach of her Matie, in the tyme of his disgrace. 36V | | Shakespeare uses "causes why" in *Henry V* (5.1.3). |
| | The causes of hatred in Leycester tovvards Her Ma. | The causes of hatred in Leyc: towardes Her Matie | The causes whie he hateth her Ma$^{tie}$ 36V | |
| 137/ 92 | The force of female suggestions. | The force of female suggestion | The force of female suggestions | |
| | An euident Cõclusion that the executiõ is meãt in the tyme of her Ma. 111 | An evident conclusion that the execution is meant in the tyme of her Ma$^{tie}$ 37 | An evident conclusion that the executnig is ment in the tyme of her Ma$^{tie}$ 37 | |
| | An error of the father novv to be corrected by the sonne 112 | An error of the father now to bee corrected by the sonne | An error by y$^e$ father corrected by the Sonne. | |
| 138/ 93 | Her Ma. lyfe and death, to serue the conspirators | Her Ma$^{ties}$ lief and Death to serue the | Her Ma$^{ts}$ death to serve the conspirato$^{rs}$ | |

|  |  |  |  |  |
|---|---|---|---|---|
|  | turn. | conspirators tourne. 37V | torne |  |
|  | A proclamation vvyth halters. | A proclamacõn w$^{th}$ Halters | proclimacõn w$^{th}$ halters |  |
|  | Papistical blessing. 113 The statute of cõcealing the heire apparent. | The statute of concealing y$^e$ heyre apparant. 37V | The sta$^{te}$ of 13° of concealnig y$^e$ heire apparant unlesse of the naturall bodie. |  |
|  | Richard going tovvards Heirusalẽ begã the custome by parliament, as Polydore noteth Anno 10 of Richard 2 to declare the next heire. | Ryc going towardes Jerusalem, began the custome by parliament, as Polyd: noteth. a° 10 R 3 to declare the next heyre. |  | A. changes the king: from RII to RIII. |
| 139/ 93 | The daunger of our countrie by cõcealing the next heire. 114 | The danger of our Countrey in concealing the next heyre. | 37V The daunger of o$^r$ Realme by concealnig of the next heire. |  |
| 139/ 94 | Great inconueniences. | great Inconveniences | imanente inconveniences upon her Ma$^{ties}$ death | Shakespeare uses 'imminent' near 'death' twice. |
|  | Sir Christopher Hattons oration. | 38 S$^r$ Xpofer Hattons oration | 38 Sir Xpõfer Hattons oracõn |  |
| 140/ 94 | 115 Intolerable treasons. | Intollerable Treasons |  |  |
|  | 116 The miseries to follovve vpon her Maiest. death. | 38V The misseries to follow vpon her Ma$^{ties}$ death. |  |  |
| 141/ 95 | The daũger to her Ma. by this statute. |  | 38V The daunger of her Ma$^{tie}$ by the sta$^{te}$ of succession |  |

| | | | | |
|---|---|---|---|---|
| 142/ 95 | 117 The hastnyng of the conspirators | 39 The hastenning of the Conspirators. | 39 The Lawe Salique ni ffraunce 39V | Only B notes "The Lawe Salique": see "the law Salique |
| 142/ 96 | The vvatchvvord of the conspirators. 119 ARE YOV SETLED? | The watchworde of the Conspirators 39V Are you settled. | The watchword of the Aspiro$^{ts}$ | that they have in France" *Henry V* (1.2.11). |
| 143/ 96 | A great misterye. 120 Assĕblyes at Communions. Straũgers vvythin the Land. The peril of oure countrie if Hũtingtons claime take place. | Great misterye Assemblies at comũnions. Strangers within y$^e$ Realme. 40 The perill of our Country if Hunt: clayme take place | straungers ni y$^e$ lande 40 | |
| 144/ 96 | 121 The read rose and the whyte The miserie of England by the cõtentiõ betvv York and Lãcaster. | The misery of Engl: by the contention betweene Yorke & Lancaster. | 40V The redd Rose and the white The calamitie of Engl: by the contencõn of York & Lancast: w$^{th}$ the contynuance ~ thereof. | Shakespeare uses this image of roses and uses 'calamity' 10 times; 'continuance' 10 times; 'contention' 9 times: note c/c/c alliteration. |
| 144/ 97 | Guelphians & Gibiline 122 Edvvard Plantaginet Erle of vvarvvik. | Guelphians & Gibelynes. 40V 15 H7 Edw: Plantagenet Earle of Warw: | Edw: Plantaginet Earl: of war: | From here on B.'s text is in Italics for emphasis. |
| 145/ 97 | The battaile by Tadcaster on palme Sŏdaye, An. 1460. 123 | The Battayle by Tadcaster on palme Sunday A° 1460 | The Battle of Tadcaster on Palme Sundaye Barnett and Tewxburie | B. notes Barnet and Tewxburie: *Henry VI* part 3: 5.3.19 |

| | | | | |
|---|---|---|---|---|
| | The daũger of Hũtingtons claime, to the Realm and to hir Ma. | The danger of Hunt: clayme, to the Realme & to her Matie 41 | Straungers to her Ma^tie and the Realme by Hunt: clayme. 41 | B. makes a mistake, changing danger to straunger. |
| 146/ 97 | Hovv Hũtington maketh his title before her Maiestie 124 | How Hunt: maketh his title before her Matie | The Queens title by Lanc: and York Huntnigtons title | |
| 146/ 98 | The moste of Hũtingtõs ancestours by vvhõ he maketh title, attainted of treason. | The most of Hunt: Ancestors by whom he maketh title, attainted of treason | The most of his Auncestors by whom he claymeth attaynted of treason. Doct Shawe | Both B & the Halle annotator spell attaynted with a 'y'. Shakespeare mentions Doctor Shaw in *Richard III* (3.5.97). |
| | The infamous deuice of K. Rich. the third allovved by Huntington | The Infamous dealing of K. Ryc 3 allowed by Hunt: | | |
| | Anno 1 Mariæ. | Anõ 1 Maria | | A. notes the Queen. |
| | A point to be noted by her Majesty. 125 The joyninge of bothe hovvses. | A point to be noted by her Matie 41V The Joyning of both Howses | The ioynnig of both howses. 41V | |
| 147/ 98 | The Line of Portugalle. | The Lyne of Portugall | Portnigall | Hand 'D' in *Sir Thomas More* spells 'portigall' with an 'i' and 'll'. |
| | The olde estimation of the house of Lancaster. | The old estimacõn of y^e House of Lanc: | Oulde estmiacõn of the howse of Lancaster The knigs of the howse of Lanc: Henr: the 7^th his descent. | Shakespeare uses 'descent' 17 times. |
| | 126 Henrie Earle of Richmõd. | Hen: Earle of Richm: 42 | 42 | |
| 148/ 99 | The line of Portugal. 127 | The Lyne of Portugall | The Lyne of Portingall | |

|   |   |   |   |   |
|---|---|---|---|---|
|   | The svvord of greate force to iustifie the title of a kingdom. | the sworde of great force, to iustifie the title of a knigdome. | the sworde a straunge ~ mayntenaunc of the title of a knigdome Judae and Israell ni England. | Shakespeare uses 'maint-enance' 3 times. |
|   | Great dangers. 128 The beginning of the controuersie betvvixt York and Lãcaster. | Great dangers 42V The beginning of the controuersie betwixt York & Lancaster | 42V The begninig of the controuersie betweene Yorke and Lancaster | Shakespeare uses 'between' more often than 'betwixt'. |
| 149/ 99 | Edmond Crookeback the beginner of the House of Lãcaster. | Edmond Crookback beginner of the House of Lanc: | Edm: crookback begnier of the howse of Lanc: |   |
|   | Blanche. | Blaunch |   | Again A. notes the woman. |
|   | Iohn of Gaunt. 129 Hovv the kingdom vvas first broght to the house of Lancaster. | Jo: of Gaunt How the Kingdom came first to y$^e$ house of Lanc: | John of Gaunt Duke of Lanc: Howe y$^e$ Kingdome was first brought nito the howse of Lancaster. Henr: 4.5 & 6 of the howse of Lan: Edw: 4$^{th}$ & Rich 3 of the howse of Yorke Hen: the firste Sonne of John of Gaunte | B. gives John of Gaunt his title: he was Neville's ancestor. |
| 149/ 100 | The issue of Iohn of Gaunt 130 | The yssue of John of Gaunt | 43 John Duke of Somerset the 2 Sonnes of John of Gaunte | B writes 'Sonne': the First Folio spells 'sonne' thus 555 times, 'son' just 68 times. (Crystal, 62) |
| 150/ 100 | The pedegree of K Henrie the 7. | The pedegree of H. 7. 43 | The pedigree of K. Henr 7th | B. noting details: see "he from John of Gaunt doth bring his pedigree" |
|   | The tvvo daughters maried to Portugal & | The 2 dawghters married to Portugall & | Daughters Phillipp By Blaunch maried to Portni:gall |   |

| | | | | |
|---|---|---|---|---|
| | Castile. | Castile. | Cathernie by Constance maried to Spayne | *Henry VI* part 1 (2.5.76) and *Henry VI* part 3 (3.3.81). |
| | Forrayne titles. | Forreyne titles | | |
| | The issue of king Edvvard the third. | The yssue of K. E. 3. | the yssue of K: Edw 3. Rich 2 | |
| | 131 Tvvoe Edmũdes the tvvoe begĩners of the tvvoe houses of Lancaster & York. | Two Edm: the two beginners of the 2 houses of Lanc: & Yorke. | William of Hatfeild 2 sonne of Edw 3 | From here B. makes his own notes: "William of Hatfield" see *Henry VI* part 2, (2.2.10) |
| | 132 | 43V | Lyonell Duke of Clarence 43V | "Lionel Duke of Clarence" 4 times in *Henry VI* parts 1 & 2. |
| 151/ 101 | The claime & title of York. | The clayme & title of Yorke. | Edmund of Langley the first duke of Yorke Edmund of Langley had a sonne named Rich: Plantag: Edw 4 sonne to Planta. & heire to Lyonell the 3 sonne of K: Ed: 3 | "Edmund Langley, Duke of York" twice in *Henry VI* parts 1 & 2. |
| | The issue of king. Edvvard the 4. | The Yssue of K: Ed: 4. | The yssue of Edw: 4th Edw 5th | |
| | The Duk of Clarence attaynted by parlament. | The Duke of Clarence attainted by Parliam$^t$ | His 2 Brothers George Duke of Clarence | "George of Clarence" see *Henry VI* part 3, twice. |
| | | | The yssue of the Du: of Clarence | |
| | | | Ed: Ea: of Warrwick & Marga: countess of Salisburie | |
| | | | the yssue of Mar: Count: of Salisb: Cardin: Poole & Henr: Poole. | |

| | | | | |
|---|---|---|---|---|
| | Huntĩgtons title by the Duke of Clarēce. 133 | Hunt: title by the Duke of Clarence | 44 Hunt: tytle by y$^e$ Du: of Clarence | |
| 152/ 101 | K. Rich. the third. | K: Ryc: 3 | Rich: Duke of Gloucester. | |
| | The happie cõiũnctiõ of the tvvoe houses | The happy coniunction of the ii howses | The ioynnige of both howses. Henrie 8$^{th}$ | Shakespeare uses "both your houses" three times in *Romeo and Juliet*. |
| | The issue of king Hẽry the seuenth. | The yssue of K: H: 7 44 | Henr: 7$^{ths}$ two daughters | |
| | The Line & title of Scotland by Margar. eldeste daughter to king Hẽry the seuenth. | The Lyne & title of Scotland by Margaret eldest daughter to H 7. | Margaret of Scotlands tytle whose sonne James 6$^{th}$ most happilie joined both kingdomes into one | B. squeezes this in at a later date. |
| | Arbella. 134 | Arbella | Arbella. after maried to y$^e$ Earle of Hartfo grandchild & dies without yssue | *Henry VIII* "if the king should without issue die" (1.2.134) *Edward III*: "died and left no issue" (1.1.9) see also Halle's annotator: "dying without yssue". f.v$^b$, Keen & Lubbock, 1954, 136. |
| 153/ 102 | The Lyne & title of Suffolke by Marie, seconde daughter to king Henry 7. | The Lyne and tytle of Suff: by Marye Second daughter of King H. 7. | the 2 daugh: of K: Henr: 7$^{th}$ by whome the howse of Suffc maketh clayme. Charles Brandon Duke of Suffc Earle of Herford Ea: of Derbye 44V | |
| | The issue of Fraũcis, eldest daughter to Charls Brandõ Duke of Suffolk. | The yssue of Fr: first dawghter to Charles Brandon | the ysue of ffraine: eldest daughter to char: Brandon | |

216

| | | | | |
|---|---|---|---|---|
| | The issue of Elenor, seconde daughter to Charls Brandõ. 135 | The yssue of Elianor Second Daughter to Charles Brandon 44V | The yssue of Elynor the 2 daug of cha: Brandon D: of Suffc 45 | |
| | Hũtingtõ behinde manie other titles. | Hunt: behinde manie other titles | | |
| 154/ 103 | 136 The policie of the Conspirators for the deceyuing of her Maiesty. Leycester variabilitie. 137 Barres pretẽded against the claime of Scotland and Suffolk. Against the Queene of Scotland & her sonne. | The policey of conspirators against her Matie. 45 Leyc: Variability Barres pretended against the clayme of Scott: & suff: | 45V Barrs p$^{re}$tended by the conspirators three barrs aganist Marie Que: of Scotts and James 6$^t$ K: of Scotts 1 fforranie birth 2 K: H: 8$^{th}$ s testam$^{te}$ 3 Relligion. | B. notes Henry VIII's will, signed by Neville's father. |
| 155/ 103 | Against Arbella. 138 Against Derbye. Against the children of Hartford 139 Leicester dealing vvith the house of Suffolk. | Arbella. 45V Against Derbye Against the children of Hertforde 46 | Aganist Arbella. aganist Suffc Aganist my Lo: Derbyes children Aganist my Lo: of Hertf: children 46 | |
| 156/ 104 | Bastardy. Forreyne byrth. 140 Bastardies lauful stops. | Bastardye Forreigne Birth Bastardies Lawfull Estoppell | Bastardie fforranie ~ birth 46V | A. notes the lawful 'estoppell' of Bastardies but |

| | | | | |
|---|---|---|---|---|
| | The impedimentes agaĩst Scotland three in number. | Impedmts against Scotl: 3 in number | the 3 barrs aganist the tytle of Scotl: and the R: of Scotts answered | B does not. |
| | A protestation. | 46V<br>A protestacon: | | |
| 157/<br>104 | Touchĩg the first impediment of forrayne byrthe.<br>141 | Touching y$^e$ first Impediment of forreyne Birth. | fforr: Birth is the i barr. | |
| | An Alien may purchasse. | An alien may purchase. | | |
| 157/<br>105 | The true Maxima against Aliens. | The true Maxime against Aliens. | 47 | |
| | The statute of K. Edvvard vvhence the Maxima is gathered | The statute of K: Ed: 3 whence the maxime is gathered | Sta$^t$ de Edw 3 Knigs children borne out of y$^e$ Realme noe Aliens. | |
| | Reasons vvhy the Scottish title is not leted by the Maxima Against Aliens.<br>142 | Reasons why the scottish title is not letted by the Maxime against Aliens | | |
| | The first reason. | The 1 reason<br>47 | the Answere to the i Barr. | |
| 158/<br>105 | The rule of thirds. | The rule of Thirds | cawses ni Lawe Dower | |
| | Tennant by courtisie. | Ten~ t by Curtesie | tenauntable curtisie | |
| | Diuision among daughters. | Division amongst daughters | copercinerie betweene daughters<br>47V | coparcenary: a legal term for a shared inheritance, OED. |
| | Executours.<br>143 | Executors<br>The Crown no such inheritance as is meant in the | Executor | A. scores through this |

218

| | | | | | |
|---|---|---|---|---|---|
| | | statute. | | | note. |
| | The secõd reason. The Crovvn no such inheritaunce as is meant in the statute. | The 2$^{nd}$ reason The Crown no such inheritance as is meant in y$^e$ statute. | 2 reason. | | |
| | The Crovvn a corporation. 144 | The Crown a Corporacon 47V | | | |
| 159/ 106 | The third reason. The Kĩgs issue excepted by name. L. Liberorum. F. de verb sign. | The 3$^d$ reason The kings yssue excepted by name. | 3. Reason Infantes de Roy ni y$^e$ Sta$^{te}$ signified is y$^e$ knigs yssue and not his children. | Shakespeare uses 'signified' 3 times. | |
| | 145 The fovvrth reason. The kĩgs meaning | 48 The 4 reason The K. meaning | 48 4 Reason | | |
| 160/ 106 | The matches of England vvyth forreyners. | The matches of Engl: with Forreyners | | | |
| | The fifte reason. Exãples of forreiners admitted | The 5. Reason Examples of Forreyners admitted | 5 Reason | | |
| | 146 Flores hist. An. 1066. | Flores Histor: Ano 1066 | | | |
| | Pol. lib. 15 Flor. hist. 1208. | 48 Polyd: Lib 15 Flo: Hist: 128. | | | |
| | King Iohn a Tyraunt. 147 | John a Tyrant. 48V | 48V Kinge John an vsurper | Shakespeare uses 'usurper' in *King John* and 3 other plays. | |
| 161/ 107 | The sixt reason. The iudgement and sentence of K. Henry the seventh. 148 The seuenth | The 6 reason The Judgement & sentence of K: H: 7. The 7. reason | 6 Reason 49 reasons and more | | |

219

| | | | |
|---|---|---|---|
| 162/ 107 | reason. The Q. of Scot. and her sonne no Aliens. 149 | | perticuler proue the Q of Scotts and her sonne noe Aliens 1 perticuler reason 2 reson stat$^{te}$ de natis Vltra Mare | B, uniquely, uses Latin. |
| | | 49 | | |
| | The second impediment against The Q. of Scot. and her sonne vvhich is K. Hĕrie the eight his Testament. | The second impedimt against The Qu: of Scotts & her son which is K: H: 8 testament 49V | The 2 ympedim$^{te}$ wch is y$^e$ testam$^{te}$ of K: H: 8. being i barr against Q: of Scotts and her Sonne 49V | |
| 163/ 108 | Forreine birthe no impediment in the iudgement of K. Henr(ie) the eight. 150 | Forryn Birth no Impediment in the Judgement of K. H. 8. | fforra: birth noe barr ni y$^e$ Judgem$^{te}$ of K. Hen: 8 | |
| | The succession of Scotland nexte by the iudgement of the cõpetitours. | The succession of Scotland next by the competitors owne Judgemt | The seconde succession of Scotl: next by the uidgm$^{te}$ of y$^e$ competitors. | |
| | The Duke of Northumberlandes drift. 151 | The Duke of North: Drift. 50 | The drift of y$^e$ D: of Northumberland. 50 | Shakespeare uses "drift of" 5 times. |
| | The mutable dealĩg of the house of Dudley. | The mutable dealing of the house of Dudleys. | | |
| 164/ 109 | The authoritie and occasion of K. Henries testamĕt. 152 The kĩgs Testamĕt forged. | The auctority and occasion of K: Hen: Testament. The K: testament forged. 50V | 50V Kinge H: testam$^{te}$ forged | |
| 165/ 109 | The first reason. Iniustice & improbabilitie. 153 | The first reason. Iniustice & Improbabilytye | 1 Reason ni probabilitie | |

|  |  |  |  |  |
|---|---|---|---|---|
|  | The example of Fraunce. | The example of France |  |  |
|  | The secõd reason. | The second reason. | 2 Reason ni |  |
|  | Incõgruities and indignities. 154 Adrian Stokes. | Incongruities & Indignities. 51 Adrian Stokes. | nicongruitis and <u>nidignities</u> 51 |  |
| 166/ 110 | The third reason. The presupposed vvill is not Authentical. | The third reason The presupposed will is not authenticall | Reason y<sup>t</sup> y<sup>e</sup> presupposed wills are not authenticall. 2 S<sup>r</sup> John Hales |  |
|  | 155 The disprouing of the vvill by vvitnesses. The Lord Pagett. | The Disproving of the will by witnesses Lo: pagett 51V | 4 Reason of dissprounige the will by <u>witnesses</u> Lo: pagett 51V |  |
|  | Sir Edvv Mõtague VVillm Clarcke. 156 A meting together about this matter of the nobility. My L. of Leycester agayne playeth double. 157 | S<sup>r</sup> Edw: Montague. W<sup>m</sup> Clarke. A meeting togither about y<sup>e</sup> matter of the Nobility. Leyc: againe playeth double. | S<sup>r</sup> Edwarde <u>Montegue</u> wm. Clearke the Lo: of Leicest: double dealnige. 52 | B. uses alliteration: see "double-dealing" in *Twelfth Night*: (5.1.27). |
| 167/ 111 | The olde Earle of Pẽbroks admonition, to the Earle his sonne yet liuĩg. The third impediment of Religiõ. | The old Earle of pem: admonicon, to his son the Earle now living. 52 The 3<sup>d</sup> Impediment of Religion. | The ould Ea: of Pembrooks adminicõn to his sonne that <u>nowe liveth</u>. 3 Barr is religion |  |
| 168/ 111 | Princes of Germanye. 158 Q. Mary. | Princes of Germany. Qu: Mary. | Qu Marie |  |

221

| | | | | |
|---|---|---|---|---|
| | Q. Elizabeth.<br>*The Dudleys | Qu: Elizabeth.<br>The Dudleys. | Q Eliza:<br>Dudleys religion<br>52V | |
| | Mõsieur. | Monsieur.<br>52V | Mounsier | |
| | King of Navarre.<br>Prince of Condye. | King of Navare<br>Prince of Condie. | K: of Navarr<br>Prnice of Condie | |
| 168/<br>112 | My L. of Huntingtons religion.<br>159 | My Lo: of Hunt: Religion. | Lo: of Hunt: his Religion. | |
| 169/<br>112 | The title of thos vvhiche ensvve the Q. of Scottes. | The Title of those wch ensure the Qu: of Scotts. | | |
| 170/<br>112 | The yõg king of Scotland<br>160 | The young King of Scotts.<br>53 | The younge K: of Scotts James y$^e$ 6.<br>53 | B adds the name:<br>James the 6$^{th}$. |
| | The deuice to set out her Ma. vvith the yong king of Scotlãd.<br>161 | The device to sett out her Matie with the young King of Scotts | | |
| 170/<br>113 | The intolerable procedinges of certayne Ministers in Scotlãd agaĩst theyr Kĩg by subornation of hys enymyes in England.<br>162 | The intolerable proceedings of certeyne ministers in Scotl: against their King by subordinacon<br>53V | The demeno$^s$ of (s)ome of his accõn in Scotl:<br>53V | (s)?: letter invisible due to binding. Shakespeare uses "demonstrations of" twice. |
| 171/<br>113 | Sir Patrick Adamson Archbishop of S. Andrevves. | of his Enemyes in Englande.<br>54 | S$^r$ Pattrick Anderson Archb: of S$^t$ Androwes<br>54 | B changes the name. |
| | Treasons Plotted Against the K. of Scottes.<br>163 | Treasons plotted against the K: of Scotts. | | |
| 172/<br>114 | Leycester cunning deuice for overthrovvĩg the Duke of Norfolke.<br>164 | Leyc: cunning device for overthrowing the Duke of Norff:<br>54V | Leic: most cunninge devise for overthrownige of y$^e$ Duke of Norffc.<br>54V | |
| | The impudencie of Iudas. | The impudency of Judas | | |

| | | | | |
|---|---|---|---|---|
| 173/ 114 | The speaches of Leices to the D. of Norfolk. 165 Ley. cousynage of the Quene. | The speeches of Leyc: to the Duke of Norff: Leyc: cosinage of her Matie 55 | 55 | |
| | The Duke of Norfolks. flyĩg into Norfolk | The danger Duke of Norff flying into Norff: | The Duke of Norff flynige nito Norff | A. deletes danger. |
| | Machauellian Sleyght 166 | Machiavillean sleights. | | |
| 173/ 115 | Leicester deuices for the over- throvv of Syr Christopher Hatton. | Leyc: devices for the over- throwing of S$^r$ xpofer Hatton 55 | his devise for y$^e$ overthrowe of S$^r$ Xpofer Hatton Hen: vmpton | Sir Henry Unton was "Neville's friend and neighbour." (James, 2008, 158). |
| 174/ 115 | Leicester deuices against the Earle of Shrevvsburie. 167 | Leyc: devices against the Earle of Shrousbury. 55V | | |
| | Ley. contempt of the anciẽt Nobility of Englãd. | Leyc: contempt of the ancient Nobility of Englande. | his contempte of Auntiente nobilitie 55V | |
| | Nevv mẽ most contẽptuous. | New men most contemptuous 56 | newe men most contumelious | B. uses 'contumel- ious': see Henry VI Part 1: (1.4.38) Part 2: (3.2.204) Timon of Athens: (5.5.173) "base and abject" see Henry IV part 2 (4.1.33) In Henry VI part 3 'downfall' |
| | D. Dudleys ieste at the Erl. of Arũdel. 168 | Dudleys insolent speeches against y$^e$ Earle of Arundell. | Duke Dudleys insolent speach of the Earle of Arundell. 56 | |
| 175/ 116 | The most abiect behauior of Duke Dudley in aduerse fortune 169 Leicester base | The base & abiect behavior of Dudley in his owne adversity Leyc: base | The base & abiect behavio$^r$ of D: Du: ni his downefall and adversitie Leic: base | |

223

| | | | | |
|---|---|---|---|---|
| | behauiour in adversitie. | behaviour in adversity. | behavioure ni adversitie | (3.3.104) (5.6.65) and 'adversity' (3.1.24). 'deluding' is used twice by Shakespeare. |
| | Leicester deceiuing of Syr Christopher Hatton. | 56V His deluding S$^r$ Xpofer Hatton | His deludenige of S$^r$ Christo: Hatton | |
| 176/ 116 | A pretie shifte of my Lorde Leyc. 170 Her Ma. speech of Leyce. to the Treasurer. | Her Maties speach of Leyc: to my Lo: Treasuror. 57 | 56V Her Ma$^{ts}$ speech to y$^e$ Lo: tresorer of my Lo: of Leyc: . | |
| | The daũger of her Ma. by oppressiõ of the fauourers of the Scottishe title. 171 A Similitude. | The danger of her Matie by oppression of the favourors of the Scottish title. A fitt comparison | The Daunger of her Ma$^{tie}$ by opressnige of y$^e$ favorites of y$^e$ Scottish tytle 57 | Shakespeare uses 'favourites' 6 times in early plays, 'favourers' once in *Pericles* (1.4.72). |
| 177/ 117 | Earle of Leicester. Earle of Hũtingt. | | Ea: of Leicester Ea: of Huntnigton | |
| | The old Coũtesse of Huntingtons speach to her sõne. 172 Nearnes in cõpetitors doth incite thẽ to aduẽture. | The old Countes of Hunt: speeche of her sonne Late Earle. 57V | The owld countess of Huntnigtons speach of her sonne nowe Earle. | |
| | Henrye Bolingbrooke after K. Hẽry the fourth. | | Hen: Duke of Lancaster an vsurper Rich: | B notes two usurpers, both in Shakespeare plays: in *Henry VIII* Richard is called a 'usurper' (1.2.197). |
| 178/ 117 | Richard Duke of Glocest. after K. Richard the third. | | Duke of gloucester an vsurper | |
| | The great vvisdom of her Ma. in cõseruĩg the next | The great wisdome of her Matie in | the greate wisdome of her Ma$^{tie}$ conc$^v$nnige y$^e$ | |

|  |  |  |  |  |
|---|---|---|---|---|
|  | heirs of Scotland. | conserving the next heire of Scotlande. 58 | next heire of Scotland 57V |  |
|  | 173 The K. of Scotlands destruction of more importance to the cõspirators then his mothers. | The King of Scotl: death of more importance to the competitors then his Mothers. |  |  |
|  | The Erle of Shreusburie disgraced by the cõpetitoures. 174 |  |  |  |
| 179/ 118 | The vigilant eye that her Ma. ancestours had to the collateral lyne | The vigilant eye of her Maties Ancestors to the collaterall Lyne. 58V | The vigelent eye of her Ma[ts] auncesto[rs] to y[e] collaterall Lyne. | Neville writes that Elizabeth has "a vigilant Eye" in a letter of 15/5/99. |
|  |  |  | Edw: Earle of war his sister Margar: countess of Salisburie of y[e] collaterall lyne exe with her sonne Henr: executed 58 | B. deletes underlined words. |
|  | Persons executed of the house of Clarẽce. 175 |  |  |  |
|  | The example of Iulius Cesars destruction. | Toe much confidence very pillous in a prince. | To much confidence verie perilous ni a Prnice. | "Your wisdom is consumed in confidence." |
| 180/ 118 | To much cõfidence very perilous in a Prince. 176 | This was Julius Caesars destrucion. 59 | This was the distruction of Julius Cesar by Marc: Brutus 58V | *Julius Caesar* (2.2.49). B notes Marcus Brutus. |
| 180/ 119 | The example of Alexãder the great, hovv he was fortolde his daunger. 177 | This was the death of Alex: the great. | the death of Alexander y[e] great by Antipater and his three Sonnes |  |
| 181/ 119 | Late executions. Fraude to be | Late Executions | the late execucõns |  |

| | | | | |
|---|---|---|---|---|
| | feared in pursueing one parte or faction onlie. 178 The comparison of vvolues & Rebels. | 59V wolves and Rebells both alike | wolves & Rebells howe alike 59 | Shakespeare uses wolves as a metaphor for rebels in *Henry VI* Parts 2 & 3. In his letters Neville spells Rebells with two lls. B deletes Marie and names John. |
| | Rychard Duke of York. | | Richard Duke of York A$^{no}$ Regni Henr: 6 | |
| 182/ 120 | Duke Dudley. A good rule of policie. 179 | Duke Dudley. | John Duke of Northumberland Anno Regni marie Edwardi 6 | |
| | The spech of a certayne Ladie of the Court. 180 | 60 The speech of a Lady of the court. | The speach of a Ladye in court | |
| 183/ 121 | More moderation vvisshed in matters of factiõ. | 60V Moderacõn wished in matters of faction. | 59V Moderacõn ni matters of ffaction | |
| | The speach of a Courtier. 181 | The speech of a Courtier. | The speach of a Courtier | |
| | This peril of diuisions & factions in a common vvealth. | The perill of factions in a comõnweal. 61 | The perrill of ffactions in comõnwealths 60 | |
| 184/ 121 | The daũgerous sequell of dissensiõ in oure Realme 182 | The sequels of Dissention dangerous in our Realme. | the sequel ~ daungers of dissention ni o$^r$ Realme | Shakespeare uses "dissension in our" 8 lines before 'realm' in *Henry VI* part 1 (4.1.139). |
| | Exãples of tolleration in matters of Religion. Germany | | tolleracõn in matters of Rellig: | |
| | The breach and re-union againe in Fraunce. | France 61V | ffraunce 60V | |
| 185/ 122 | 183 Flaũders. | 62 | fflaunders 61 | |

| | | | | |
|---|---|---|---|---|
| | 184
Moderation impugned by the cõspirators.
Cicero.
Cateline.
The conspirators opportunytie.
185 | | | |
| 186/
122 | Leycester to be called to accompt. | Leyc: to be called to an Accompt | Lo: of Leic: to be called to an Accompte. | |
| | | 62V
Inordinate affection by the prince to a peculier and wicked person. | 61V
Inordinat affeccõn by the Prnice to a peculier and wicked person. | Shakespeare uses 'inordinate' 3 times, 'peculier' 8 times. 'wicked' 60 times, 'affection' 78 times: all these words are in *The Rape of Lucrece.* |
| 187/
123 | 186
The death of K. Philip of Macedonie & the cause therof.
187
Pausanias. | The Cause of the death of Phillip of Macedone
63 | The cause of the death of Phill: of Macedon
62 | |
| | Kinges of Englãd ouerthrovven by to much fauoring of some particular men. | 3 Kings of England overthrowne by toe much favouring of some particular psones | these K. of England overthrowne by to much favoringe of some pticuler persons (vs) | |
| 188/
123 | K. Edvvard. 2. | Edw: 2 | Ed: 2 | |
| | K. Richard. 2.
188
K. Henrie. 6. | Ryc: 2
Hen: 6 | R: 2
Henr: 6
62V | |
| 188/
124 | Pol. lib. 23.
hist. Angl.
189 | Polyd: Lib: 23
Histor:
63V | Polidore Lib: 3
Historian | A names de La poole. |
| 189/
124 | The punishemẽt of VVilliã Duke of Suffolke.
190 | The punishmt of Wm de La poole Duke of Suff: | The punishm^te of W^m Duke of Suff: | Shakespeare names "William de la Pole" 5 times in *Henry VI* |
| | An. 30 of Kinge | Ano 30. H. 6. | An° 30° Hen: 6. | |

|  |  |  |  |  |
|---|---|---|---|---|
|  | Hẽrie. 6. | 64 |  | parts 1 & 2. |
|  |  |  | 63 |  |
|  | The punishmẽt of Edmond Dudley. | The punishment of Edm: Dudley. | The punishmt of Edm: Dudley. |  |
|  | 191 |  |  |  |
| 190/ 125 | The causes vvhie Princes vvere chosen & do receyve obediẽce. | Why Princes are chosen & doe receuie obeydiences. | wherefore Prnices are chosen and receave obedience |  |
|  |  | 64V |  |  |
|  | Leycest. Theftes. 192 | Leyc: thefts | His thefte 63V |  |
|  | Leycest. murders. |  | Murder |  |
| 191/ 125 191/ 126 | A heape of Leyces. enormities that vvould be redie at the daye of his trial. 193 | His murthers A heape of his enormities that would be readie at the day of his Triall. 65 | A heap of enormities y$^t$ would be readie at the day of his triall. 64 |  |
| 192/ 126 | Her Ma. tẽder hart tovvardes the Realme. | Her Matie tender harte towards the Realme | Her Ma$^{ts}$ tender harte towards her subiects & Realme |  |
|  | 194 Lei desire, that men should think her Ma. to stand in feare of him. 195 Cicero in Officio. | 65V His desire To have men thinke her Matie doth stande in feare of him. | 64V His desire to have y$^e$ people to think y$^t$ her Ma$^t$: doth stand ni feare of hmi: for 2 causes 1 2 |  |
| 193/ 126 | A rule of Machiuel obserued by the Dudleys. | A rule of Matchiauel | A rule of Machevell observed by y$^e$ Dudleys. |  |
|  | Lei. strõg onlie by her Ma.fauour. | His strength onely by her Mats fauour. | His strength - only by her Ma$^{ts}$ fauor |  |
| 193/ 127 | An offer made for taking & tyeĩg the Beare. 196 | An offir made by the Author for y$^e$ taking & tying the Beare. | An offer made by y$^e$ Author for the taknige & tynige of y$^e$ Beare 65 |  |

228

| | | | | |
|---|---|---|---|---|
| 194/ 127 | Lei. vvhat he receyueth frõ his ancestours.<br><br>197<br>The comparyson of Leices. vvyth his father. | His Ancestors qualities<br>66<br><br><br>His comparison with his father<br>66V<br>His oath prophaned. | His Auncestors qualities <u>Jo: Du</u><br>John Dudley<br>Edm: Dudley<br>Ro: Dud:<br>65V<br><br><br>66V<br>his oathes profaned | B deletes <u>Jo: Du</u>.<br><br><br><br>.<br>See *Richard III* for 'oath' near 'profaned' (4.4.289). |
| 195/ 128 | The vveaknes of Ley. yf her Ma. turne but her countenaunce from him<br>198<br><br>The end & departure from the Gallerie. | His weakness yf her Matie turn but her favour fro$^m$ him.<br><br>67<br>The end of the Conference & departure fro$^m$ the Gallery. | His weaknes if her Ma$^{t:}$ turne but her fauor from hmi.<br>66<br><br>The end of y$^e$ conference. | Shakespeare uses 'favour' 123 times, 'countenance' 59 times. |

229

## Appendix 2

## The Northumberland Manuscript Annotations

The Northumberland Manuscript is famous because on the cover there are what seem to be signatures by William Shakespeare. In fact at the top of the page is Neville's name and family motto and scholars have agreed it once belonged to him. The Northumberland Manuscript version of *Leicester's Commonwealth* is not complete, is fire damaged and has been cut. It starts on Folio 63 (equivalent to Peck 92/*64*) from the words "a third cause of this manner".

On Folio 64 there is a change in the writing style: it is not clear whether this is one writer changing his style or two different writers.

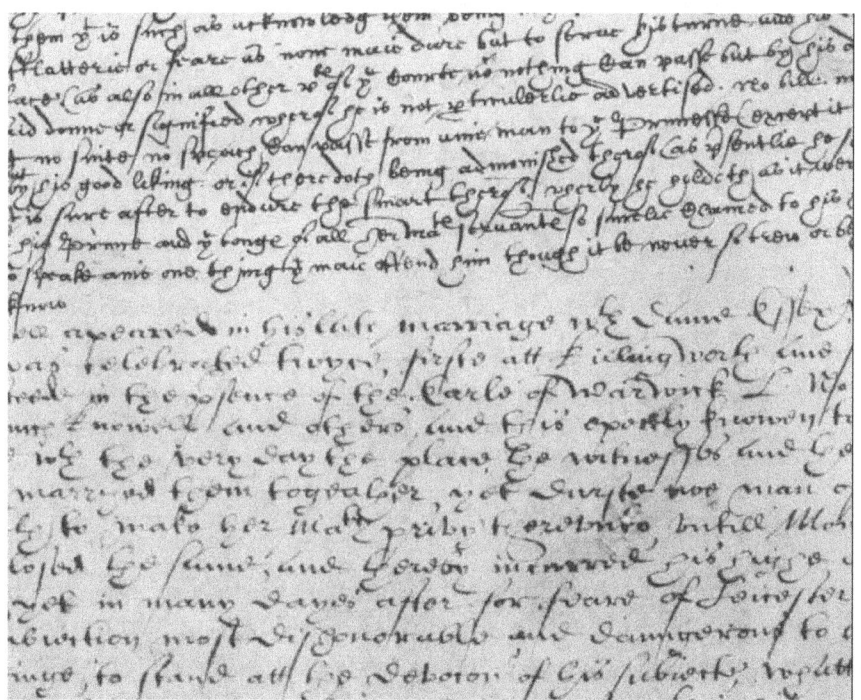

Folio 69 = Peck 95/*66*

The vast majority of the annotations are lost, either through the fire or through the trimming of the edges of the paper: occasionally it is possible to make out single last letters that the trimmer left on the edge of the text.

Of those that do survive a number are fragmentary, illegible or in poor condition. The following annotations can be made out.

Folio page:           Annotations

73:                    Licences

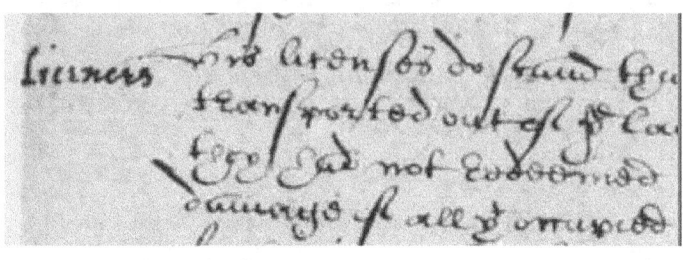

77:                    (a) most ter(rible) reveng (e upon a) tyrant

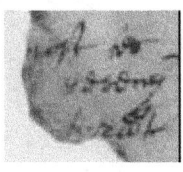

79:                    as yett

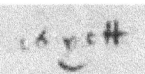

(This is not actually a true annotation but an insertion by the writer of a fragment of text he has missed out of the main body which should read: "I think that **as yet** his ability serveth not…" Peck 125/*85*.)

79:       a philosophicall argumt to prove Leyc: intent of soueraigntie.

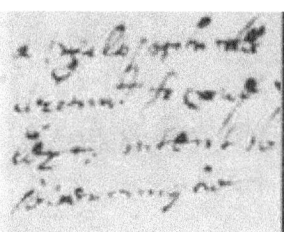

81:       meaning for him self before Hunt

          1 ye nature of ambition

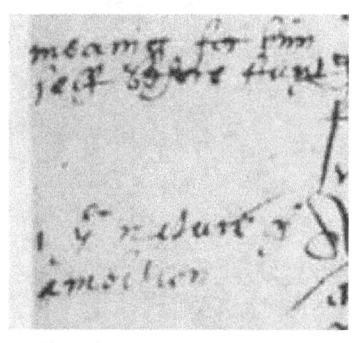

81:       his pticuler positiõ

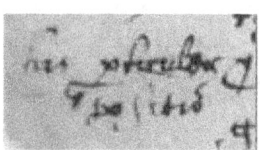

83:       yᵉ practice of K.R.3. for dispatching of his wief

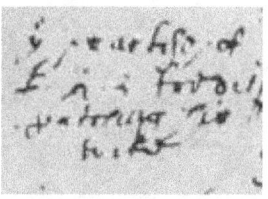

83:  a new triuni = between Leyc Talb & y^e old Coun of
Shrew

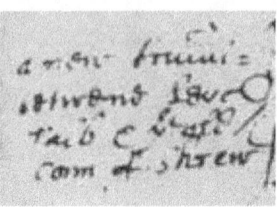

83:  his sleight to bring ye crowne to himself

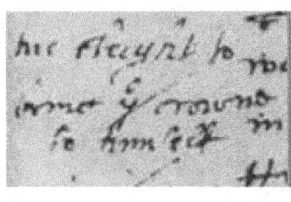

83:  (R)ych: D of Gloc
(Ano 1.) Ed (5).

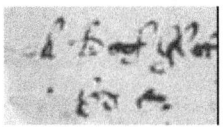

85:  An error of ye fa: now to be corrected by the sonne

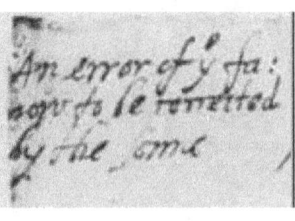

85:                    her ma: Lyfe and death to serve ye conspirators
tourne

85:                    pclamatyon wth halters
                      (Pa)pisticall blessing
                      lawy:
                      (sta)tate of (con)cealyg
                      (hei)re appa:

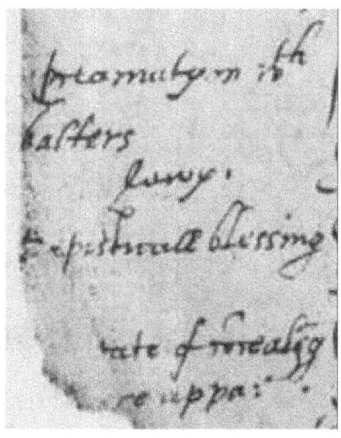

87:                   ye watchword of y\ :sup:`e` conspirators

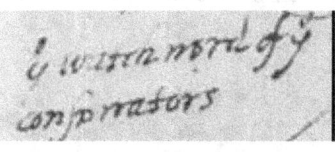

87:                   are you settled

great mistery

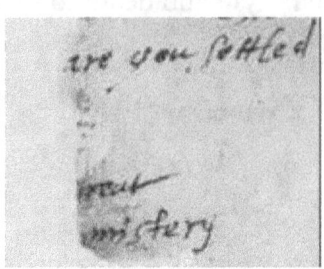

Perhaps it is appropriate that the last annotation is "great mistery".

In chapter 4 I noted the similarities between the handwriting of the abbreviated 'proclamation' in Worsley 47, the Halle and *Sir Thomas More*. When we compare these with this word in the Northumberland Manuscript annotation on folio 85 we can see it is by a different writer and is spelt with a 'y': 'pclamatyon'.

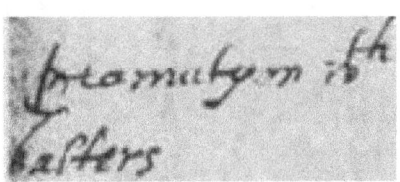

Northumberland Manuscript annotation on folio 85

This annotation is "pclamatyon w$^{th}$ halters". Both MSS 36 and 37 spell this word fully on this occasion:

MSS 36, A:  A proclamacõn w$^{th}$ Halters
MSS 47, B:  proclimacõn w$^{th}$ halters

Thus it seems more likely that the annotator of the Northumberland Manuscript was a scribe. In chapter 6 I offered evidence that he was copying Worsley MSS 36.

# Appendix 3

## The Annotations in Halle's *Chronicle* and Worsley 36 and 47

Some words are used more than once in the Halle annotations. To avoid confusion I have usually only listed the first usage. In the Notes column I have also noted the occurrence of these words in the Northumberland Manuscript annotations of *Leicester's Commonwealth* (see appendix 2).

| Halle Folio K & L page | Halle Annotator D | Worsley 36 Annotator A | Worsley 47 Annotator B | Notes |
|---|---|---|---|---|
| f.ii, 127 | Howses | Howses 41V & 43V | Howses 41 & 44 | |
| f.iii | The duke of Herford | | Earle of Herford 44 | D & B |
| f.iv<sup>a</sup> | Kynge | King 17, 44, 52V, 53, 53V, 58, | Kinge 48V, & 50V | |
| f.iv<sup>b</sup> | Duke of Norfolk | Duke of Norff: 54, 54V, 55 | Duke of Norffc. 54, 55 | |
| | John of gaunt | Jo: of Gaunt 42V John of Gaunt 42V | John of Gaunt Duke of Lanc: 42V John of Gaunte 42V, 43 | |
| f.iv<sup>b</sup> 128 | Edmund duke (of) yorke | | Edmund of Langley the First duke of Yorke 43V | D & B |
| | murther | His murthers 64V | | D & A |
| | assur(ed) | | assurance 30V | D & B |
| | friendly | freinds. | frnds 4V, 31V | |
| f.v<sup>a</sup> f.ix<sup>b</sup> 138 f.x<sup>b</sup> 138 | embassie embassadors embassadours | Embassadresse 9 | Emba: 10V | |
| f.v<sup>a</sup> 128 | Arundell | Arundell 24V, 55V | Arund 24V Arundell 55V | |
| | archebishop of cant' | Archbishop Of Cant: 9 Archbyp of Cant: 30 | Archb: Of Canter: 10V Archb: Of Caunterb: 30 | |

236

| | | | | |
|---|---|---|---|---|
| | Henry duke of (la)ncaster | | Hen: Duke of Lancaster 35V | D & B |
| f.vi[b] | Kynge Richard Kinge Ric' | | Ric 2 35V Rich 2 43 | D & B |
| f.vii[a] | (To)wer at london | Tower 21V y[e] Tower 26 | the Tower: 25V | |
| | the parliament a parliament | parliament 37V Parliam[t] 43V | | D & A |
| f.ix[a] | the crowne | The Crown 25, 35, 47 the crowne 32 | the crowne. 25 | |
| | pleasure | pleasure. 27V | pleasure 27V | |
| f.ix[b] | money | Money 13, 23 | money 14V, 23 | |
| f.x[a] | Dyvisyon | Division 47 | | D & A |
| | heares male | heire 37V | heire 37, 37V, 43V, 57 | |
| | bothe (t)he howses yorke and lancastre | both Howses 41V Yorke & Lancaster. 40, 42V the 2 houses of Lanc: & Yorke. 43V | both howses. 41V, 44 York & Lancast: 40V, Yorke and Lancaster 42V | |
| | a sleight counsel | sleight 35 sleights. 55 counsaill 19, 24V | councell 24V | D & A C (NHMS) has 'sleight'. |
| f.x[b] | Kinge henry | K: Hen: 6 | K.Hen: 35V K. Henr: 7[th] 43, 44 | |
| f.xii[a] 129 | henry the iiiith | | Henr: 4. 42V | D & B |
| | at oxford | Oxforde. 26V, 27 | in Oxford 13V, 26 | |
| f.xiii[b] | the treason | Treason 3, 41 | treason 3V, 41 | |

| | | | | |
|---|---|---|---|---|
| f.xiv[a] | ancestor | Ancestrors. 9, 41, 58 | ancesto[rs] 57V | In Halle's text the word 'conspirator' is not used. D & A |
| f.xvii[a] 129 | conspiratowes conspiratour | conspirators 35V, 37, 39, 44V | conspirato[rs] 35 conspirators 37 45V | |
| | execution | execution 36V Executions 59 | | |
| f.xviii[a] 130 | scottes | Scotts 48, 52V, 53, 54 | Scotts 45V, 49, 52V | |
| f.xviii[a] & fxx[a] f.xviii[b] | lord percey The Pearcyes | The Perrceys 36 | The Peirceyes 35V | |
| | into Wales | Wales 21 in Wales 29 | In Wales 21V, 29 | |
| fxix[b] fxii[b] 139 | practize of Rebells rebelles | practice 5, 14, 34V; Rebells 59V | practices 6, 34V Rebells 58V | C (NHMS) has 'practice'. A remarkable coincidence: that the words 'rebells' and 'wolf' occur so close together in Halle & in Worsley MSS 36 & 47 we find "wolves & Rebells". C (NHMS) has 'death'. |
| fxx[a] 130 | The wolf | wolves 59 | wolves 58V | |
| fxxii[a] | The clayme of | clayme, 40V the clayme of 43V | clayme. 40V, 44 | |
| | the deathe of | The death of 9V, 10, 11, 59, 62V, | The death of 10V, 11, 14, 58V, 61V | |
| fxxii[b] 131 | the battayle | The Battayle 40V | The Battle 40V | |
| fxxiii[a] | a good corage | A good wishe 4V; good 6, 13 | good 14V | |
| | gret | great 17, 28, 37V, 39V, 42, 57V, 59 | great 27V, 58V greate 57 | C (NHMS) has 'great'. |
| fxxiii[b] | the castell | castell 22 | | D & A |
| fxxiv[a] fxxv[b] | of Calyse calice | of Callice 24V | of Callis 24 | |
| fxxv[a] | englisshe | English 5 | Engli: 6 | |

| | | | | |
|---|---|---|---|---|
| | | sonne | sonne 37, 57, | sonne 37, 42V, 43, 43V, 44, 49, 52, 57, 57V | Crystal (2008), states that Shakespeare's preferred spelling is sonne not son. C (NHMS) has 'sonne'. |
| fxxv[b] | | earle of northumberland | Duke of Northumberland 31V | the Duke of Northumberland 31, 34, 49V, 59 | |
| fxxvi[a] | | execution | execution 36V | execucõns 58V | |
| fxxvi[b] 132 | | the prince of | the prince 20V, 26V, 31, 52V, 58V, 62V | the Prince 20V, 23V, 30V, 52V, 58, 61V | |
| | | duke of yorke | | duke of Yorke 43V, 59 | D & B |
| | | Scotland | Scotland 21V, 44, 49V, 57V | Scotland 57 | |
| | | the scottes | Scotts 49, 52V, 53, 54 | Scotts 45V, 46V, 49, 52V | |
| fxxviii[b] 132 | | foren | forreyn 3V, 24, 46V<br>Forreyne 43<br>Forreigne 46<br>Forryn 49V | forraine 4V<br>fforraigne 24<br>fforraine 45V, 46 | |
| f.xxix[a] 133 | | rebellyon | rebellion 7, 19 | Rebellion 8 | |
| | | spoyle of a towne | spoyling of Oxforde. | | D & A |
| f.xxix[b] | | mariage | mariage 7, 7V | marriage 8<br>mariag 9<br>mariage 18 | |
| f.xxx[a] | | fraunce | France 3V, 7V, 9, 50, 61 | ffraunce 4V, 10V, 39, 60<br>ffrance 9 | |
| | | slayne | slayne 19V | | D & A |
| | | doctor | D. 9, 16V; 27V<br>Do: 10, 14 | Doct 41;<br>Do[r] 11V<br>Do: 16, 18, 27 | Several doctors are listed in MSS 36 & 47 listed as D. |
| | | An othe taken and not regardyd | His oath prophaned 66V | his oaths profaned 65V | Broken oaths are a theme of early plays. |

| | | | | |
|---|---|---|---|---|
| fxxx[a]<br>fxxx[b] | discention, civil discenscyon | Dissention 61 | dissention 60 | Shakespeare uses 'dissension' in *Henry VI* part 1 (4.1.139). |
| fxxxi[a] 134 | Guyen | Guineans 5 | Gunians 6 | |
| fxxxii[a] | England | Engl 5, 40, 48, Englande. 19, 53, 55V<br>England 63 | England 6, 20, 42, 62<br>Engl: 40V | |
| | abrode | abroade 17V, 21V | abroade 21 | |
| fxxxii[b] | favour | favour 24 | favor 2, 23V<br>favour 65V | |
| fxxxii[b] 135 | enemye | Enemies 34<br>enemyes 53V | enimi: 34 | |
| Henry V<br>fxxxii[b] | counsel | counsaill 19, 24V | councell 24V | |
| fii[a] | counsellers | counsellor 34 | | D & A |
| | calamitye | | calamitie 40V | D & B |
| fiii[a] 136 | persones | persons IV<br>person. 15V, 62V | persons 2, 62<br>person 61V | |
| | favourer | favourors 57 | | D & A |
| fiii[b] | traytors. | Traytors 4 | trayt: 5 | |
| | hanged | hanged 19V, 27V | hanged 20, 27V | |
| fiv[b] | tytle | tytle 44<br>title 31V, 41, 42, 43V, 44, 46V, 52V, 57 | tytle 31V, 44, 46V, 56V<br>title 41, 42 | |
| fv[a] | an usurper | | an vsurper 48V, 57 | D & B |
| fv[b] | The lawe | The Law 6V | The Lawe 39<br>Lawe 7V | |
| | boke | booke 20, 25V | booke 25V | |

|  |  | successy(on) | succession 31V, 49V | succession 31V, 33V, 38V, 49V |  |
|---|---|---|---|---|---|
|  |  | dog(hter) to Kinge | daughter to | daughter to 44V daugh: of K: 44 |  |
| fv[b] 137 |  | diverse | Divers 8V, 10 | diverse 9V, 11V |  |
| fvii[b] |  | testament | testament 49, 50 | testam[te] 45V, 49, 50V |  |
| f.viii[a] |  | secunde | Second 44, 48V, 50 | seconde 49V |  |
| f.viii[b] |  | pleasure | pleasure 27V | pleasure 27V |  |
| f.ix[a] |  | oration | oration 38 | oracõn 38 |  |
| f.ix[b] 138 |  | Julius | Julius 58V | Julius 58 |  |
|  |  | bankett |  | banqueting 25 | D & B |
|  |  | straungers | Strangers 39V | straungers 39V, 40V | D & B agree on spelling. |
| f.x[a] |  | agayne | again 18 V againe 51V | againe 19 |  |
| f.x[b] |  | policie | Policy 5V policey 44V | pollicie 6V |  |
| f.xi[b] |  | realme | Realme 39V, 40V, 61, 65 | Realme 37V, 40V, 47, 60, 64 |  |
| f.xii[b] 139 |  | attaynted | attainted 41, 43V | attaynted 41 |  |
| f.xxi[b] 142 |  | religyon | Religion 5, 8, 51V, 52V | Relligion 6 religion 52, 52V |  |
| f.xxv[b] 143 |  | power | power 16V, 20V | power 17V, 21 |  |
| f.xxvi[b] 144 |  | subiectes | subiects 6 | subiects 64 |  |
| f.xxvii[b] |  | daungerose | danger 18V | daunger 19, 38V | D & B agree on spelling. |
| f.xxix[a] 145 |  | pitiuse | pitiful 12, 28V | pittifull 14, 28 |  |

241

| | | | | |
|---|---|---|---|---|
| f.xxxvi<sup>b</sup> 146 | wiff | wief 8, 9V, 14, 34V | wief 10V, 15V, 34V | C spells wife 'wief' in NHMS. |
| f.xli<sup>a</sup> 147 | descende | | descent 41V | D & B |
| f.xlii<sup>a</sup> | pedigree | pedigree 42V | pedigree 43 | |
| f.xlv<sup>a</sup> 148 | The duke of Clarence | The Duke of Clarence 43V, 31V | Duke of Clarence 43, 43V, 44, 31V | |
| Henry VI | | | | |
| f.i<sup>a</sup> | duke of Bedford | Earle of Bedforde 21 | Earl of Bedd: 21V | |
| | duke of glocester | Du: of Glou: 35, | Duke of Gloucester 44, 57, 35 | C (NHMS) has D of Gloc. |
| | preparation | preparations 7 preparacõn 22 preparacõns 31 | p<sup>r</sup>paracõn 8 preparacõn 22 preperãcon 31 | |
| f.ii<sup>b</sup> 150 | proclam(ed) | proclamacõn 37V | proclimacõn 37 | |
| | himsellf | himselfe 8V, 32V, 35, himself 26, 32 | himselfe 26, 35 himself 32V | |
| | name | name 47V | named 43V | |

D & B match annotations 12 times, twice more on spelling, indeed B's spellings are closer to D than A's are to D.

D & A match annotations 10 times.

D & B's matches are of more substance, of named figures, such as Edmund Duke of York and Henry Duke of Lancaster, whereas D & A agree on individual words such as 'slayne', 'castell' and 'division'. The closer match between D and B are suggestive of Henry Neville being the annotator of both documents.

Perhaps it is purely coincidence that the last of the shared annotations should be the word 'name'.

# Appendix 4

## The Vocabulary of *Look About You*

If *Look About You* is a very early work by the bard we would not expect the vocabulary to be so well developed as in later plays but could reasonably expect there to be tell tale habits, such as using 'un-', 'dis-' and hyphenated words. I also look at the incidence of words used in the Phaeton sonnet which I have previously used to examine the vocabulary of early works (Casson, 2009).

**'Un' Words in *Look About You***

There are 22 'un' words used 27 times; of these 16 are to be found in the Shakespeare canon [frequency in square brackets]; there are 5 words that are not used by the bard but of these, 3 have close equivalents, such as 'untrussing' instead of 'untruss'd'.

Unrestful: [0] (unrest x [8])
Unpeopled: [4]
Untainted: [7]
Unchaste x 3: [4]
Uncase x 2: [1] *Edmund Ironside*
Uncased: [0] (uncase: *The Taming of The Shrew*)
Undefiled: [0]
Unjust x 3: [23] *Thomas of Woodstock*
Unjustly: [8] *Troublesome Raigne*
Unkind: [29] *Arden of Faversham, Locrine, Edmund Ironside*
Unsent for: [0]
Untutor'd: [5] *Edmund Ironside* (untutored x 2); also in dedication of *Rape of Lucrece*
Untruss'd: [0] (untrussing: *Measure for Measure*)
Unblest: [1]
Unthrift: [3]
Undeserved: [5] *Arden of Faversham, Edmund Ironside*,
Unlucky: [6] *Arden of Faversham, Troublesome Raigne* (unluckily: *Thomas of Woodstock*)
Unlawful: [11]
Unlookt-for: [1]
Unheard-of: [1] *Thomas of Woodstock*; *Edward III* (without hyphen)

243

Unheard: [4] *Edmund Ironside*
Uncivil: [8] *Locrine, Troublesome Raigne, Edmund Ironside, Edward III*

22 'un' words (used 27 times) is the same number as in *Locrine* (22 words used 30 times). In *The Troublesome Raigne of John* there are 38 'un' words used 52 times. Sams (1986, 351) stated that the average was 40 occurrences in each Shakespeare play. I have also listed the frequency of these words in the apocryphal plays I have found are early works by Neville (see Casson, 2009). Of the words used in *Look About You* the following numbers occur in these plays:

*Edmund Ironside*: 6
*Arden of Faversham*: 3
*Troublesome Raigne*: 3
*Thomas of Woodstock*: 2/3
*Locrine*: 2

In my concluding chapter 9, I have suggested the early works were as follows:

*Mucedorus* 1584-5 (published anonymously 1598, revised 1610)
*Look About You* 1585-6 (published anonymously 1600)
*Arden of Faversham* 1586-88, (published anonymously 1592)
*Locrine* 1586-89 (published as by W.S. in 1595)
*Edmund Ironside* 1587-8 (never published: one manuscript)
*The Troublesome Raigne of John* 1587-8 (published anonymously 1591)
*Thomas of Woodstock* 1592-3 (never published: one manuscript)

It is therefore interesting to see how the 'un' words increase through these works. I have listed the number used later by Shakespeare and then in [square brackets] the number the bard did not use in later works:

*Mucedorus* 15 used 24 times; Shakespeare canon 7, [7]
*Look About You* 22 used 27 times; Shakespeare canon 16, [6]
*Arden of Faversham* 19 used 23 times; Shakespeare canon 16, [3]
*Locrine* 22 used 31 times; Shakespeare canon 16, [5]
*Edmund Ironside* 36 used 39 times, Shakespeare canon 30; [6]
*The Troublesome Raigne*: 39 used 51 times; Shakespeare canon 34, [6]

This might be used as evidence for dating *Arden of Faversham* earlier. Holinshed is a source of all these except *Mucedorus*.

**Dis - words: 18**
dishonoured [3] *Arden of Faversham* (dishonour: *Arden of Faversham, Edmund Ironside* and *Troublesome Raigne*)
disdaine [41] *Troublesome Raigne, Edmund Ironside*, (disdainer, disdained *Mucedorus*; disdain'd and disdained *Troublesome Raigne*;)
disgrace [52] *Mucedorus, Troublesome Raigne* (disgraced *Edmund Ironside*)
displeasure [42] *Mucedorus, King John* (displeased: *Arden of Faversham*)
dislike [18] *Mucedorus, Arden of Faversham* (and in Neville's letter 27/6/1599)
disquiet [3]
dispos'd [0] (disposed 27: *King John*), (disposed *Mucedorus*; dispose *Edmund Ironside*)
discharge [30] *Arden of Faversham, Troublesome Raigne*, (discharged: *Arden of Faversham*; discharging *Troublesome Raigne*)
dismaying [0] (dismayed *Mucedorus*, dismay 6, *Edmund Ironside*)
dispatch [70] *Troublesome Raigne, Edmund Ironside, King John* (dispatch'd *Arden of Faversham*)
dispaire [59] *Edmund Ironside, King John,* (dispairing: *Arden of Faversham, Edmund Ironside*)
dispight [0] (despite 56: *King John*)
disguise [19], *Mucedorus* (disguised x 2, disguisement *Edmund Ironside*)
discovered [9] *Troublesome Raigne*, (discover *Arden of Faversham, Edmund Ironside*)
distrest [0] (distressed 10), (distress, distressed *Mucedorus*; distress'd and distressed *Troublesome Raigne*, distress *Troublesome Raigne*; distressful: *Arden of Faversham*)
dismist [0] (dismissed 3)
disturb [13] *Troublesome Raigne*, (disturbance, disturb'd *Mucedorus*; disturbing/disturbed: *Arden of Faversham*; disturber *Troublesome Raigne*) (disturbance, disturbed, *Edmund Ironside*)
dispute [5] *Troublesome Raigne*

This list shows that *Look About You* is closest to *The Troublesome Raigne*:

*Mucedorus* 4 (5 near misses)
*Arden of Faversham* 3 (7 near misses)
*Edmund Ironside* 3 (8 near misses)
*Troublesome Raigne* 7 (5 near misses)
*King John* 5

**Hyphenated words:** (in the 1600 Quarto)
I have put the number of times a hyphenated pair of words is used in canonical works in [square brackets]. I have then listed when they are used in apocryphal works and put other uses in brackets.

High-way [0: 5 with no hyphen] *Thomas of Woodstock*
Bed-fellow [3: 10 with no hyphen] *Mucedorus*
Run-awaies [0: 3 with no hyphen] runaways x 2: *Edmund Ironside*; (run away *Mucedorus*; *Arden of Faversham*; *The Troublesome Raigne*; *Edmund Ironside*; *Edward III*; *Thomas of Woodstock*)
Newes-thirsting [thirsting 1] (according to LION, unique)
Unheard-of [0: unheard 1] *Thomas of Woodstock*; (unheard of *Edward III*)
Low-priz'd [0] (high-prized *Thomas of Woodstock*)
Home-bred [3] *Edmund Ironside*
hayre-brain'd [2: hare brain'd and hair brain'd in *Henry VI* part 1] (harebrain *Arden of Faversham*; hare-brain *Thomas of Woodstock*; hare brained *Edward III*)
Weather-cocke [1]
bloud-sucker [1] (bloodsucker *The Troublesome Raigne*; blood-sucking *Locrine*; sucked their blood *Thomas of Woodstock*; suck thy blood *Mucedorus*; suckst her blood *Edward III*)
halfe-penny [1: 6 with no hyphen] half-penny-worth *Henry IV* part 1 (halfpenny *Edward III*; *Sir Thomas More* section by Hand D = Shakespeare)
Apron-strings [0] (apron-men *Coriolanus*)
Mile-End's [Mile-end x 2]
Graves-end [0] (mentioned by Neville in a letter dated 27/6/1599)
heart-sigh's [0] ("heart-sore sighs" twice in *Two Gentlemen of Verona*)
birth-right [0: 4 with no hyphen] (birthright *The Troublesome Raigne*; *Thomas of Woodstock*)
never-changing [0]
hate-corrupted [0] (according to LION, unique)
fore-telling [0: foretell x 5] (foretelling *Locrine*; foretelleth *The Troublesome*

*Raigne*; foretells *Thomas of Woodstock*; foretold *Edward III*)
hel-hound [2: hell hound] hell-hound *Mucedorus*; (hellhound *Thomas of Woodstock*)
Blacke-heath [0: 1 with no hyphen] also in the annotations of Halle's *Chronicle*
Golde-smith [0: 9 with no hyphen, all in *The Comedy of Errors*]
Out-fac'd [4] ("I'll face her out" *Mucedorus*)
fore-spoken [0]
over-seer [0] (overseer *The Troublesome Raigne*)
hob-goblin [0: 2 with no hyphen]

For this list I added the words used exactly to those that are near misses.

*Mucedorus* 5
*Arden of Faversham* 3
*Locrine* 2
*The Troublesome Raigne* 5
*Edmund Ironside* 3
*Edward III* 6
*Thomas of Woodstock* 9

*Edward III* has now been accepted into the canon of Shakespeare's works and it can only be a matter of time before *Thomas of Woodstock* is likewise accepted. Given that, as I have previously suggested, *Look About You* followed after *Mucedorus*, it is not surprising to find a relatively high number of these words being used in that play. I have already shown there is a strong relationship between *Look About You* and *The Troublesome Raigne* (in chapter 7).
In *Look About You* there are "home-bred brawles"; in *Richard II* "home-bred hate"; in *Venus & Adonis* "home-bred strife". I suggest this is the same poet writing. In *Look About You* the writer coins a hyphenated "never-changing". The bard hyphenates 'changing' twice: speaking of Richard Neville, Edward IV says, "Wind-changing Warwick now can change no more." (*Henry VI* part 3: 5.1.57); the Bastard Faulconbridge (another hidden Neville) in *King John* speaks of Commodity as, "this all-changing word" (2.1.582) and in the same speech hyphenates "purpose-changer" (2.1.567).

**Phaeton sonnet words**
In my previous book I examined the 1591 Phaeton sonnet and found there

was good evidence not only for it being an early work by the bard but also for Neville (Casson, 2009). I noticed that Spring, Summer and Winter were mentioned but NOT autumn. The same is true of *Look About You*.
The words "**flowrie pleasance**" occur in the sonnet. In *Look About You* Prince John asks:

> What shall olde winter with his frosty jestes,
> Crosse **flowry pleasure**?          (451)

When comparing the numbers of Phaeton sonnet words in these texts I have also listed near misses, where a comparable word such as 'wit' instead of 'wits' is present. I have listed the number of these after the totals, as 17:7 in the case of *Look About You* (17 direct hits and 7 near misses). Whilst the following chart does not provide any conclusive evidence it points towards *Look About You* being one of the early works of Shakespeare-Neville.

## Phaeton sonnet words in Apocryphal Plays:

| Word↓ | Mucedorus | Look About You | Arden Faversham | Troubles. Raigne | Locrine | Edmund Ironside | Downfall | Death |
|---|---|---|---|---|---|---|---|---|
| sweet | √ | √ | √ | √ | √ | √ | √ | √ |
| friend | √ | √ | √ | √ | √ | √ | √ | √ |
| name | √ | √ | √ | √ | √ | √ | √ | √ |
| agrees |  | agree | agree | √ | agree/d | agree/d | agree |  |
| **increase** | √ |  |  | √ |  |  |  |  |
| **rival** |  |  | √ |  |  |  | √ |  |
| Spring | √ | √ | √ | √ | √ | √ | √ | √ |
| **branch** | √ |  |  | √ | √ |  |  |  |
| flourishing |  |  | flourished | flourish |  |  |  |  |
| Summers/'s |  | summer | √ | √ | summer | √ |  |  |
| shady | shadow | shadow | shadows | shade/ow | √ |  | shade |  |
| pleasures | √ | √ | √ | pleasure | √ | √ | pleasure | pleasure |
| cease | √ |  | √ | √ | √ |  |  | √ |
| Winters/'s |  | winter |  | √ |  |  | √ |  |
| storms |  |  | storm/y | storm | √ | √ | √ | storm |
| repose |  |  | √ |  |  |  |  |  |
| peace | √ | √ | √ | √ | √ | √ | √ | √ |
| spends | spend | √ | spend | spend | spend |  | spend |  |
| franchise |  |  |  |  |  |  |  |  |

| | | | | | | | | |
|---|---|---|---|---|---|---|---|---|
| living | √ | √ | √ | √ | live/s/d | √ | √ | livings |
| thing | √ | √ | √ | √ | √ | √ | √ | √ |
| daisies | | | | | | | | |
| sprout | | | | | √ | | | |
| little | √ | √ | √ | √ | √ | √ | √ | √ |
| birds | √ | | bird | √ | √ | bird | √ | |
| sing | √ | √ | | √ | √ | | √ | √ |
| **herbs** | √ | | | | √ | | | |
| plants | plant | | plant | plant | | plant | | |
| **vaunt** | √ | | | √ | avaunt | | | |
| release | | √ | | | | | | |
| English | England | √ | England | √ | | √ | | √ |
| wits | witless | wit | wit/ted | √ | | √ | √ | √ |
| dead | √ | √ | √ | √ | √ | √ | √ | √ |
| laurel | | | | √ | √ | | | |
| except | √ | √ | √ | √ | √ | √ | √ | |
| green | √ | √ | | √ | √ | √ | √ | √ |
| fruits | | | fruit | fruit | fruit | | | |
| barrenness | | | | barren | √ | barren | | |
| o'erspread | spread | spreads | | | over-spread | spread | over-spreade | |
| flowery | | √ | flowers | flower | flowering | flower | flower | flowers |
| pleasance | pleasures | pleasure | pleasure | pleasant | pleasant | pleasant | | pleasure |
| flowerets | | flowring | flowers | flower | flowers | flower | flowring | flowers |
| morality | | | | | | | | |
| Italy | | | √ | √ | √ | | | |
| Total: | 19: 7 | 17: 7 | 16: 13 | 22: 11 | 22: 10 | 17: 8 | 17: 7 | 13: 6 |

At first this seems to suggest a close relationship between *Look About You* and Munday's *The Downfall* but when we compare the former to other earlier plays we can see that there are a number of near misses that ally it more to them, such as 'shadow' and 'summer'. Furthermore *Look About You* contains specific rare words such as 'release' and 'flowery' that do not occur in *The Downfall* whereas words that appear in the latter and not in *Look About You* are more commonplace, such as 'storms' and 'birds', though the two rarer words, 'rival' and 'over-spread' do occur. When we compare the texts of *Look About You*, *The Troublesome Raigne* and *The Downfall* (as I do in chapter 7) we find however that the relationship is much closer between the first two. This list also shows a relationship between *The Troublesome Raigne* and *Locrine*.

I chose especially to notice the incidence of five particular Phaeton sonnet words: **rival, branch, herbs, increase, vaunt**.

| Play/Poem | Total number of words: | Rare words: |
|---|---|---|
| *Richard II* | 27 | rival, branch, herbs |
| *Henry VI* part 2 | 23 | increase, herbs |
| *Locrine* | 22 | increase, branch, herbs |
| *Henry VI* part 3 | 22 | increase, branch |
| *Edward I* (Peele) | 22 | vaunt |
| *Richard III* | 21 | increase, herbs |
| *Dr. Faustus* (Marlowe) | 21 | branch, herbs, vaunt |
| *The Spanish Tragedy* (Kyd) | 21 | increase, branch |
| *Tamburlaine II* (Marlowe) | 21 | rival, herbs |
| *Titus Andronicus*: | 20 | increase, herbs |
| *The Troublesome Raigne* | 20 | branch, vaunt |
| *James IV* (Greene) | 20 | increase, herbs |
| *The Rape of Lucrece* | 20 | vaunt |
| *Mucedorus* | 19 | increase, branch, herbs, vaunt |
| *Astrophil & Stella* (Sidney) | 18 | increase, herbs |
| *David and Bethsabe* (Peele) | 18 | increase, branch |
| *Two Gentlemen of Verona* | 18 | rival |
| *Love's Labour's Lost* | 18 | branch |
| *Venus & Adonis* | 17 | increase, herbs |
| *Jew of Malta* (Marlowe) | 17 | increase |
| *The Downfall of Robert Earle of Hunt* | 17 | rival |
| *Edmund Ironside* | 17 | |
| *Thomas of Woodstock* | 17 | |
| **Look About You** | **17** | |
| *Taming of The Shrew* | 16 | rival |
| *Henry VI* part 1 | 16 | branch |
| *Arden in Faversham* | 16 | rival |
| *Tamburlaine I* (Marlowe) | 15 | vaunt |
| *The Death of Robert, Earle of Hunt* | 13 | |

What this shows is how *Look About You* falls within a group of early works.

## Appendix 5

## The Date of *Look About You*

*Look About You* is not mentioned in Henslowe's Diary and there are no other records of its stage history, so a definite date for the composition of the play cannot be established. Begor (1965, 61, 83) wondered whether "its author was too daring in his political didacticism, and the work was forcibly removed from the stage." If this was the case the play can be seen to sit alongside *Edmund Ironside* and *Thomas of Woodstock* which were perhaps too politically controversial to be printed. It may simply be that relevant records are missing.

Porohovshikov (1955, 44) pointed out that 20 plays had never been printed in Shakespeare's lifetime, "among which were such matchless productions as Julius Ceasar, Twelfth Night, As You Like It, Measure for Measure, Macbeth, and Anthony and Cleopatra." Thus these works were not published until 20 years after they had been written. There is nothing therefore to preclude *Look About You* being written 15 years before it was finally printed, as I have suggested in chapter 7. However, as Begor dated the play to 1598, let us look further at what she said on the dating.

There are two possible explanations for the relationship of *Look About You* to the Chettle and Munday Robin Hood plays: either *Look About You* was written before or after them. Begor prefers to latter, stating it **must** have been written after *The Downfall of Robert the Earl of Huntington* and *The Death of Robert Earl of Huntington*. An alternative which I have proposed is that it was written before. *Look About You* was definitely published before them, in 1600, whereas *The Downfall* and *The Death* were printed in 1601.
To be fair to Begor, who may be regarded as a major authority on the play, I will review her arguments for a late date.
Begor (1965, 70) found many plot parallels between *Look About You* and *The Downfall* and *The Death*. She therefore thought that *Look About You* depended on them rather than the other way round. She thought all the Shakespeare parallels were evidence of it being written after 1597 as the majority of the parallels were with *Henry IV* part 1. She pointed out that *The Downfall* was completed by February 1598 and *The Death* by March 8[th] (according to Henslowe's diary, when final payments were recorded).

Both plays were licensed for performance on March 28th 1598. She then stated that *Look About You* "**must** have followed actual performances of *The Downfall* and *The Death* of 1598" (Begor, 1865, 50) and therefore be dated between the end of March 1598 and the late fall of 1600. However Begor (1965, 38) pointed out that *Look About You* (LAY) has a much closer relationship with *The Troublesome Raigne* (TR) than with the text of *King John* (KJ), giving four examples of this:

1) In both TR and LAY, Lady Faulconbridge is a virtuous, modest woman; in KJ "she shows little remorse for her adultery with Richard, blaming the king rather than herself".
2) In both TR and LAY, the youth of Lady Faulconbridge and Richard are emphasised: in KJ age is not mentioned.
3) In both TR and LAY, Faulconbridge has been a crusader in the Holy Land.
4) Lady Faulconbridge is named Marian in LAY; she is called Margaret in TR; she is nameless in KJ.

Despite this relationship with a play printed in 1591 Begor (1965, 54) stated that, "All evidence points to a late 1598 or early 1599 date for LAY more probably the former, **though nothing can be proved**." Therefore Begor's insistence that the play **must** have followed the *The Downfall* and *The Death* cannot be said to be proven.

Begor (1965, 53) argued that, "*Look About You* was probably written before October 1599, when *Sir John Oldcastle* was composed; for the escape of Sir John from the Tower of London in *Oldcastle* IV. v. and vi., very closely resembles the escape of Gloster and Skink from the Fleet in *Look About You* and the Oldcastle scenes **seem** derivative rather than original. Secondly the relationship of *Look About You* to *The Downfall* and *The Death* suggests that LAY was written within at least a year and a half of the two Munday-Chettle plays; this would place the comedy between March 1598 and the summer of 1599. Thirdly, there was a tendency among Henslowe's dramatists to produce close together in time a number of plays on a given historical era and thereafter to ignore the period: the only other known Admiral's Men plays dealing with the reign of Henry II, Richard I and John are *The Downfall* and *The Death*, and the non-extant *Funeral of Richard Coeur de Lion*, all written in the spring of 1598, and possibly the non-extant *William Longsword*, entered in Henslowe's Diary in January

1599. Fourthly, the parallels between I *Henry IV* (late 1597) suggest that LAY was written not long after Shakespeare's play – within a year or so at the most – which would place it no later than mid 1599. Finally we have already seen that LAY is deeply involved in Elizabethan politics, its author commenting on current affairs through general historical parallels and there is **perhaps** a deliberate parallel in the play to a specific, domestic political situation existing in England in the summer and early fall of 1598. LAY features an actual quarrel between the English monarch and his favourite; and in the summer of 1598 a bitter quarrel between Elizabeth and Essex occurred, during which Essex drew his sword on the queen. If, therefore, as is **extremely** likely, the quarrel between the Young King and his father in LAY is to be taken as a specific comment upon the Elizabethan political picture when LAY was written, the play **must** have been composed shortly after the quarrel between Essex and Elizabeth probably in the late summer of (or) early fall of 1598." (my added emphasis)

Begor's argument is plausible, although to describe the Young King as the monarch's favourite is stretching it a bit far! However Begor entirely missed the references to *Leicester's Commonwealth* and Mary Queen of Scots. Let us reflect on each of her arguments in turn.

Any copying of Gloster's escape by the writer of *Sir John Oldcastle* could have been done at any time: it provides a date before which the play was written but that is all. The second point is not proven. The third is persuasive but then *The Troublesome Raigne* had been on the stage for a decade. The fourth point is not certain and I have suggested the alternative explanation is that *Look About You* predated *Henry IV* just as *Locrine* did and the latter contains many more parallels to the speeches of Falstaff (see Casson, 2009, 112). The last point is not as certain as Begor suggests. Whilst the quarrel between the Queen and Essex might be analogous to incidents in *Look About You* it is certainly not as definite a source as Begor insists: her frequent resort to '**must**' is an attempt to strengthen a case that is not as certain as she suggests. Begor's case for the date she has chosen is mainly based on the relationship between *Look About You* and the two Munday-Chettle plays. However I have shown there are in fact stronger links between it and *The Troublesome Raigne* which was written ten years before.

Begor (1965, 589) traced the origins of the multiple-disguise comedy to Italian Commedia Dell'Arte. Neville had been to Italy in 1581.

# Appendix 6

*The Famous History of George Lord Fauconbridge*

As stated in chapter 7, a fantastical novel, embroidering the Faulconbridge legend, *The Famous History of George Lord Fauconbridge* appeared in 1616. This is the very year William Shakespeare from Stratford died. I provided evidence that Neville outlived William in appendix 10. Whilst I doubt it is by Shakespeare-Neville I have examined this rare, forgotten work to see whether there is any evidence referring to Shakespeare or Neville in it. I am grateful to Peter Jarvis of the Manchester University John Rylands Library for providing me with a copy of this document, (downloaded from www.lion.chadwyck.co.uk). The novel is comic and serious by turns. Let us begin with an outline of the story.

## The Plot of *The Famous History of George Lord Fauconbridge*

Richard I, on his way to the Holy Land, visits the court of Duke Don John of Austria. Being challenged to a tournament by John's son, Prince Phillip, he kills him. Richard, wounded in the fight, is imprisoned and his knights sent back to England. Two Earls, Arundell and Oxford, disguised as friars, visit Richard, who recovers from his wounds. Clarabel, Don John's daughter, falls in love with Richard. Don John sentences Richard to fight with a lion. Richard tears its heart out, so gaining the title 'Cœur de Lion'. Richard and the Earls leave Austria, Clarabel accompanying them dressed as a page. On the journey back to England she becomes his lover, gaining "the title of a King's Concubine". Clarabel becomes pregnant and whilst she awaits the baby's arrival, Richard sets off secretly to revenge himself on Austria. A boy is born: he is named George Faukonbridge because on his chest is a birthmark of "a golden Faulkon, soaring over a most dangerous bridge". One night the Queen of the Fairies steals the baby. Clarabel and the three nurse maids are grief stricken. Clarabel finds out that Richard has gone to attack her father and now is further distressed by her abandonment and the conflict in her feelings about her father and lover.

Richard is killed in the war in Austria. The defeated army returns to England and crowns John who expels Clarabel from the court. She wanders as a disgraced beggar. Meanwhile Faukonbridge grows up with the Fairies in the forest to be a fine young man. The Queen of the Fairies gives him three gifts: the lion skin his father wore which confers on him courage and victory, a purse of gold which forever renews the wealth inside it and a ring that heals all ills. At the age of fifteen he meets King John in the woods. The King arranges for him to be educated. Faukonbridge "having the lofty spirit of knight-hood springing in his brest" then asks permission to go adventuring. His first knightly encounter is with his own rejected, miserable mother whom he rescues from penury and heals with his ring. At this stage neither recognises the other. They travel together and meet the three destitute nurses who have become dumb, blind and lame. Faukonbridge heals them with his ring. Clarabel asks him to give her the ring and the purse. Chivalrously Faukonbridge gives her these fairy gifts. Whilst she sleeps under a tree on a hot day, a raven flies down and steals the ring. Faukonbridge chases after it but the bird flies out to sea and drops the ring into the waves. Faukonbridge is then taken on board a Moorish ship and transported to Morocco whilst his mother is left desolate. She wanders along the sea shore and with her endless supply of gold from the fairy purse, sets up a monastery and a hospital. A fisherman called Peter gives her a dolphin he has caught and she finds the healing ring in its belly. She has many guests, pilgrims and visitors whom she heals and feeds. However she presumes, because the ring was found in the dolphin, that Faukenbridge is drowned. Grieving, she sets up a golden Falcon on the top of the monastery, naming it St. Peter's Hermitage after the fisherman.

Meanwhile Faukonbridge becomes the prized possession of the Moroccan King. One day he is shocked by a Mohammedan festival and his Christian zeal causes him in a fury to attack and kill 26 nobles. The Moroccan King sends him away on a ship. The ship is becalmed and the crew are nearly starving when they finally arrive at a desert island. Faukonbridge goes in search of food but is abandoned on the island when the crew sail away. Eventually rescued, he ends up at Clarabel's monastery where, seeing the birthmark of the golden falcon over a bridge, she recognises him and they are joyously reunited.

**Sources**

The main source for *The Famous History of George Lord Fauconbridge* is *The Troublesome Raigne of John* which was first published in 1591 and again in 1611. "The Scythian Tamberlaine" is mentioned in a description of massed armies. "The Scythian Tamburlaine" is referred to in the Prologue to *The Troublesome Raigne*. (*King John* was not published until the First Folio in 1623, though it is mentioned in Meres 1598 list of Shakespeare's plays and is believed to date from 1595-6.) However there are a large number of changes and distortions of the original Fauconbridge story: in

*The Troublesome Raigne* Philip Fauconbridge wins the lion skin by killing Limoges, the Austrian Duke, whereas in *The Famous History* it is given to George by the Queen of the Fairies. *The Troublesome Raigne* is a history with one character who is fictional. *The Famous History* is a romantic fiction with almost no real history. Traditional folk tales of fairies and stolen babies are also sources.

**The date**

It is very unlikely that the piece was written and immediately published. It is more likely that it was written some time before. What evidence is there in the text suggesting a date? The date of publication is very mysterious: being published immediately after the death of the writer who invented the Fauconbridge family we must suspect that someone published it at that time because they felt free to do so. As a romance where a parent and a long lost child are reunited it fits themes of Shakespeare's late plays. As such perhaps it was written between 1611 (when *The Troublesome Raigne* was republished) and 1612. The last plays of Shakespeare are dated as follows:

*Pericles*: 1608-9
*Cymbeline* 1609-10
*The Winter's Tale* 1610-11
*The Tempest* 1611-12
*Cardenio/Double Falshood* (with Fletcher) 1612
*Henry VIII* (with Fletcher) 1613-14
*The Two Noble Kinsmen* (with Fletcher) 1613-14

*The Famous History of George Lord Fauconbridge* has more in common with the plays 1608-1612 than the last two. The story of an illegitimate boy who lost his mother and was finally reunited with her would appeal to Neville, the illegitimate boy who lost his mother when aged just ten. He wrote three plays, *The Comedy of Errors*, *Pericles* and *The Winter's Tale* about children being reunited with long lost mothers. He used the Faulconbridge name in six plays:
*Henry VI* part 1 (4.7.67); *Henry VI* part 3 (1.1.239) *Love's Labours Lost* (2.1.42); *The Merchant of Venice* (1. 2. 66); *Henry V*, (3.5.44 and 4.8.100) and of course *King John*.

**Hints of Shakespeare's plays**

The imagery of the baby being stolen by the Fairy Queen recalls *The*

*Midsummer Night's Dream* and the argument between Oberon and Titania over the Indian boy.
Fauconbridge, aged 15, is found in the woods, "like vnto a sauage satyr". This recalls the unrecognised princes in the woods in *Cymbeline*.
The desert island recalls *The Tempest*.
The Moors remind one of *Othello*.
The reunion with the mother recalls *Pericles* and *The Winter's Tale*.

## Disguise
The Earls of Arundell and Oxford visit the imprisoned Richard disguised as friars. Clarabel disguises as a page boy to elope with Richard.

## Chastity before marriage
This is an important theme in *The Famous History* and much of Shakespeare. *George Lord Fauconbridge* is a bastard and his mother is called the "King's Concubine".

## Characters and names
Rosamund is mentioned in *Look About You* which also tells a story of a Faukenbridge, see chapter 7.
Claribel is the name of the King Alonso's daughter in *The Tempest*. She marries the King of Tunis before the play starts.
Don John is the villainous bastard brother of the Prince of Aragon in *Much Ado About Nothing*.
Adonis is to be found in *The Taming of The Shrew*, Sonnet 53 and *Venus and Adonis*.

## Vocabulary
There are some rare words used in *The Famous History*. These might of course simply be due to coincidence, or evidence that the writer had read Shakespeare.

'hunger-starved': Shakespeare uses this once with a hyphen in *Henry VI* part 3 and once without in *Pericles*. The word 'hongersterv(ed)' is in a Halle's *Chronicle* annotation (Keen & Lubbock, 1954, 132).
'inthronised': the rare word 'enthronized' is in *Locrine* (2.2.24) and Neville wrote 'inthronize' in a letter dated 2/11/1600 (James, 2008, 158). Whilst the word is not used in any canonical work it is recalled in *Thomas of Woodstock* when Richard II says, "this day we will be new enthronished" (2.2.114).

'clip': 'clipping' is used in *Look About You*.
"unlookt for" (twice): is also in *Look About You*.
'tirannous': Shakespeare uses 'tyrannous' 14 times. Neville used the word 'tirannous' (spelt with an 'i') in a letter dated 20/3/1600 (Winwood, 1725, Vol 1, 161).
"bereaved of, bereave me of life, bereft of": these phrases were often used by Shakespeare and in the early works and were used by Neville in a letter dated 27/6/1599 (see Casson, 2009, 121-2 and Winwood, 1725, Vol 1, 52).
"seas of blood covered the green fields": the image of red blood on green grass is often found in early works such as *Locrine* and in *Richard II* where Richard says, "Her pastures' **grass** with faithful English **blood**." (3.3.100).
"collop of her own flesh": see *Henry VI* part 1, "a **collop** of my flesh" (5.4.18)

Three words also occur in Worsley MSS 47 (see chapter 3): 'banqueting', 'contrarieties', "great grief".

Whilst this list is short and these words might simply occur by chance or be the result of the writer reading Shakespeare's works, their occurrence together is suggestive of some connection. At the least it seems that the writer probably knew *Look About You*. There are also some elements of blot cluster: "spotting her name, stain, blemisheth, staind with shame, blotted her good name, that spot", but these lack the other words usually associated with the cluster so it is highly unlikely that Neville himself wrote *The Famous History*. I note however that all these references to shame are to a woman: was the writer of this novel a woman familiar with Shakespeare/ Neville's vocabulary?

### Who was the anonymous writer?
There is some evidence that this piece may have been written by a woman. The writer describes Clarabel's pregnancy, the birth of Faukonbridge and her grief at the loss of the child with an eye for emotional detail that suggests some experience. Is *The Famous History* by Anne Neville (Killigrew)? She had at least one child die young. The story is of a shamed woman with an illegitimate child: Anne may well have had an illegitimate child, Edward (who scribbled in the Halle *Chronicle*, see chapter 4) when Neville was in the Tower. Whilst Neville expressed his guilt and shame in a series of plays in

which the women are innocent *(Othello, Pericles, Cymbeline, The Winter's Tale, The Tempest, Cardenio/Double Falshood* and *Henry VIII)*, Anne might have used this novel to explore her guilt as a woman in relation to a knightly, noble, suffering man. This however must remain purely speculation until more evidence is available. However it is not simply empty speculation. The alternative, namely that an unknown writer, with no connection to the Nevilles, would embroider the Faukonbridge legend and publish the work immediately after the deaths of Henry Neville and William Shakespeare, is perhaps more far fetched than the secret connections I have suggested.

**Is this a tribute to Neville?**
The name George is very obviously not accurate to *The Troublesome Raigne* or *King John* where the Bastard Fauconbridge is called Phillip. I wonder whether G (for George), being the previous letter in the alphabet to H (for Henry), is as close as the writer felt she could get without identifying Neville by his first name. Whilst this may at first seem too speculative, the Muses are said to have danced at Faukonbridge's birth: surely this identifies him as a poet? Faukonbridge is described as "noble minded" and having "a lofty spirit of Knighthood". Neville was regarded as a "noble knight" and actively hoped for a revival of chivalric values in his involvement with James I's son, Henry. Shakespeare's last play (written with Fletcher) was based on Chaucer's *Knight's Tale* and is about two chivalrous knights.

**Conclusion**
Was this the plot of a play that never was written? Was it Anne's way of saying goodbye to Henry Neville? As the only piece of writing about a fictional bastard Fauconbridge that is not by Shakespeare-Neville, I suspect some connection to him but at this point nothing can be proved and this remains speculation.

## Appendix 7

### *Mucedorus* and *Leicester's Commonwealth*

This is a section of a chapter, with updated additions, from my previous book: *Enter Pursued by a Bear* (Casson, 2009, 54 - 57) in which I showed that *Mucedorus* was Neville's first comedy, written in about 1584-5, almost a decade before he began using the Shakespeare pseudonym.

In *Mucedorus* a bear appears on stage. This was probably an actor in costume: Mouse describes the bear as "some devil in a bear's doublet" (1.2.4). The bard refers to bears 49 times. The bear was a symbol for the Earls of Warwick, who were Henry Neville's ancestors. In *Henry VI* part 2, Warwick says:

> Now, by my father's badge, old **Nevil's** crest,
> The rampant **bear** chain'd to the ragged staff…        (5.1.202)

Here Warwick (Richard Neville) by his father, means his father-in-law, Richard Beauchamp: it was through his wife, Anne, Beauchamp's daughter, that Richard became the Earl of Warwick. The mistake however reveals the **Nevil** connection. Earlier in the same play The Duke of York, (who married Cecily Neville) says:

> Call hither to the stake my two brave **bears**,
> That with the very shaking of their chains
> They may astonish these fell-lurking curs:
> Bid **Salisbury** and **Warwick** come to me.        (5.1.144)

The Earl of **Salisbury** was Richard Neville (1400-60) and his son the Earl of **Warwick** Richard Neville (1428-71: the King Maker). Clifford replies:

> Are these thy **bears**? We'll bait thy **bears** to death.
> And manacle the **bear**-ward in their chains,
> If thou darest bring them to the baiting place.        (5.1.148)

Again in *Henry VI* part 3 King Edward refers to: "two brave **bears**, **Warwick** and **Montague** that in their chains fettered the kingly lion" (5.7.10). Both men were Nevilles: Richard Neville (The King Maker) the Earl of **Warwick** and his brother, John Neville, Marquis of **Montague**. Richard, Duke of Gloucester, (soon to be King Richard III, a Plantagenet-Neville (who will marry Anne Neville), calls himself, "an unlicked **bear-whelp**" in *Henry VI* part 3 (3.2.161). Edmund the bastard in *King Lear* says he was born under Ursa Major (the Great **Bear** constellation: 1.2.127). Bears continue to appear occasionally in other plays: in *The Comedy of Errors* (written between 1589-94) Dromio of Syracuse says,

> As from a **bear** a man would run for life,
> So fly I from her that would be my wife.    (3.2.153)

This, in one of Shakespeare's earliest plays, sounds like a memory of Segasto and Mouse fleeing the bear in *Mucedorus* or of Dametas fleeing the bear in the *Arcadia*. All this is comic but there may be a serious reason for fleeing a bear if that bear is murderous. In *Leicester's Commonwealth* (1584) Robert Dudley, the Earl of Leicester, is referred to as such directly: "my Lord of Leicester (whom you call the **Bearwhelp**)..." (Peck, 2006, 61). Neville had two copies of this banned document, which were discovered by Brenda James amongst the Worsley Manuscripts at the Lincolnshire Archives. Neville annotated *Leicester's Commonwealth* with references that link up with Shakespeare's history plays. Two of these annotations pick out the bear. The text reads:

"You know the bear's love, said the gentleman, which is all for his own paunch, and so this **Bearwhelp** turneth all to his own commodity, and for greediness thereof will overturn all if he be not stopped or muzzled in time." (Peck, 2006, 53)

Worsley MSS 47, 6V

Here, in the margin, Neville has written '**Beares**'. Furthermore the politics of this **bear** image are further developed in the document:

"my Lord of Leicester is very well known to have no title to the crown himself, either by descent in blood, alliance, or otherways... he **will play**

**the Bear** when he cometh to dividing of the prey and will snatch the best part to himself." (Peck, 2006, 86)

Robert Dudley was not only linked with a bear by the authors of *Leicester's Commonwealth*. The prey Dudley was after was of course Queen Elizabeth herself. In 1573 Dudley gave Elizabeth I "a fan of white feathers set in a gold handle decorated with emeralds, diamonds and rubies, on each side a **white bear** and two pearls hanging a lion ramping with a white bear at his feet." Dudley had received a gift of "**white bears**" from the Muscovy Company in 1571 (Haynes, 1987, 100). In *Mucedorus* we find:

Segasto:  Thou talkest of wonders, to tell me of **white bears**.
          But, sirra, didst thou ever see any such?

Mouse:    No, faith, I never saw any such, but I remember
          My father's words: he bade me take heed I was
          Not caught with a **white bear**.       (1.4.39)

This dangerously political warning (the play was performed before Elizabeth I) is disguised in a pun on 'wight' = person/woman = white and bear = bare/naked, and is delivered by a seemingly innocuous clown. Neville's father did warn his son about Robert Dudley's ambitions. Dudley was believed to have poisoned the Earl of Essex, murdered his own wife and to have ambitious designs to take over the kingdom. Mucedorus saves the princess Amadine from a dangerous bear and from the unwanted suitor Segasto: the princess stands in for Elizabeth I. This identification is further suggested by the following from *Leicester's Commonwealth* which describes Robert Dudley's "hasty preparation to rebellion and assault of her Majesty's royal person and dignity… she should once fall within the compass of his furious **paws**, seeing such a smoke of **disdain**…" (Peck, 2006, 92). Just ten lines later the name Amadis occurs in the text. Is this a possible source then for the name of the princess Amadine? She speaks of:

> that ugly bear,
> But all in vain, for, why, he reached after me,
> And hardly I did oft escape his **paws**…(2.4.53)

Furthermore at the start of the play Comedy (a woman) confronts Envy (a man):

> Thou, **bloody,** Envious, **disdain**er of men's joy,
> Whose name is fraught with **bloody stratagems**,
> Delights in nothing but in spoil and death,
> Where thou maist trample in their luke warm blood,
> And grasp their hearts within thy cursed **paws**...
(Induction, 41)

In *Leicester's Commonwealth* the words '**disdain**', '**paws**', '**bloody**' and '**stratagems**' all relate to Robert Dudley. In the Shakespeare canon a **paw** just once belongs to a baited **bear** – who is none other than Richard Neville, the Earl of Warwick (in *Henry VI* part 2, 5.1.153). Ambrose, Robert Dudley's brother, became Earl of Warwick in 1561 and so the bear and ragged staff were his emblems. Neville had an argument with Ambrose in 1583. I have suggested *Mucedorus* was written 1584-5. A story in which a bear is killed and a proud, unwanted suitor is displaced might well express Neville's feelings towards the Dudleys.

Furthermore the writer of *Leicester's Commonwealth* warns: "**Hastings**, for aught I see, when he cometh to the scambling is like to have no better luck by **the Bear** than his ancestor had once by **the Boar**" (Peck, 2006, 90). As William Hastings the Lord Chamberlain goes to his execution in Shakespeare's *Richard III*, he recalls a dream of a **boar** (3.4.87). Richard III is symbolised by the **boar** repeatedly in the play. Bremo, the wild man in *Mucedorus*, asks:

> Who knows not Bremo's strength,
> Who like a king commands within these woods?
> The **bear**, the **boar**, dares not abide my sight,
> But **hastes** away to save themselves by flight. (2.3.6)

Another creature that may possibly link *Mucedorus* and *Leicester's Commonwealth* is a mouse: the clown in the play is called Mouse. In the tract I find Leicester described thus: "as for valor, he hath as much as hath a mouse," (Peck 194/*127*).

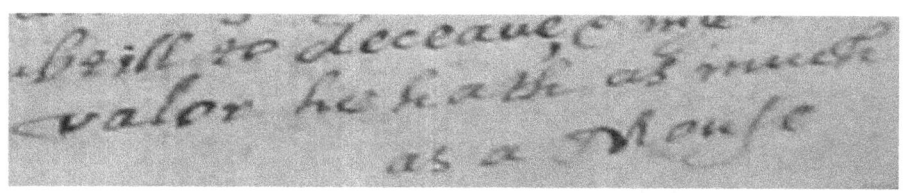

Worsley MSS 47, 65

Neville writes 'Mouse' with a capital, as if it were a name. Indeed this suggests that the characters of Segasto, Bremo, the bear and Mouse may all hold elements of Leicester. Mucedorus overcomes all to win Amadine.

Shakespeare's most famous stage direction is "Exit pursued by a bear" in *The Winter's Tale* (3.3.57). In the play *Mucedorus*, written up to 25 years earlier, there is a stage direction: "Enter Segasto running and Amadine after him, being pursued with a beare" (1.3). The bear is the most obvious link between these two plays. In the First Folio the spelling of this famous stage direction is: "Exit pursued by a Beare" Thus the spelling is the same in Worsley MSS 47.

Worsley MSS 47, 65

# Appendix 8

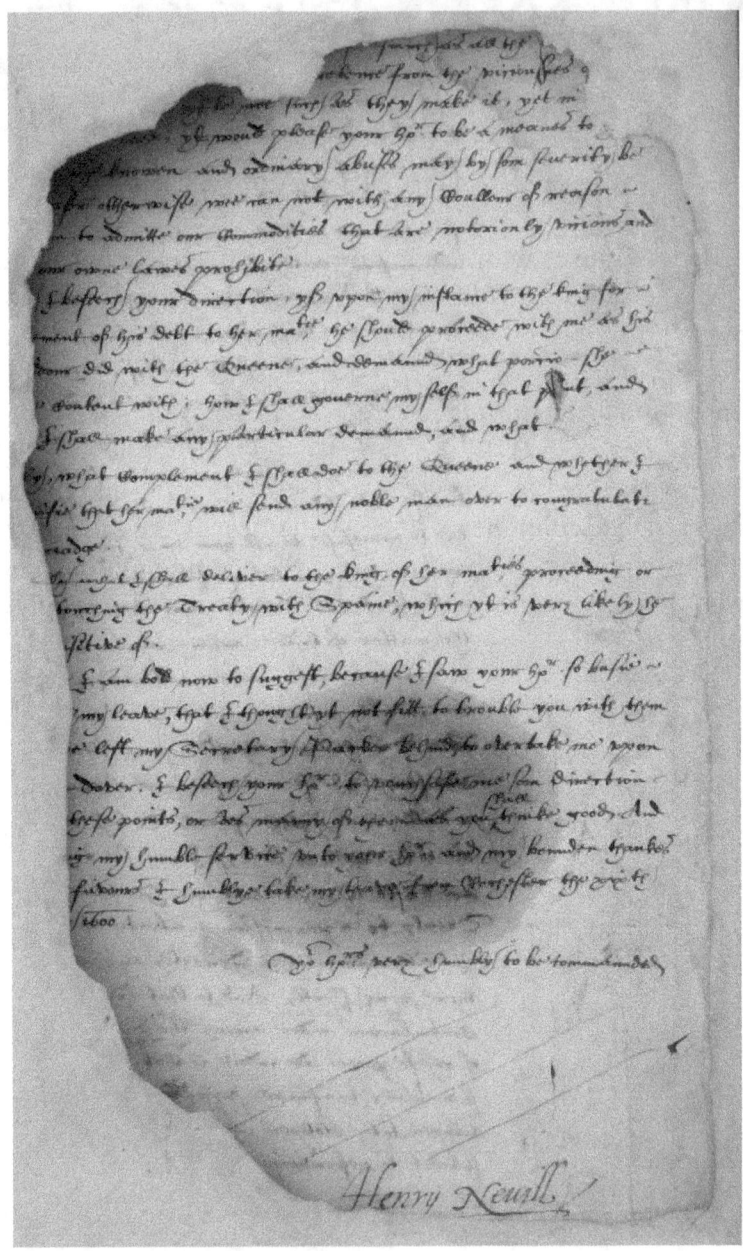

Henry Neville's letter, 19th February, 1601

Cotton Manuscripts, Caligula EX folio 21V, © The British Library Board. This is the second page (the verso) of the letter. The stain in the centre is the remains of the wax seal. The letter was singed in a fire on October 23rd 1731 when Ashburnham House went up in flames. Much of the Cotton Library was saved and is now at the British Library in London.

**A transcription** (by Anne Cole and John Casson)

…as much as all the
… retence from the viciousnes of…
…yt be not such as they make it, yet in
… yt would please your ho$^r$ [Honour] to be a meanes to
the knowen and ordniary abuses may by som severity be
for otherwise wee can not with any Coullour of reason ~
n to admitte our Commodities that are notorionly vicious and
our owne lawes prohibite.

I beseech your direction, yf upon my instance to the knig for ~
ement of his debt to her ma$^{tie}$ [Majesty], he should proceede with me as his
dour did with the Queene, and demand what porcio[n] she
Content with; how I shall governe myself ni that p..nt, and
I shall make any particular demand, and what.
y, what Complement I shall doe to the Queene and whether I
fie that her ma$^{tie}$ [Majesty] will send any noble man over to congratulate
{mar}riadge.

what I shall deliver to the knig, of her ma$^{ties}$ [Majesty's], proceednig or
towchnig the Treaty with Spaine, which yt is very likely he
isitive of.

I am bold now to suggest, because I saw your ho$^r$ [Honour] so busie ~
my leave, that I thought yt not fitt, to trouble you with them
e left my Secretary Parker behnid, to overtake me upon
Dover. I beseech your ho$^r$ [Honour] to vouchsafe one some direction
these points, or ues manny of them wch you shall thnike good. And
in my humble service unto your ho$^r$ [Honour] and my bounden thankes
favours I humblye take my leave from Rochester the xix$^{th}$
1600
Your ho$^{rs}$ [Honour's] very humbly to be commanded
Henry Nevill

**The date of the letter**
"The recipient of the letter is not identified, but Neville addresses him as 'your honour' and asks him for 'som direction' on various points of Anglo-French diplomatic relations, so Robert Cecil seems a likely candidate. Neville returned to England on 6 August 1600, and I assume this letter was written early the following year, on 19 February 1600-1, just as he was preparing to return to France. (For some reason our catalogue gives the date as 19 January, but the letter is quite clearly docketed 19 February.) The volume also contains letters addressed to Sir Thomas Parry, Neville's successor as ambassador in Paris, so it is possible that Neville's letter was filed with other French diplomatic material and ended up in Parry's papers." (Personal communication from Dr Arnold Hunt, Curator of Historical Manuscripts, British Library, 4/6/2009.)

The confusion of the date 1600/1601 is due to the old style calendar in which the new year began in March (so a letter dated February 1600 would actually be written in 1601).

The letter then was written on the very day of Robert Devereux, the Earl of Essex's treason trial. Just six days later he was executed. The letter was written in Rochester, on the road to Dover. It is evidence that, on the day of the trial, Neville was preparing to return to France to take up his ambassadorship again, as if nothing had happened. His cover was blown by Henry Wriothesley, the Earl of Southampton, who, on February 21[st], hoping perhaps to save his own life, confessed and implicated Neville in the Essex Rebellion (James & Rubinstein, 2005, 145). Neville was arrested in Dover and they were both imprisoned in the Tower for the remainder of Elizabeth I's reign.

## Appendix 9

### *Edward IV*, Thomas Falconbridge, Essex and Neville

As mentioned in chapter 7, a two part play on the reign of Edward IV appeared in print in 1599 (Q1) and 1600 (Q2). The second quarto was therefore printed the very same year as *Look About You* and both plays featured a bastard called Falconbridge. Also in 1600 two other plays which included a Falconbridge were printed for the first time: Shakespeare's *The Merchant of Venice* and *Henry V*. In two of these plays the Falconbridge is fictional; in two he is a real historical figure. In *Look About You* and *The Merchant of Venice* the Falconbridges are imaginary characters; in *Edward IV* and *Henry V* they are Thomas Neville and a French nobleman, (spelt Fauconberge in Holinshed) who was killed at Agincourt (3.5.44; 4.8.100). Thomas Heywood has been accepted as the main author of *Edward IV* with some revising help from Henry Chettle (Rowland, 2005, 6, 9). Both these authors had been involved in the *Sir Thomas More*. I accept this attribution.

This appendix focuses on the first part of *Edward IV*, looking at the role of Thomas Neville-Falconbridge and suggests, for the first time, a possible hidden connections between the play, the Earl of Essex and Henry Neville. Edward IV was the son of Richard Duke of York and Cecily Neville. Her brother Edward was the great, great grandfather of Henry Neville.

### Thomas Falconbridge

Thomas, the Bastard of Fauconberg, was an illegitimate son of William Neville, Lord Fauconberg, the first Earl of Kent. William was another of Cecily's brothers. Shakespeare mentioned William in *Henry VI* part 3: "Stern Falconbridge commands the narrow seas" (1.1.241), though Cairncross (1964, 15 footnote) suggested that Shakespeare, following Halle's *Chronicle*, had conflated William with his son Thomas, who was also a sailor. Thomas, the Bastard of Fauconberg, had received the freedom of the City of London in 1454 for his part in removing pirates from the North Sea and the English Channel[46]. He was made Vice-Admiral of the Fleet by his cousin Richard, Earl of Warwick (another Neville) of whom he was a zealous supporter. He had played an active part in placing Edward IV on the throne in 1461 and stayed with Warwick when the 'Kingmaker'

---

46    From: http://en.wikipedia.org/wiki/Bastard_of_Fauconberg accessed 6/7/2009

changed allegiance. In the ensuing debacle he was arrested and finally beheaded in 1471.

Not only was Falconbridge mentioned in *Henry VI* part 3 but it was in that play that the name 'Nevil' was mentioned more times than in any other Shakespeare play (seven in the First Folio version, eight times in the 1595 quarto, *The True Tragedy of Richard Duke of York*). Edward IV is crowned in the play. *Henry VI* part 3 is clearly a source for *Edward IV*. Twice in *Henry VI* part 3 the myth of Phaethon is used, referring to the Duke of York (Cecily Neville's husband). This same myth is used by the bastard Fauconbridge in *The Troublesome Raigne* and I have shown this has connections with the Phaeton sonnet and Henry Neville (Casson, 2009). In *Edward IV* the king uses this myth when speaking of Thomas Falconbridge:

> Well, let this Phaethon that is mounted thus,
> Look he sit surely, or, by England's George,
> I'll break his neck. This is no new evasion.
> I surely thought that one day I should see
> That bastard Falcon take his wings to mount
> Into our eagle aery… (1.1.146)

The writer makes sure the audience knows that Falconbridge is a Neville, repeatedly identifying him as Thomas Neville and using the name Neville 15 times. He is not the only Neville in the play, which ends with Richard III speaking to his Queen, Anne Neville, though she not identified by that surname but as "Anne of Warwick", (being the daughter of Richard Neville, Earl of Warwick, the 'Kingmaker').

**Neville and Essex**

In chapter 2 I showed how Shakespeare and other playwrights used history as a metaphor for the present, enabling them to explore dangerously topical issues through the safely distanced stories of past kings. Rowland (2005) in his definitive edition of *Edward IV*, teases out the hidden contemporary references to Robert Devereux, the Earl of Essex, and the threats to England's peace. The Falconbridge rebellion is depicted as a time of social unrest due to economic distress: this was a contemporary concern as a series of poor harvests had resulted in food shortages and price rises. Likewise the play *Sir Thomas More* had also shown unrest resulting partly from the price of bread.

In 1599 when the play was first published, Essex had been sent to Ireland to quell rebels. Rowland (2005, 25) makes a direct link to the indiscriminate awarding of knighthoods mentioned twice in *Edward IV* and Essex awarding them in the field (much to Elizabeth I's displeasure). Rowland also shows there are many other covert links between the play's locations and characters and Robert Devereux, the Earl of Essex.

Devereux was not the only person sent abroad by Elizabeth in 1599: Henry Neville went to France as ambassador, principally charged with getting France to pay back money borrowed from the Queen and also to negotiate a peace treaty. It is therefore startling to find that not only is a peace deal agreed with France in *Edward IV* but the French also agree to pay the English large amounts of money! This of course was wishful thinking as Neville was in fact unable to get any money from the French. However if history is metaphor it suggests the writer of *Edward IV* was not only pointing to the contemporary Earl of Essex but also the coming negotiations with France. Furthermore he did so with clear warnings of the dangers to the realm of a rebellion by a bastard Neville. Within two years Robert Devereux and Henry Neville were both on trial for their lives after the abortive Essex rebellion. Is this purely coincidence, a case of Life imitating Art, or was the playwright aware of the links between Essex and Neville and the dangers they might pose? He had worked on *Sir Thomas More*, in which I have shown Neville himself was secretly involved. Was he warning him that ambition leads to a fall? The Phaethon image then would be no hackneyed accidental reference. The portrait of Thomas Falconbridge in the play is not attractive but shows him as a desperate rebel in bad company: unlike all the other Falconbridges in Shakespeare's plays this is no flattering or attractive portrait. The rebel Spicing, in defeat, attacks his leader:

> Art thou that Neville whom we took thee for?
> Thou art a louse, thou bastard Falconbridge!
> Thou baser than a bastard, in whose birth
> The very dregs of servitude appears! (1.10.3)

After this Shakespeare never again used the name Falconbridge.

# Appendix 10

## Arbella

"seeking death, find life"
*Measure for Measure* (3.1.43)

One of the annotations in Worsley MSS 47 reads, "Arbella after maried to y$^e$ Earle of Hartfo grandchild & dies without yssue" (44). Arbella was aged about 9 when *Leicester's Commonwealth* appeared. She was a possible successor to Elizabeth I being a descendant of Henry VII. She married William Seymour, the grandson of Edward Seymour, 1$^{st}$ Earl of Hertford in 1610. Arbella's died on September 27$^{th}$ 1615 so this annotation must have been made after that. The annotation seems to be in the same handwriting and is immediately after an annotation referring to the accession of James I which reads, "whose sonne James 6$^{th}$ most happily joined both kingdomes into one". In chapter 3 I suggested this showed that Neville continued to refer to Worsley 47 into the 17$^{th}$ Century and indeed the document that follows *Leicester's Commonwealth* is dated 15/7/1613.

The printed annotation simply reads 'Arbella'. In Worsley MSS 47 Neville has put a dot and forward slash ( . / ) after 'Arbella' and then continued on. This suggests that he first copied the printed annotation verbatim and only later added "after maried to y$^e$ Earle of Hartfo grandchild & dies without yssue". This is squeezed in before the next note which states "the 2 daugh: of K: Henr: 7$^{th}$ by whome the howse of Suffc maketh clayme" and is Neville's version of the next printed annotation (see Appendix 1). The words after 'Arbella . /' are clearly inserted later as 'dies' invades the main text and 'yssue' partially covers the word 'daugh(ter)' of the next annotation.

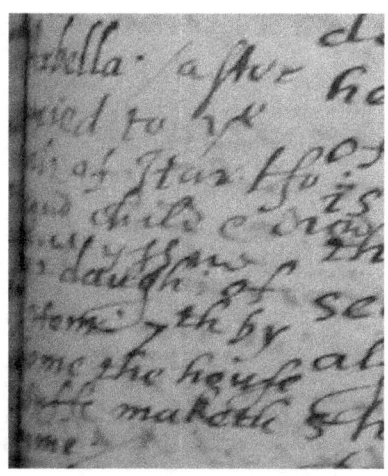

Worlsey MSS 47, 44

But this note poses a problem indeed! Neville is believed to have died on July 10th 1615 (James & Rubinstein, 2005, 201). This annotation must have been written after September 27th 1615. There is evidence that Neville may have been alive after his reported death. On November 14th 1616 John Chamberlain wrote in a letter that "Sir Harry Nevill" was at supper with Sir Ralph Winwood in the company of Sir Henry Savile, Sir Robert Killigrew, Sir Arthur Throckmorton and numerous others (Rowse, 1962, 309; McClure, 1939, Vol. 2, 34). It has been presumed this was Neville's son who shared his father's name. The above annotation suggests that the man in the company of his close friends could have been Neville himself. It was however Chamberlain himself who first reported Neville was seriously ill on Febuary 9th 1615, and dead, in a postscript to his letter of 13th July 1615 (McClure, 1939, Vol. 1, 577, 607). Neville must have been dead by 1619 when Chamberlain reported that his widow Anne was to marry Bishop George Carleton (McClure, 1939, Vol 2, 270).

One implication of this is that Neville might have lived longer than William Shakespeare from Stratford who died in April 1616. With his front man gone and himself officially dead, Neville could not write anything more under the Shakespeare nom-de-plume. This increases the tantalising mystery of the anonymous *Famous History of George Lord Fauconbridge* which appeared in 1616 (see appendix 6). In that story the bastard Faulconbridge travels to another country: did Neville leave England? He had been to the Netherlands in 1613 (Winwood, 1725, Vol 3, 467).

I pointed out, in chapter 4, that in *Henry VIII* we hear, "if the king should **without issue die**" (1.2.134). The above annotation reads, "Arbella after maried to y^e Earle of Hartfo grandchild & **dies without yssue**" (44). *Henry VIII* was on stage in 1613. We can see then that this annotator of c1616 uses a phrase Shakespeare (or Fletcher) used just three years earlier. In reviewing the authorship of scenes in *Henry VIII* Act 1, scene 2 has been assigned to Shakespeare.

We can compare the handwriting of 'Hartfo' in the above annotation with another occasion when Neville writes this name on a previous page:

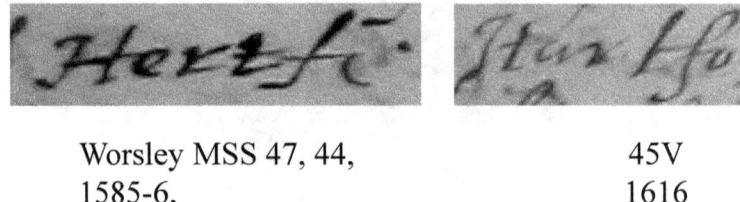

Worsley MSS 47, 44,               45V
1585-6,                                      1616

If the dating I have suggested for the original annotations, circa 1585-6, is correct, then we are looking here at the writing of the same person 30 years later. A handwriting expert will perhaps be able to tell us whether this annotation was inserted by different writer. If it was not Neville who was it?

# References

Internet resources:

The text of *Look About You*:
www.archive.org/details/lookaboutyou160000londrich

The text of *Leicester's Commonwealth*:
http://www.dpeck.info/write/leic-comm.pdf

The text of *The Famous History of George Lord Fauconbridge*:
www.lion.chadwyck.co.uk

First Folio spelling from:
http://etext.virginia.edu/etcbin/toccer-new2?id=ShaR3F.sgm&images=images/modeng&data=/texts/english/modeng/parsed&tag=public&part=5&division=div1
accessed 2008 - 9

Books:

Adams, S. (1995) Household Accounts and Disbursement Books of Robert Dudley, Earl of Leicester, Camden Fifth Series, Volume 6, Cambridge University Press

Additional MS 33594, Ralph Sadler letters, British Library.

Armstrong, E.A. (1979) Shakespeare's Imagination, A Study of the Psychology of Association and Inspiration, London, Landmark Edition, University of Nebraska Press

Barber, R. (2003) Richard Plantagenet, Woodbridge Suffolk, Boydell Press

Bate, J. (2006) Titus Andronicus, The Arden Shakespeare, London, Thomson Learning

Begor, A.C. (1965) Look About You, a Critical Edition, PHD thesis, Harvard University, Cambridge Press (DA 32 [1971]: 907A)

Bevington, D. (1968) Tudor Drama and Politics: Critical Approaches to Topical Meaning, Cambridge, MA., Harvard University Press

Bullen, A.H. (1891) Antient Drolleries (No 2) Pimlyco, or, Runne Red-Cap, Tis a Mad World at Hogson, 1609, Facsimile, Oxford University Press

Campbell, L.B. (1968) Shakespeare's Histories, Mirrors of Elizabethan Policy, London, Methuen & Co. Ltd.

Cairncross, A. S. (1964) The Third Part of Henry VI, The Arden Edition of the Works of William Shakespeare, London, Methuen & Co. Ltd, Harvard University Press

Casson, J. (2009) Enter Pursued by a Bear, The Unknown Plays of Shakespeare-Neville, London, Music for Strings

Cotton MSS, Caligula EX and EXI, manuscripts in the British Library, London

Craik, T.W. (ed) (2005) King Henry V, The Arden Shakespeare, London, Routledge

Crystal, D. (2008) Think on my Words, Exploring Shakespeare's Language, Cambridge University Press

Dover Wilson, J. (1923) The Spellings of the Three Pages (of Sir Thomas More) with Parallels from the Quartos, Appendix, pp 132-141, in Shakespeare's Hand in The Play of Sir Thomas More, papers by Pollard, A. W., Greg, W. W., Maunde Thompson, E., Dover Wilson, J. & Chambers, R. W., Cambridge University Press

Dutton, R. & Howard, J.E. (Eds), (2006) A Companion to Shakespeare's Works, he Histories, Oxford, Blackwell Publishing

Egan, M. (2006) *The Tragedy of Richard II* Part One: a newly authenticated play by William Shakespeare, four volumes, Lewiston, The Edwin Mellen Press

Farmer, J. S. (1910) Sir Thomas More, Tudor Facsimile Texts, Malone Society

Fields, B. (2006) Players, The Mysterious Identity of William Shakespeare, Stroud, Sutton Publishing Limited

Foster, M. (1981) Gloucester Hall and the Survival of Catholicism, Oxoniensia 46, Oxfordshire Architectural and Historical Society

Gabrieli, V. & Melchiori, G. (1990) Sir Thomas More, The Revels Plays, Manchester University Press

Given-Wilson, C. & Curtles, A. (1984) The Royal Bastards of Medieval England, London, Routledge & Kegan Paul

Greg, W. W. (ed) (1913) Look About You, The Malone Society Reprints, Oxford University

Greg, W. W. (1923) Special Transcript of the Three Pages in Shakespeare's Hand in The Play of Sir Thomas More, papers by Pollard, A. W., Greg, W. W., Maunde Thompson, E., Dover Wilson, J. & Chambers, R. W., Cambridge University Press

Guy, J. (2009) A Daughter's Love, London, Harper Perrennial

Hadfield, A. (2005) Shakespeare and Republicanism, Cambridge University Press

Halle, E. (1550) Chronicle, Hesketh Collection, Lancaster University Library

Halliday, E. F. (1977) A Shakespeare Companion 1564-1964, London, Gerald Duckworth

Harley MSS 7368, Sir Thomas More, manuscript in the British Library, London

Hattaway, M. (1993) The Third Part of King Henry VI, The New Cambridge Shakespeare, Cambridge University Press

Haynes, A. (1987) The White Bear, Robert Dudley, The Elizabethan Earl of Leicester, London, Peter Owen

Hazlitt W. C. (1874) A Select Collection of Old English Plays (originally published by Robert Dodsley in 1744) including *Look About You*, London, Reeves and Turner

Helgerson, R. (2006) Shakespeare and Contemporary Dramatists of History, chapter 2 in A Companion to Shakespeare's Works, The Histories, edited by Dutton, R & Howard, J, Oxford, Blackwell Publishing

Hicks, L. (1964) An Elizabethan Problem, Some Aspects of the careers of Two Exile-Adventurers, London, Burns & Oates

Holinshed, R. (1976) Chronicles, Volume 2, Reprint of 1807 edition, New York, AMS Press Inc

Humphreys, A.R. (1981) Much Ado About Nothing, The Arden Shakespeare, University Paperbacks, London, Routledge

James, B & Rubinstein, W.D. (2005) The Truth Will Out: Unmasking The Real Shakespeare, Harlow, Pearson Longman

James, B. (2008) Henry Neville and the Shakespeare Code, Bognor Regis, Music for Strings

Jupin, A.H. (1987) A Contextual Study and Modern-Spelling Edition of Mucedorus, The Renaissance Imagination, Vol 29, London, Garland Publishing Inc.

Keen, A. & Lubbock, R. (1954) The Annotator, London, Putman

Malone Society Reprints, (2003) Titus Andronicus, 1594, Vol. 166, Oxford University Press

Melchiori, G. (2001) King Edward III The New Cambridge Shakespeare, Cambridge University Press

Lemon, R. (Ed), (1865) Calendar of State Papers, Domestic 1581-1590,

Dept of MSS British Library London, Longman, Green, Longman, Roberts and Green

LION: Literature on Line database: http://lion.chadwyck.co.uk accessed at Manchester University

Logan, T. P. & Smith, D.S. (eds) (1975) The Popular School, A Survey and Bibliography of Recent Studies in English Renaissance Drama, Lincoln, University of Nebraska Press

Lovell, M. S. (2005) Bess of Hardwick, First Lady of Chatsworth, London, Abacus

McLaren, M (1949) "By Me…" a report upon the apparent discovery of some working notes of William Shakespeare in a sixteenth-century book, London, John Redington

McClure, N. E., (Ed.) (1939) The Letters of John Chamberlain, Two Volumes, Philadelphia, The American Philosophical Society

Meagher, J.C. (1980) The Huntington Plays, A Critical Edition of The Downfall and The Death of Robert, Earl of Huntington, New York, Garland Publishing, Inc

Mears, N. (2004) Stubbe [Stubbs], John (c.1541–1590), Oxford Dictionary of National Biography, Oxford University Press, 2004 [http://www.oxforddnb.com/view/article/26736, accessed 11/2/2007]

Melchiori G. (2001) Edward III, The New Cambridge Shakespeare, Cambridge University Press

Michell, J. (2000) Who Wrote Shakespeare? London, Thames & Hudson

Muir, K. (1960) Shakespeare as Collaborator, London, Methuen

Munday, A. (1909) Fidele and Fortunio or The Two Italian Gentlemen, Chiswick Press, The Malone Society Reprints

Munday, A. (1965) The Downfall of Robert the Earl of Huntington, Oxford

University Press, The Malone Society Reprints

Nelson, M. (1962) Look About You and the Robin Hood Tradition, Notes and Queries, 141-143

Nosworthy, J.M. (1955) Shakespeare and Sir Thomas More, RES new series, VI, 12-25

Peck, D.C. (1985) Leicester's Commonwealth, The Copy of a Letter Written by a Master of Art of Cambridge (1584) and Related Documents, London, Ohio University Press

Peck, D.C. (ed.) (2006) Leicester's Commonwealth, The Copy of a Letter Written by a Master of Art of Cambridge (1584) and Related Documents, Ohio University Press,
Athens, Ohio, London, (Reprinted in PDF format, 2006):
http://www.dpeck.info/write/leic-comm.pdf

Porohovshikov, P. S. (1955) Shakespeare Unmasked, London, Henderson & Spalding

Price, D. (2000) Shakespeare's Unorthodox Biography: New Evidence of an Authorship Problem, Greenwood Publishing Group

Ribner, I. (1965) The English History Play in the Age of Shakespeare, London, Methuen & Co. Ltd.

Rowland, R. (2005) The First and Second Parts of King Edward IV, Thomas Heywood, Manchester University Press

Rowse, A. L. (1962) Raleigh and the Throckmortons, London, Macmillan & Co Ltd

Sadler, Vol IV, Additional MS 33.59A, in the British Library, London

Sams, E. (1986) Shakespeare's Edmund Ironside: The Lost Play, Aldershot, Hants, Wildwood House

Sider, J.W. (1979) *The Troublesome Raigne of John King of England*,

New York & London, Garland Publishing, Inc.

Sokol, B.J. & Sokol M. (2004) Shakespeare's Legal Language A Dictionary, London, Continuum

Spurgeon, C. (1958) Shakespeare's Imagery and what it tells us, Cambridge University Press

Stallworthy, J. (ed) (1994) Wilfred Owen, The War Poems, London, Chatto & Windus

Stowe, 156, 174, miscellaneous letters and documents in the British Library, London

Taylor, G. (1986) Some Manuscripts of Shakespeare Sonnets, Bulletin of the John Rylands Library of Manchester, Vol 68

Thorndike, A. H. (1902) The Relation of As You Like It to the Robin Hood Plays, Journal of English and Germanic Philology 4, 59-69

Trace, J. (1968) Shakespeare's Bastard Faulconbridge: An Earl Tudor Hero in Shakespeare Studies III edited by J. Leeds Barroll, University of Cincinnati

Ubaldino, P. (1590) Discourse Concerning the Spanish Fleet Invading England in the Year 1588. Reprinted in The Harleian Miscellany, Vol 1, 119-132, London, 1809

Vendler, H. (1999) The Art of Shakespeare's Sonnets, Belknap Press, Cambridge, Harvard University Press

Warren, R. (ed) (2003) *Henry VI* part 2, The Oxford Shakespeare, Oxford University Press

Wentersdorf, K. P. (1965) The date of *Edward III*, Shakespeare Quarterly, 16

Winwood, R. (1725) Memorials of State in the reigns of Q. Elizabeth and K. James, 3 Volumes, London, T. Ward

Yelverton MS XXXIX, Additional MS 48035, miscellaneous letters and documents in the British Library, London

1594 quarto text of The First Part of the Contention Betwixt the Two Famous Houses of York and Lancaster,

1595 The True Tragedy of Richard Duke of York and the death of good king Henry Sixt, Shakespeare Quarto Facsimiles No 11, Oxford Clarendon Press, 1958

## Authors' Index

Adams, S. 55
Armstrong, E.A. 36, 117
Barber, R. 101, 103
Bate, J. 23, 110
Begor, A.C. 109, 110, 111, 118, 126, 129, 210 - 212
Bevington, D. 15, 82, 129, 132, 133
Bullen, A.H. 102
Campbell, L.B. 126
Cairncross, A. S. 145
Casson, J. 10, 13, 15, 22, 29, 30, 36, 40, 41, 43, 54, 58, 69, 80, 98, 99, 104, 105, 110, 114, 112, 115, 116, 120, 121, 122, 123,125, 130, 132, 133, 145, 147, 204, 207, 211, 215, 218, 223, 225
Craik, T.W. 17
Crystal, D. 58, 60, 121, 136
Dover Wilson, J. 74
Dutton, R. & Howard, J.E. 129
Egan, M. 30, 40, 110, 115, 132,
Farmer, J. S. 60
Fields, B. 108
Foster, M. 55, 56, 108
Gabrieli, V. & Melchiori, G. 79, 129, 132, 134, 141
Greg, W. W. 102, 136
Guy, J. 83, 134, 135
Hadfield, A. 23, 33, 113
Halle, E. 9, 10, 11, 29, 33, 38, 60, 64, 65 – 80, 94, 111, 116, 125, 128, 132, 141, 142, 144, 145, 153, 159, 175, 178, 196 – 203, 206, 215, 216, 225
Halliday, E. F. 36
Hattaway, M. 88
Haynes, A. 55, 213,
Hazlitt W. C. 114
Helgerson, R. 133
Hicks, L. 108
Holinshed, R. 9, 33, 110, 114, 122, 123, 131, 142, 146, 205, 225
Humphreys, A.R. 10
James, B & Rubinstein, W.D. 9, 13, 17, 26, 33, 35, 53, 65, 80, 91, 101, 105, 111, 149, 224
James, B. 26, 28, 35, 36, 37, 55, 66, 85, 88, 102, 108, 114, 121, 146, 148,

185, 215, 219,
Jupin, A.H. 122
Keen, A. & Lubbock, R. 9, 29, 33, 60, 65 - 80, 94, 111, 128, 178, 215
Lemon, R. 108
Logan, T. P. & Smith, D.S. 99, 109, 111, 130
Lovell, M. S. 108
McLaren, M. 65
McClure, N. E. 8, 229
Mears, N. 115
Melchiori G. 22, 141-3
Michell, J. 7
Muir, K. 115, 117
Munday, A. 10, 15, 79, 99, 102, 109, 118, 120, 122, 127, 128 – 129, 132, 209, 210, 211, 212
Nelson, M. 99, 102, 109, 130
Nosworthy, J.M. 132
Peck, D.C. 11 – 32, 34, 44, 48, 51, 52, 53, 54, 56, 81 - 90, 91, 101, 106, 107, 120, 124, 133, 150 – 193, 219, 220
Porohovshikov, P. S. 210
Price, D. 7
Ribner, I. 105, 132
Rowse, A. L. 149
Sams, E. 37, 47, 116, 123, 148, 204
Sider, J.W. 27, 32, 47, 86, 111, 123
Sokol, B.J. & Sokol M. 53
Spurgeon, C. 47
Stallworthy, J. 16
Taylor, G. 105
Thorndike, A. H. 118
Trace, J. 105
Ubaldino, P. 143, 145
Vendler, H. 121
Warren, R. 109
Wentersdorf, K. P. 143
Winwood, R. 10, 14, 35, 37, 40, 42 - 49, 52, 54, 73, 74 – 76, 86, 104, 112, 120, 121, 153, 123, 149, 151, 159, 215

# INDEX

Abbreviations 35, 64, 65, 89, 91, 107, 111, 115, 171, 184
Allen, Dr. Thomas 61, 132, 204
Alliteration 28, 45, 53, 212, 221
Arbella 77, 108, 178, 208, 216, 217, 271 - 273
Beauchamp, Richard 9, 260
Blot image cluster 93, 137, 142 - 144, 163, 258
Bodley, Sir Thomas 181
Brandon, Charles, Duke of Suffolk 168, 216, 217
Carew, Sir George (Lord Hunsdon, Lord Chamberlain) 108, 199
Cecil, Robert 84, 85, 123, 139, 184, 267, 165, 223
Chamberlain, John vii, 108, 272
Chettle, Henry ix, 91, 119, 123, 128, 134, 146, 157 - 161, 164, 251 - 253, 268
Clifford, George, Baron of Westmoreland 154
Davenant, Sir William 34
Dee, Dr. John 61 - 62, 204
Dekker, Thomas ix, 91, 164
Devereux, Walter, Earl of Essex 60
Devereux, Robert, 2[nd] Earl of Essex 18, 19, 127, 179, 267, 269, 270
Devereux, Robert, 3[rd] Earl of Essex 34
Donne, John 74
Dudley, Ambrose, Earl of Warwick 3, 11, 131, 263
Dudley, John 60, 191, 203, 229
Dudley, Edmund 191, 203, 228, 229
Dudley, Robert, Earl of Leicester xi, 12, 36, 46, 50, 114, 191, 196, 202, 223, 261, 262, 263
Dudley, Robin, (illegitimate son of Leicester) 32, 59 - 60, 192, 194
Elizabeth I 1 - 3, 5, 9, 11, 12, 15, 18, 19, 25, 26, 39, 40, 41, 62, 82, 122, 131, 133, 134, 136, 140, 141, 160, 180, 222, 225, 253, 262, 267, 270, 271
Falconbridge 27, 105, 146, 165, 268 - 270
    Fauconberg 27, 28, 105, 127, 128, 129, 268,
    Fauconbridge 13, 56, 126, 128, 138, 139, 145, 253 – 259, 269, 272, 274
    Faukenbridge 120 - 121, 125, 126, 127, 132, 136, 138, 139, 140, 141, 143, 144, 150, 154, 161, 255, 257,
    *The Famous History of George Lord Fauconbridge* 128, 254 – 259, 272, 274

First Folio vii, 16, 37, 55, 62, 65, 74 - 76, 78, 85, 92, 127, 136, 186, 214, 255, 264, 269, 274
Foxe, John 183
Gaunt, John of, Duke of Lancaster 28, 51, 52, 53, 54, 80, 126, 133, 165, 214, 236
Geoffrey of Monmouth 125, 126, 163, 183
Gloucester Hall xi, 11, 59 – 61, 132, 192, 194, 204
*Gorboduc* (see Sackville)
Grafton, Richard 123, 163
    *Chronicle* 123
Greene, Robert 123, 249
    *George a Greene* 123
    *Friar Bacon and Friar Bungay* 155
Gresham, Elizabeth (Neville's mother) 3, 138
Gresham, Thomas (Neville's uncle) vi, 3
Guise, Duke of, 180
Halle's *Chronicle* ix - xi, 25, 30, 31, 37, 67, 72, 73 – 94, 113, 136, 143, 144, 155, 159,
    164, 176, 180, 183, 184, 189, 197, 213, 216, 235, 236 – 242, 257, 258, 268
Hatton, Sir Christopher 5, 26, 53, 112, 211, 223, 224
Henslowe's Diary 123, 160, 251, 252
Henry VIII viii, 4, 20, 28, 56, 99, 137, 165, 168, 217
Herbert, William, Earl of Pembroke 74
Heywood, Thomas ix, 91, 128, 164
    *Edward IV* 128, 176, 268 - 270
Holinshed *Chronicles* vi, viii, 31, 53, 134, 135, 140, 152, 153, 163, 177, 179, 183, 245, 268
Huntington, Earl of, 9, 120, 122, 136, 199, 207, 209, 213, 222
    Henry Hastings 9, 121
    David of Huntington 122
    see also Munday for:
    *The Downfall of Robert the Earl of Huntington*
    *The Death of Robert Earl of Huntington*
James I vii, 63, 126, 135, 259, 271
Jermin, Sir Robert 4, 110, 207
Jonson, Ben v, vii
    *Bartholomew Fair* 154
Killigrew, Anne see Neville, Anne (nee Killigrew)

Killigrew, Henry, Sir (Anne's father) vi, 4, 135
Killigrew, Robert, (son of William) 34, 272
Killigrew, Thomas (son of Robert) 34
Killigrew, William 4, 34, 196, 158
Knollys, Bess 109
Knollys, Lettice, Countess of Essex and Leicester 5, 11, 60, 111, 131, 193, 204, 207
Knollys, Sir William 109
Leighton, Sir Thomas 33, 109, 207
Lodge, Thomas, *The Wounds of Civil War* 96
Marlowe, Christopher 147, 250
    *Ovid's Elegies* 147
    *Tamburlaine* 147, 156, 162, 250, 214
    *Dr. Faustus* 162, 250
    *Jew of Malta* 250
Mary Queen of Scots 2, 3, 4, 109, 126, 131, 134, 154, 180, 253
Meres, Francis 74, 255
Merton College, Oxford x, xi, 59, 61, 181, 184
Miniature superscript letters 64, 65
Munday, Anthony 119, 134, 146, 159, 160, 161, 164, 251, 252, 253
    *Fedele and Fortunio* 123, 159, 160
    *Sir John Oldcastle* 252, 253
    *Sir Thomas More* ix, 91, 102, 132, 164
    *The Downfall of Robert the Earl of Huntington* 6, 123, 146, 149, 157, 158 – 9, 160, 161, 248, 249, 250, 251, 252
    *The Death of Robert Earl of Huntington* 123, 151, 157, 158 – 9, 160, 250, 251
Nashe, Thomas 147
    *Summer's Last Will and Testament* 147
Navarre, Henri of 179, 180, 222
Neville, Alan de 132
Neville, Anne (nee Killigrew, Neville's wife) 4, 34, 117, 258, 259
Neville, Anne (Richard III's wife) 4, 9, 17, 70, 162, 261, 269
Neville, Catherine, daughter of John, Baron Latimer 126
Neville, Charles, sixth Earl of Westmoreland 4
Neville, Cecily 10, 55, 260, 268, 269
Neville, Edward (Neville's grandfather) 137, 155, 165, 167
Neville, Edward (Neville's son) 92 – 93
Neville, Frances (Neville's daughter) 73, 108

Neville, George, Baron Bergavenny 167
Neville, Henry (the hidden bard, Shakespeare-Neville) v, vi - x, 2 - 4, 13, 19, 21 – 24, 27, 31,
  32, 34 - 36, 40, 41, 43, 44, 45, 47 - 49, 51, 52, 53, 56 - 59, 61, 62, 64, 65, 68, 69, 72
  -74, 76, 78, 79, 82, 84 - 87, 91 - 109, 111, 112, 114, 117, 119, 122 - 127, 129, 131,
  132, 134 - 141, 145, 146, 149 - 153, 155, 159, 163 - 167, 169, 171, 174, 175, 176, 179
  - 186, 189, 197, 198, 202, 203, 214, 222, 225, 226, 230, 242, 244, 245, 246, 248, 253
  -260, 262 - 265, 267, 268 - 273
Neville, Sir Henry (Neville's father) vi, 4, 5, 8, 20, 33, 56, 91, 92, 99, 108, 109, 131, 207,
  217, 262
Neville, Sir Henry, 6th Baron Abergavenny (Neville's uncle) 4
Neville, Sir Henry, 7th Lord Abergavenny 133
Neville, John, Baron of Essex 127
Neville, John, Marquis of Montague 261
Neville, John, 4th Baron, Lord Latimer 82
Neville, Ralph, 6th Baron of Raby and 1st Earl of Westmoreland 51
Neville, Ralph, Earl of Westmoreland 10, 50, 82
Neville, Richard, Earl of Warwick (the Kingmaker) 4, 9, 16, 26, 36, 42, 46, 55, 105, 150, 166,
  247, 260, 263, 268, 269
Neville, Richard, Earl of Salisbury 49, 55, 101, 139, 260
Neville, Sir Thomas, Speaker of the House of Commons 168
Neville, Thomas (the bastard, see also Faulconbridge) 27, 105, 128, 268, 269
Neville, William, Lord Fauconberg and Earl of Kent 27, 105, 268
Northumberland Manuscript ix, x, xi, 3, 32, 33, 69, 70, 72, 83, 84, 115 – 117, 164, 183, 184, 230 – 235, 236
Paulet, Sir Amias 109, 131, 132, 200
Peele, George
  *Edward I* 123, 162, 250
  *David and Bethsabe* 250
Percy, Henry, Earl of Northumberland 51, 82
Percy, Henry, 8th Earl of Northumberland 126
*Pimlyco or Runne Red-cap* 124

Rastell, John 98, 167
> *Graunde Abridgement* 98, 167

Robin Hood 120, 122 - 123, 127, 132, 160, 161, 251
Robsart, Amy (Leicester's first wife) 60, 64
Sackville, Thomas, *Gorboduc* 7
Sadler, Sir Ralph 109, 122, 131
Salique law 37 - 38, 72, 76, 212
Savile, Henry 61, 62, 181, 272
Shakespeare canonical works:
> *A Midsummer Night's Dream* 11, 124, 125, 148, 163, 257
> *All's Well That Ends Well* 136, 189
> *Anthony and Cleopatra* 13, 19, 81, 191, 251
> *As You Like It* 28, 122, 123, 161, 251
> *Coriolanus* 19, 30, 45, 100, 148, 155, 246
> *Cymbeline* 81, 96, 106, 137, 256, 257, 259
> *Edward III* viii, 8, 13, 15, 16, 22, 26, 28, 44, 47, 50, 77, 79, 138, 141, 149, 156, 165, 174, 176 - 182, 184, 186, 216, 243, 244, 246, 247
> *Hamlet* 7, 13, 21, 30, 36, 49, 81, 133, 152
> *Henry IV* part 1  1, 8, 9, 28, 41, 51, 79, 80, 81, 82, 135, 149, 150, 161, 162, 164, 207, 246, 251, 253
> *Henry IV* part 2 10, 50, 80, 81, 82, 142, 147, 223
> *Henry V* vi, 8, 9, 25, 37, 39, 43, 44, 49, 73, 75, 76, 80, 81, 82, 98, 128, 136, 143, 165, 181, 185, 210, 212, 256, 268
> *Henry VI* part 1  8, 9, 11, 14, 26, 36, 42, 44, 53, 55, 74, 78 - 82, 91, 100, 103, 118, 128, 136, 140, 149, 153, 166 – 167, 182, 185, 186, 215, 223, 226 - 228, 240, 246, 250, 256, 258
> *Henry VI* part 2  vii, x, 8 - 13, 16, 19, 24, 36, 37, 45, 46, 49, 51, 54, 55, 74, 79 - 82, 100, 104, 118, 123, 126, 133, 136, 140, 148, 153, 155, 164, 166 – 167, 185, 186, 215, 223, 226 - 228, 250, 260, 263
>> *The First Part of the Contention* 11, 12, 45, 51, 166, 186
> *Henry VI* part 3  8 - 11, 16, 17, 22, 23 - 27, 42, 46, 50, 52, 53, 55, 74, 79 - 82, 85, 105, 127, 128, 136 - 138, 147, 148, 150, 153, 166 – 167, 185, 186, 208, 212, 215, 223, 226, 247, 250, 256, 257, 260, 261, 268, 269, 269
>> *The True Tragedy of Richard Duke of York* 26, 55, 56, 147, 186, 269
> *Henry VIII* viii, 8, 28, 43, 77, 80, 81, 82, 127, 133, 137, 164, 165,

167, 168, 216, 224,
256, 259, 272, 273
*King John* vi, 8, 13, 19 – 21, 30, 36, 43, 59, 79, 80, 101, 126, 127, 128, 132, 139, 142,
146, 148, 150, 156 – 159, 161, 165, 204, 219, 245, 246, 247, 252, 255, 256, 259
*King Lear* 19, 28, 58, 81, 97, 139, 140, 147, 165, 185, 261
*Julius Caesar* 8, 14, 16, 18 – 19, 27, 38, 39, 42, 119, 136, 162, 164, 185, 225
*Love's Labour's Lost* 32, 79, 128, 147, 250, 256
*Macbeth* vii, 3, 15, 162, 185, 251
*Measure for Measure* 138, 243, 251, 271
*Much Ado About Nothing* x, 137, 139, 164, 257
*Othello* 50, 53, 93, 257, 259
*Pericles* 14, 30, 47, 124, 206, 224, 256 - 257, 259
*Richard II* 7, 8, 23, 42, 80, 81, 82, 91, 126, 133, 142, 147, 152, 165, 247, 250, 257, 258
*Richard III* 8, 9, 10, 13, 17, 25, 62, 70, 78, 80, 81, 82, 95, 96, 97, 138, 148, 155, 162,
164, 168, 191, 201, 213, 229, 250, 261, 263
*Romeo and Juliet* 43, 57, 73, 78, 79, 147, 151, 205, 207, 216
*Sonnets* vi, 25, 34, 46, 47, 48, 127, 128, 132, 142, 150, 152, 159, 186, 201, 205, 257
*The Comedy of Errors* 44, 124, 137, 140, 141, 142, 165, 247, 256, 261
*The Merchant of Venice* 44, 128, 144 - 146, 256, 268
*The Rape of Lucrece* viii, 8, 13 - 16, 18, 46, 63, 101, 107, 133, 138, 142, 143, 148,
150, 154, 182, 185, 190, 207, 227, 243, 250
*The Taming of The Shrew* 24, 53, 136, 149, 164, 186, 243, 250, 257
*The Tempest* vii, 61, 183, 256, 257, 259
*The Two Gentlemen of Verona* 11, 41, 52, 79, 122, 137, 149, 161, 164, 180, 246, 250
*The Winter's Tale* 28, 93, 101, 151, 256, 257, 259, 264
*Timon of Athens* 8, 36, 223
*Titus Andronicus* 13, 14, 16 - 18, 19, 23, 25, 29, 30, 47, 48, 79, 87, 139, 141, 142,
148, 159, 185, 186, 205, 250

*Twelfth Night* 53, 176, 221, 251
*Venus and Adonis* 24, 133, 148, 182, 207, 247, 250, 257
Shakespeare apocryphal works:
*Arden of Faversham* x, 5, 16, 79, 141, 153 - 4, 156, 164, 185, 243 - 250
*A Yorkshire Tragedy* x, 64, 93, 128, 185
*Cardenio (Double Falshood)* x, 164, 256, 259
*Edmund Ironside* x, 14, 22, 26, 29, 36, 43, 49, 50, 79, 143, 149 - 156, 185, 243 - 251
*Hardicanute* 185
*Locrine* x, 22, 44, 48, 49, 50, 74, 79, 123, 126, 134, 143, 151 - 153, 156, 159, 162,
181, 182, 184, 185, 243 - 250, 253, 257, 258
*Look About You* x, 119 – 163, 166, 167, 185, 243 – 253, 257, 258, 268, 274
*Mucedorus* x, 6, 41, 43, 48, 123, 134, 150 – 151, 157, 162, 183, 185, 244 - 250, 260 –
264
*Sir Thomas More* ix, xi, 65, 68, 70 - 72, 85, 86, 87, 90, 91, 100, 107, 123, 150, 164 –
175, 183, 184, 186, 189, 213, 235, 246, 268 - 270
*The Taming of A Shrew* 185
*The Troublesome Raigne of John* x, 13, 14, 16, 19, 20, 21, 23, 29, 37, 49, 56, 59, 74, 79,
80, 81, 87, 101, 126, 127, 132, 134, 135, 137, 138, 139, 143, 144, 145, 146, 149, 152,
156 – 159, 161, 185, 243, 244 - 247, 249, 250, 252, 253, 255, 256, 259, 269
*Thomas of Woodstock* x, 8, 27, 40, 80, 82, 126, 164 – 167, 186, 243, 244, 246, 247,
250, 251, 257
Shakespeare, William (from Stratford) v, vi, 73, 128, 175, 254, 259, 272
Sidney, Sir Henry 199
Sidney, Mary, Countess of Pembroke 74
Sidney, Sir Philip 3, 5, 61, 250
Sidney, Robert 3
Sheffield, Lady Douglass 21, 32, 59, 60, 192
Spelling 32, 37, 41, 46, 48, 55, 56, 65, 69, 70 - 72, 75, 76, 79, 84 – 91, 92, 105, 108 - 110, 115, 116, 120, 127, 136, 139, 150, 159, 169, 176, 181, 183,

188, 196, 197, 201, 210, 239, 241, 242, 264, 274
Stubbe, John, *The Discoverie of a Gaping Gulf* 141
Tilney, Sir Edmund 165
Vaux, Sir Nicholas 133
Vaux, Thomas (poet) 133
Vaux, William 133
Walsingham, Sir Francis 2, 3, 139, 190, 191
West, Anne 111, 207
Wilkins, George, *The Miseries of Enforced Marriage* 128
Wilson, Robert, *The Three Lords and Three Ladies of London* 36
Worsley, Sir Richard (Neville's son-in-law) 65
Worsley, Sir Robert 73
Worsley manuscripts viii, x, xi, 128, 131, 261,
    Worsley MSS 36 ix, xi, 2, 3, 8, 11, 34, 59, 77, 79, 108 – 118, 188 – 229, 235, 236 – 242,
    Worsley MSS 47 ix, 3, 8 - 12, 18, 21, 26, 29, 30, 32 – 107, 122, 130, 133, 139, 149, 154, 159, 164, 166 - 168, 171 - 175, 181, 183, 184, 188 – 229, 235, 236 – 242, 258, 261, 264, 271, 273,
    Worsley MSS 40 (The Tower Notebook) ix, 79, 127, 184,
Wriothesley, Henry, The Earl of Southampton vii, 58, 108, 132, 133, 134, 267
Yarborough, fourth Earl of, 128
Yarborough, eighth Earl of, x, 73,
Yarborough, second Baron of 73

www.ingramcontent.com/pod-product-compliance
Lightning Source LLC
Chambersburg PA
CBHW071222080526
44587CB00013BA/1460